OCR

D1049913

Turning Away From Technology

Turning Away From Technology

Turning
Away From
Technology

A New Vision for the 21st Century

℘ Edited by *Stephanie Mills*

with a foreword by *Theodore Roszak*

Sierra Club Books · San Francisco

The Sierra Club, founded in 1892 by John Muir, has devoted itself to the study and protection of the Earth's scenic and ecological resources—mountains, wetlands, woodlands, wild shores and rivers, deserts and plains. The publishing program of the Sierra Club offers books to the public as a nonprofit educational service in the hope that they may enlarge the public's understanding of the Club's basic concerns. The point of view expressed in each book, however, does not necessarily represent that of the Club. The Sierra Club has some sixty chapters coast to coast, in Canada, Hawaii, and Alaska. For information about how you may participate in its programs to preserve wilderness and the quality of life, please address inquiries to Sierra Club, 85 Second Street, San Francisco, CA 94105. http://www.sierraclub.org/books

Library of Congress Cataloging-in-Publication Data
Mills, Stephanie.
    Turning away from technology : a new vision for the 21st century / by Stephanie Mills.
        p.   cm.
    Includes bibliographical references and index.
    ISBN 0-87156-953-1
        1. Technological forecasting.   2. Twenty-first century—Forecasts.
    3. Technology—Social aspects.   I. Title.
    T174.M56   1997
    303.48'3—dc21   97–8045

Production by Susan Ristow
Cover and book design by Amy Evans
Printed in the United States on acid-free paper containing a minimum of 50% recovered waste paper, of which at least 10% of the fiber content is post-consumer waste.

10 9 8 7 6 5 4 3 2 1

Contents

In Defense of the Living Earth

Theodore Roszak

Pity the poor Luddites! No movement in history has done more unde-served service as an ideological whipping boy. For nearly two centuries, this small contingent of the doomed and desperate men who struggled across the pages of English history in a few brief outbursts between 1811 and 1816 has been a favorite target for the contempt of fanatical futur-ists and technological enthusiasts. The Luddites are indeed held in such contempt that their critics have never felt the least need to find out who they really were and what they wanted. Recall the famous Groucho Marx quip: "I'd never join a club that admitted people like me." I sus-pect many of those who are out to bash the Luddites would invoke the same paradox: "I wouldn't waste my time studying people as crazy as that." As "crazy" as what? It doesn't really matter. If the Luddites had never existed, their critics would have to invent them. Those who favor indiscriminate industrial growth need an opposition that is just as indis-criminate in its hostility to industrialism—the better to score easy points.

Briefly, then, for the record: There has never been a movement that simply and unthinkingly hated machines and set about destroying them. There has never been a movement that called all technology evil and demanded its repeal in favor of reverting to fingernails and incisors. There has never been a movement that suggested that we live in caves and do without running water. The original Luddites were not such peo-ple. The Neo-Luddites who have produced this book are not such peo-ple. The Ur-Luddites of the English Industrial Revolution were angry weavers who had been "downsized" out of their jobs by factory owners who ousted them in favor of power looms and knitting frames. The weavers, the first victims of technological unemployment, with no union to speak for them and no welfare benefits to draw upon, understandably found this unfair. They appealed for justice, first to the owners, then to Parliament. Their petitions, regarded as illiterate and presumptuous, went unanswered. Only then did they go underground and resort to guerrilla tactics. As followers of the mythical General Ned Ludd, they declared themselves an "Army of Redressers" and threatened to sabotage any owner who refused to bargain with them. That is how they got involved in machine wrecking. Yes, they did burn down a few machine sheds. But there is only one instance of violence against people—an owner who was killed. The Redressers never harmed the person or property of those who negotiated with them. In any case, they were soon suppressed by armed force; several were hanged for destroying private property; the rest dispersed.

That small, futile gesture of defiance at the outset of the Industrial Revolution was enough to earn the original Luddites a place in history. They were the first to make it clear that industrialism is not an unmixed blessing, that technology is not neutral. They had learned in the school of hard knocks that there can be such a thing as inappropriate technology: machines and systems of machines that sacrifice the public good to enrich a selfish few. A simple point, but one that continues to get buried in the propaganda of "progress." Beyond that, the first Luddites were, in fact, so moderate in their demands that I suspect the Neo-Luddites you will find in this collection would be sorely disappointed in them if they once more walked among us. I think the Luddites of 1811 would have settled for a living wage and some job security. Their protest arose not from philosophical first principles, but from the anxiety and indignation of the hungry men. Had their grievances been met with a fair response, they might well have deemed steam technology beneficial. The new power looms, after all, did a good job of producing cheap cottons. Cheap cottons meant clean underwear, and clean underwear meant healthier people.

Neo-Luddites, who are mainly academics and writers, take a vastly more critical view of technology. As they should. Two centuries into the Industrial Revolution, we have far more experience to draw upon—especially the experience of megatechnology and multinational corporate control, forces that go far beyond the struggling little textile mills of

Manchester and Leeds. Above all, we have the experience of rampant biospheric degradation, an issue that belongs distinctly to our time. The first reports we find of environmental impact in the industrial records describe the pall of smoke that could be seen at a distance over the factory towns of the English midlands. At the time, some observers identified that as an exciting sign of progress, and so, too, the railroads that put the steam engine on wheels and soon took it across the landscape at ten, twenty, thirty miles an hour. These were wonders of the world in their time and not easily dismissed with philosophical disdain.

Today, the inhumanity and destructiveness of industrialism take different and subtler forms and have reached global proportions. One has to be on the far side of the Industrial Revolution to see such issues clearly. And what those issues illuminate is the problem of *scale* in human affairs. *Bigness:* That is the devil that lies waiting in the details of every good thing we invent or merchandise. A program, a project, an invention may seem benign and constructive. But build it on too big a scale—as is bound to be the case where profit is the measure of progress —and it will turn on you like Frankenstein's monster.

In confronting that monster, some of my fellow Neo-Luddites can be sweeping in their prescription for technology withdrawal. Perhaps they are right in their absolutism. Maybe our species cannot be trusted with anything that gets much beyond water wheels and windmills. But then there are those in the conflicted middle, who, for all their principles, boarded a 747 to attend the conferences where these discussions took place, who employ word processors to write their critiques, and who use e-mail to keep in touch across the world. I count myself among these. I have no choice but to be conflicted. The only reason I am alive to write this essay today is because several years ago an ingenious new surgical procedure saved my life. Some years later, another medical miracle saved my wife's life. For this, I am grateful. Without pharmaceutical support for my asthma, I would probably stop breathing tomorrow— though I more and more suspect that the industrial pollutants that come with the pharmaceuticals were responsible for the disease in the first place.

And beyond dire necessities, I confess to finding both pleasure and fascination in much modern technology. I think motion pictures are a magnificent art form, I believe electricity is a marvelous convenience. I even enjoy good television—when I can find it. I regard the science behind that technology as the most enthralling intellectual adventure of our age. I can even admire the genius that built the word processor I am using to keystroke this essay, though I live in fear that our growing computer dependence will spell disaster at some point not far down the line.

I say all this to raise an issue. Can a Neo-Luddite make so many compromises with Modernity? I would say yes, because I believe wisdom in these matters lies precisely in the conflict. Tearing as it is, the conflict comprehends the whole of human nature, the compassionate and the demonic, the mad and the magnificent. The talents of *Homo faber* are not the whole of human culture, but they account for many of our greatest achievements. I cannot write them off. But nothing debases those talents more readily than the arrogance of insisting that they, and the corporate forces that control them, can be trusted to prescribe their own values and limits.

The Neo-Luddite critique is utterly rational and realistic. Owning machines is a form of power. Using those machines to drive people off the land or out of a job, to cheat them in the marketplace, or to desecrate the natural environment is an abuse of power. Neo-Luddites know that true progress—improvements in the quality of life, not the quantity of goods—never grows from machines, but from the judgment and conscience of our fellow human beings. Technological enthusiasm clouds that judgment; profiteering corrupts the conscience. By way of an alternative, Neo-Luddites opt for prudence and the human scale. Theirs is a simple program: scale down, slow down, decentralize, democratize. Sound views, humane values, but hardly as thrilling as the promise that corporate chieftains and technophiliac enthusiasts make to those who will sell them their souls. At the beginning of the modern era, Sir Francis Bacon authored the mission statement of "the New Philosophy." It was nothing less than "to establish and extend the power and dominion of the human race itself over the universe." The oldest temptation in the world. *"And ye shall be as gods."*

High tech, the subtlest and most seductive stage of industrialism, has sweetened that temptation to the maximum. It has made so much seem so possible! It seems to offer us nothing short of magic. By clicking buttons and flicking switches, we can create our own virtual universe and bend nature to our will. Breed perfect babies, enjoy medical immortality, redesign the plants and animals to our specifications, globe-trot the planet on economy fares, lunch at the Ramada Antarctica, tune in to a thousand channels of nonstop entertainment, colonize the cosmos. There has never been so intoxicating, nor so deluded, a program.

There is a note of extremity to much of the discussion in this volume.

That is understandable. What have Neo-Luddites to hold against the Titanic powers and infantile obsessions of the industrial establishment? Not much, it would seem. A plea for living within limits, an appeal for loyalty to place, a respect for the natural order of things that was here before us and never needed us. These are easily drowned out by Promethean sound and fury. But to despair is to overlook the fact that Neo-Luddites have a powerful ally. She is called Earth. Her life-enhancing capacities are robust and deeply rooted; they have triumphed over numerous planetary emergencies: the taming of the oxygenated atmosphere, innumerable meteor collisions, ice ages, "Great Dyings." The environmental limits that Neo-Luddites would have us respect are Earth's, not ours, and they will not long be violated. Some postmodernist thinkers, hopelessly sunk in the dazzling theatrics of the urban world, believe we are as free to fabricate values as to change last year's fashions or pick numbers in a lottery. They are wrong. Life and mind emerge from an evolutionary history and remain ecologically contextualized. There are limits to our "dominion over the universe." Those limits are, I suspect, generously broad, but they are not infinite. Eventually our excesses will be balanced out. Does that sound consoling? It shouldn't. When the balance is struck, the casualties of the adjustment may include *us*, our species as a whole, the innocent and the guilty alike. We do well to recall that no species, not even our two-legged, wordy-headed own, can live beyond the means afforded by the biosphere, and none are exempt from extinction.

The Neo-Luddites, the spiritual descendants of St. Francis and William Blake, Tolstoy and Kropotkin, William Morris and Martin Buber, Black Elk and Gandhi, are the only biocentric political movement we have. Theirs is a defense of the living Earth. They alone have bravely faced the great moral challenge of our time: the creation of a sustainable postindustrial culture, a culture that will serve all people for all time. It is the one movement in the world today that transcends the mystique of progress and links us to life at large on the planet. The task is great, but we are not alone in undertaking it.

Artifacts/Considerations

Stephanie Mills

Spending two years distilling the transcripts of the 1993 and 1994 Megatechnology conferences—which constitute the body of this book—and with transcripts and papers from the 1980 conference "Technology: Over the Invisible Line?"—which was their direct ancestor—has kept me in an ongoing, imagined dialogue with the scores of participants. These were pretty cosmopolitan assemblies. While over half of the participants were from the United States, the balance came from Austria, Canada, England, Germany, India, Ireland, Malaysia, Mexico, the Netherlands, Norway, Sweden, and Thailand. Admirable folks, each and all, sometimes daunting in their brilliance. In the solitude of my writing studio, though, I've been asking them the begged questions. What might the intelligent, unconverted reader's response to the ideas, experiences, and analyses expressed herein be? Relief or denial, excitement or skepticism, perhaps, along with wondering what are the functional implications of this analysis? Does this thinking lead to a life that you or I would actually want to live? John Mohawk has sagely alerted us to the catastrophe of Utopian thinking. No one-size-fits-all blueprint for a future in which technology and trade are not masters, but servants, could—or should—be drawn. Movements are better at proscribing than prescribing. Diversity is the cardinal virtue.

Nevertheless, it seems important to confront the question of whether our activities and technologies have brought us and the biosphere to a condition in which some aspects of survival are contingent upon mass technology. Has technology become the infrastructure without which we perish? There are doubling billions of us. Much of the world's soil is exhausted, eroded, or blanketed by asphalt. Feeding the hungry masses is an end that's justified such means as applying industrial models to agriculture (the upshot of which has been to contaminate soils, poison pollinators, emphasize monoculture, make farming capital-intensive and commodity-oriented; *sic transit* family subsistence). Still, should biotechnology, as a possible emergency measure, be renounced altogether? Martha Crouch's good wisdom on the subject—that there are always better small-scale, indigenous alternatives to the proposition of genetically engineering the manufacture of vast quantities of synth chow—certainly sounds more laborious than a fast-pseudo-food fix.

Or, to take a trickier hypothetical question: Scattered around the world are little research institutes figuring out bioremediation, biological design, engineering waste and pollution out of mass production, working for the preservation of genetic diversity, and the like. All of these offer some hope for regenerating the Earth and sustaining communities. Shall we question the information technologies that allow such experimenters to assess and refine their practices and to communicate their achievements quickly to colleagues around the world? It's both a serious question with no easy answer, and, for the foreseeable future, a moot point, for electronic communications media are achieving hegemony. Yet if we persuade readers of nothing else, it should be clear that for every gain from even the most judicious utilization of modern technology, there will be certain losses. All the curmudgeonly inventors, activists, and gardeners who lack, or forego, computers will be out of the electronic loop, for one thing.

In San Francisco nearly twenty years ago, I had a salon. On one occasion John Todd and Raymond Dasmann were guests. Todd, a founder of the New Alchemy Institute and now president of Ocean Arks International, has been one of the pioneers in ecological design, creating what he calls "living machines" for food production and water purification, sail-powered work boats for Third World fishing communities, and designs for urban "green-newal" that are at once rigorous and lyrical. Dasmann, a distinguished zoologist, conservationist, ecologist, and author, would, a year or so later, be a participant in the 1980 conference. At that event he would remark on *Homo faber*'s innate tendency to disrupt ecosystems, evident since the Pleistocene, elegizing the time before the neolithic Earth as "the old, wild world." There is a thread of mourning in Dasmann, a wildlife biologist who has referred to contemporary ecosystems as "tattered remnants." Nevertheless, he, like Todd, has addressed the problem of envisioning a livable future for our species and others, and also has written usefully on that vision.

Among the few bits of conversation that I recall, Todd waxed enthusiastic about new instrumentation that allowed a careful monitoring of conditions in the greenhouse and aquaculture systems—dubbed "arks"—that he and his associates were then developing. Dasmann, I believe, wondered what acuity of senses and powers of observation were being supplanted by these cybernetic means of data collection and collation, wondered whether it might not be better to cultivate the ability to sniff the air and touch the soil and observe the water in the tanks and then articulate these findings out of direct experience. These two visionary biologists, each devoting his life to the planet's flourishing, would seem to be on different sides of the technological line. How important are such differences, finally?

Chellis Glendinning says it may be a question of time frames. Maybe those of us who cleave to the vision of a localized subsistence, to be achieved independently of capital- and research-intensive industrial products, are talking about our hopes for 200 years from now. Maybe our friends who would not now forego their silicon chip technologies figure that a return to the local can't happen now or ever. Or are they, like Helena Norberg-Hodge, thinking in terms of a strategic and transient embrace? Whichever, says Chellis, "We'd better get that out of the unconscious and into full view." Those differing assumptions may imply wholly different objectives, perhaps different worlds.

Figuring out which, trying to discern the ultimate politics of a given technology, or technological complex, impelled the discussions in '93 and '94 that led to the "78 Reasonable Questions to Ask About Any Technology." Jerry Mander's pursuit of some basic criteria for judging technology, however, was well underway by the mid-seventies (nor was he alone in such pursuit). In the conclusion to his 1978 book *Four Arguments for the Elimination of Television*, Jerry wrote, "In the case of technology, we might wish to seek a line beyond which democratic control is not possible and then say that any technology which goes beyond this line is taboo."

The radicalness of Jerry Mander's critique of television and the challenge of describing the invisible line so intrigued Diana Dillaway, then Director of Promotion for *Mother Jones* magazine, that she approached Jerry with the idea of holding a national conference to try to survey that line. In 1979 Jerry convened a planning committee consisting of himself; Diana; Lee Swenson, a longtime peace and community activist; and me. Filmmaker Toby McLeod was our wildly overqualified intern.

The conference aimed "to examine technology as a social force." Jerry, with Lee and me collaborating, stated our premises: "Technological society may have unwittingly entered an era in which most new technologies and technological development are beyond control, inevitably producing negative effects on human biology, planetary ecology, and the direction of political processes."

Given the then-current resistance efforts around dozens of areas of technological innovation—the movements to stop nuclear power, to ban supersonic air transport, to abandon hormonal contraception, to oppose the use of chemicals in food and agriculture, to outlaw microwave technology, to restrict the use of computer technology and to eliminate television—we thought it possible that we would witness the emergence of a vocal new protest movement that would question technology itself. Then along came the eighties, and the nineties. Consequently we're still waiting. If you take the longer view, however, we haven't been waiting long.

Consider this. The elimination of the slave trade, advocated in England as early as 1671 by the Quaker visionary George Fox, became law there only in 1808. John Adams and other founders of the American republic rhetorically abhorred the slave trade, but it was not until 1865 that Amendment XIII to the United States Constitution prohibited slavery throughout the nation. Abolition takes time and persistence and is achieved by degrees. Slavery still goes on, but without legal countenance.

In 1980, as in 1993 and 1994, venturing into waters navigated by the likes of Mumford and Ellul, we conference organizers were curious to discover whether the kind of analysis that demonstrates particular technologies cannot be reformed might also be extended to technological society as a whole.

We asked, "How many people place new technologies (television, electric light, cars, and computers, for instance) in historical perspective? Or have an image of a world without them?"

"Technological, mainstream society denies its alternatives, presenting us with the choice between nuclear power and a return to the Stone Age," we wrote, and pointed to a middle way. "There are other possible answers being raised by individuals working in human-scale communities, using appropriate technologies with a sense of limits." Among them, then as now, were simple living, Native American sovereignty, and bioregional movements.

After a year's preparatory work, "Technology: Over the Invisible Line?" was held over a March weekend at the Mills College campus in Oakland, California. Scores of notable authors and activists participated: Leopold Kohr, Wes Jackson and Dana Jackson, John McKnight, Barry Lopez, Murray Bookchin, David Brower, Ernest Callenbach, and Richard Grossman among them. A handful of the participants—Jerry Mander, Langdon Winner, Susan Griffin, Fritjof Capra, Godrey Reggio, John Mohawk and I—turned up at the "Megatechnology and Development" conference in 1993 and resumed the discussion. At that meeting, thanks in part to Kirkpatrick Sale and Charlene Spretnak, we came to see our criticism as part of a lineage and historic tradition. Our immediate intellectual ancestors, some of them alive and kicking, included Gandhi, Mumford, Schumacher, Roszak, Illich, and Ellul. Traditional native peoples, of course, are the originators of this critical understanding of technology, and have been resisting the takeover for 10,000 years.

Indigenous struggles for cultural and territorial self-determination have been the deepest rooted, least intellectualized, longest running, and most spiritually lucid opposition to sedentary life and imperial, and then industrial, civilization. Indian leaders today give eloquent witness that what is at stake in the confrontation with mass technology, ultimately, is the sacred.

By 1980 there had already been a plethora of horrific technological fiascoes: Teton Dam had burst, Thalidomide had deformed babies, the Three Mile Island nuclear plant had released radiation, the Italian town of Seveso had been poisoned by its chemical plant, the Amoco *Cadiz* had spilled oil on the Breton coast, and in the epidemic blights killing chestnut and elm trees and the munchings of gypsy moth caterpillars we had some hint where the introduction of exotic, genetically engineered lifeforms might lead. Ample grounds for doubting that technology makes progress. In those days, the U.S. also had a modestly effective body of environmental and workplace safety regulations, connoting official recognition of technological excess. Our politicians had not yet openly adopted high tech, economic growth, and free trade as the official state religion. This may be only nostalgia, but it seems like there was still the possibility of measured and respectful (if not consequential) debate about these concerns, and perhaps less tendency to reduce or vilify holders of dissenting views. Yes, children, back in the good old days, the soundbites were whole mouthfuls!

However civil or uncivil the discussion, the most serious version is and was carried on by the noncommercial publications of citizens' groups and activist organizations. Not long before work on "Technology: Over the Invisible Line?" I'd spent a year editing such a periodical —Friends of the Earth's *Not Man Apart*. Substantive, sometimes decisive criticism of nuclear power was one of FOE's long suits. As a romantic and a technophobe, however, I'd become averse to the copy we were getting from our crack atelier of nuclear intervenors. In terms of sensibility, they fought fire with fire (which, as any smoke jumper will tell you, can work). "Techno-twits," FOE's brilliant Amory Lovins, scout of soft energy paths, dubbed himself and his analytic ilk. Through their diligent, painstaking number-crunching—and beyond the pale, a great deal of organized civil disobedience by various alliances with mollusks (such as Clamshells and Abalones) for totems—things nuclear got worse less quickly. Still, it took Chernobyl to begin to nail the lid on the casket of, if not drive the stake through the heart of, the nuclear industry.

Very briefly, the Techno-twits and soft energy proponents had the ear of the governor of California, because the governor was Jerry Brown. Brown's receptivity to alternative intelligence meant California had an Office of Appropriate Technology complete with a community gardening program. There was a whole slew of state initiatives that promoted ecologically sensible measures like solar energy and watershed restoration—not Camelot, in prospect, but Ecotopia, much of which withered with changes in administrations.

In the fifteen years since that first conference, through computer-accelerated communications and the proliferation of trade agreements, transnational corporations made quantum progress toward world domination, as we have heard. There were portents in the eighties, but the cold ruthless megalomania of the World Trade Organization beggars my worst paranoid fantasies. The points of leverage for citizen-activists have been shifted radically by this commercial abrogation of national sovereignty. Technology does seem to accelerate history. In the last decade or so personal computers became nearly as commonplace as television; and corporate and government networking of computers further invaded privacy and rocketed financial manipulation past the sound barrier, as David Korten described, bringing the crash of the global economy ever nearer. Mechanism has restructured the inner life. We now commonly apply machine metaphors to our consciousness, imagining ourselves to be "programmed" in certain ways, possessing buttons that can be pushed, circuits that can be blown, and tapes to be changed.

As of this writing former Governor Brown is part of a communal household in Oakland, California, living in monastic simplicity, doing community work and hosting a radio talk show. Amory Lovins and his colleague and wife, Hunter, along with their associates, have created the successful Rocky Mountain Institute, a think tank doing advanced number crunching and advocating social and industrial strategies that aim at sustainability through material parsimony. RMI researches, publishes, and advises communities, governments, and businesses on the skillful and profitable conservation of resources—whether the resource happens to be energy or the community's earnings. Like Langdon Winner, Lovins believes in reasoning from ends to means in devising energy strategies. His baseline assumption for U.S. energy policy, in quip form, is that people want cold beer and hot showers. Lovins and company maintain that those amenities—and much good life besides—can be provided without overloading the atmosphere with CO_2 or nuclear waste leaking into the groundwater. What's more, the Lovinses think that given adequate accounting (a big caveat, they acknowledge), market forces are the likeliest means of rationally allocating resources. These Techno-twits are not necessarily technocrats: Genuine zeal for community self-reliance informs their work. Relying on the markets and the sophisticated modes of production required to produce many of the most advanced energy-conserving devices, though, leaves humanity dependent on the continuing existence of a complex of high technologies and centralized manufacture. What about the low-tech cultural alternatives of smelling funky, taking sweat baths, and (once we've restored our watersheds and water tables) drinking spring water?

J. Baldwin, longtime technology editor for *The Whole Earth Catalog and Review*, possesses countless skills and some thoroughbred horse sense, along with a store of life experiences that have finely honed his wits and design sense. These days he, like John Todd, is busy articulating the tenets of ecological design. J. attended that 1980 conference, contributing a paper titled "Armageddon Chic," which was a plea for honest realism, and a bit of a slap. Like the Lovinses, Baldwin, who was a student of Buckminster Fuller, does not predicate his designs for the future on humanity's sudden mutation into a race of Gandhis, or future primitives. A sage and remarkable guy, J. is heading for one of those different worlds, confident high technology can be tamed if people will only quit gassing and roll up their sleeves.

While reliving and reconsidering all that was said at these conferences, I've found myself wondering what J. might think of our positions. Not known for mincing words, Baldwin has zero patience with proponents of scenarios—like a carless society—which he deems impossible. In kindred spirit Steve Baer, a *Whole Earth* contemporary of Baldwin, a solar inventor, and energy philosopher, sharply declined the invitation to the 1980 conference. "You're talking about taking away my television set," he wrote. "Why don't you just turn off your own?" At that time, the libertarian position had some merit, and the whole body of Baer's work argued for taking him seriously. But today as the consequences of global broadcasting of MTV and Baywatch or its ilk are manifest—millions of individuals united in viewing the same trashy image—it looks impossible for television to be a private matter. It's a major factor in subverting the cultural context in which many of us would prefer to live.

What to do about it that doesn't entail a sincere Green dictatorship isn't immediately obvious. Here and there, communities are having TV fasts—"Tune-Outs," weeks during which everyone's encouraged to leave the television off and investigate other entertainments, like conversation or visiting. Neither individual abstinence nor state sanction but community consensus may be the best approach toward paring away megatechnologies and restoring self-reliance.

The Baers and Baldwins of this world are dealing concretely with specific problems of technology, also with real concern for the common weal. Their criticism of technology helps hone a keener argument and keeps before us the question of reform: Are there megatechnologies and developments that must be accepted? Can they somehow be subjected to democratic control?

Hazel Henderson, a futurist, author, and global citizen-activist, was one of the contributors to "Technology: Over the Invisible Line?" By 1980, Hazel had pioneered the ideas of corporate responsibility and public assessment of technology, enthusiastically promoted an epochal shift to solar energy, and was evolving more-meaningful-than-economic standards for assessing a country's well-being. The paper she sent to the conference, titled "Science and Technology: The Revolution from Hardware to Software," included a prototypical set of questions that would echo forward to our systemic technological assessment. Following are "Hazel Henderson's Questions":*

1. Is it labor intensive, rather than capital- and energy-intensive?
2. How much capital is required to create each workplace?
3. Does it dislocate settled communities and cultural patterns, and if so, at what social cost?

*Published in *Technological Forecasting and Social Change*, 12, 317–324 (1978).

4. Is it based on renewable or exhaustible resource utilization?
5. Does it increase or decrease societal flexibility?
6. Is it centralizing or decentralizing?
7. Does it increase human liberty and widen the distribution of power, knowledge, and wealth in societies or concentrate them?
8. Does it embody multidisciplinary thinking and global interactions, or is it parochial and one-dimensional?
9. Does it favor self-reliance or create further dependency on large institutions?
10. Does it make maximum use of existing infrastructure, or will it entail costly or duplicative infrastructure?
11. Are its cost, benefits, and risks equally borne by all groups in society, and if not, who will be the winners and who the losers?
12. What risks does it pose to workers, consumers, society at large, or future generations, and can they be assessed by current probability calculations?
13. If it is irreversible and poses massive intergenerational transfers of risk (e.g., breeder-reactor technology), it should be assumed socially unacceptable until proven otherwise.

Like Jerry Mander, Hazel Henderson has been a longtime friend. We first met in 1969 as members of a Citizens Council for Public Broadcasting, whose purpose was to defend public broadcasting from funding cuts (*plus ça change . . .*) and have stayed in touch ever since.

Not long ago, telephone lines connected Hazel in St. Augustine with me in Maple City, making possible one of our semi-annual long-distance visits. I mentioned working on this book and told her a bit about the conferences' sweeping critique of technology and economic globalization. As our chat progressed, Hazel, in a passing remark, included me in the category of "globalist."

"I'm not so sure I'm a globalist," I said. Like Wendell Berry—who says, "Properly speaking, global thinking is not possible" —I know that I have no wisdom applicable to affairs at that scale. Hazel remonstrated with me a little, arguing that to ignore the global is to default concern with that level of society to the tender mercies of the likes of the International Monetary Fund (IMF) and the transnational corporations. Non-globalists she referred to as "romantic localists."

I acknowledged the apparent necessity for local activists to use electronic networks. She agreed that such networks are vulnerable to rate hikes, surveillance, and, in the Third World, rudimentary problems like energy shortages or difficulty in obtaining or repairing the hardware. I also wondered to what extent reliance on these nearly instantaneous media would supplant older, cheaper modes of organizing like mail, pilgrimage, printing presses, pamphleteering, study groups, and oratory. We talked a little further. Hazel was impatient with advocates of the abolition of television, defying them (or me) to propose a plausible scenario whereby such a thing might be accomplished. She spoke out loud another one of the kinds of questions that have quietly piqued me throughout this project, in fact throughout my career as an ecologist. If we mount a critique, are we obliged to follow with a campaign? Or can there be, as Hazel herself once nicely put it, "different roles for different souls?" The brief of these conferences was not merely to stake out the frontiers of technology criticism, thereby making all the other activists look reasonable and realistic, but to state the depth and urgency, for our species among others, of the problem of technology.

It occurred to me that one thing remarkable about the Megatechnology conferences of the nineties was the variety and quantity of megatechnology that we didn't mention (which is less a reflection of our lack of comprehensiveness than of the encompassing scope of the subject). We didn't talk much about synthetic chemicals and their hormone-disrupting effects on vertebrates (including us) throughout the biosphere. Heavy equipment is another monstrous technology. Its politics is almost always violence to terrain: earth movers, steamrollers, backhoes, road graders, all of the juggernauts on up to the monstrous draglines used in stripping coal, with buckets large enough to accommodate a couple of pickup trucks. These machines, whose development was spurred by world wars, are no more neutral than land mines. Many of these behemoths are integral to roadbuilding, and, as the ecological evidence increasingly shows, roads are a technology that fragments landscapes, massacres wildlife (causing fatalities in the millions), and invites abuse into previously undisturbed terrain, to say nothing of serving as the subsidized sinew of commerce.

It was not our aim, however, to make a full catalogue of catastrophic technologies, but to adduce some analytical principles from a specimen handful of current brainstorms, like biotechnology, that threaten an irrevocable distortion of, and traffic in, life itself.

ʊ ♀ ♪

At times I thought we conferees were like the blind groping to describe the elephant, as in the Sufi tale. Is technology only devices? If technology—or technique, to use Ellul's term—transcends machines, how encompassing is it? Are megatechnology and the global market one system? Is the technologized life just the terminal stages of a Cartesian-Baconian brain fever, reductionism materialized as sterile excess? Where to draw the line—visible or invisible—around the problem of technology? Excess cerebration may be an occupational hazard of the technology critic. It is for this one, anyway. My biocomputer has been known to crash. Conscious attention to the physical necessities of everyday life is a good corrective, but still can spawn conundrums.

Here in northern Michigan and in most of eastern North America the winter of '95 was the longest and coldest in a decade. Deep snows blanketed the ground from November through April. I heat my home with wood and was unprepared for the winter's severity or duration. By February it looked like I might not have enough firewood to make it through to spring. A little late, this physical necessity got my attention. If, lacking wood, I resort to the electric heater, the bills outrun my budget and I wind up with acid rain and radwaste on my conscience.

None of it is abstract in the least. My nouveau-woodsy comfort seeking is a low-tech but real form of what Chellis Glendinning calls "technological encasement." There's a sense in which, as Godfrey Reggio says, "I don't use technology: I live technology." In a climate with serious winter, living technology is where it's at: Woodstoves, heavy rubber and leather boots, and synthetic fleece are technology, as are double-glazed windows and fiberglass insulation, neither of which is readily produced by cottage industries. Another Luddite hoisted by her own petard.

This private struggle for authenticity, for simplicity and integrity, really comes down to a question of how we spend our time, how we think we can or should spend our time. How specialized are our occupations? How much labor saving do we think we need? What virtues or evils do those choices feed? Beth Burrows's plaint, "The more I advocate for the splendor of the Earth, the more my garden dries up," is my experience, too. The more I confer, write, speak, volunteer, and edit, the less I dig in the dirt.

My friends nearby, Rod and Sarah, living off the grid, do find time to tend their food garden, can, knit, craft their house, earn some cash, and as citizens try to defend such integrities of landscape as remain in this neck of the woods. It's hopeful work. It entails no small amount of ingenuity, resourcefulness, and—technology—pulleys to lower their perishables into a cold storage well under their "domestead"—a geodesic tent on a wooden platform, a telephone, the indispensable kerosene technology of the Aladdin lamp. Although Sarah drives to her waitressing job in a car, she and Rod are headed for a world somewhat different from that anticipated by J. Baldwin, the Lovinses, and Hazel Henderson. They live the way they do as the most meaningful possible strategy to achieve a car-less, TV-less, nuke-less future, a reality that is not merely virtual.

Far from being eccentric, these friends of mine are right in line with the human continuum. Our experience has always included tools, *ritual technologies*—to invoke Frédérique Apffel-Marglin's eloquent formulation. Domestic necessity spurred technological development, and for millennia tools were fraught with craft and relationship to place, qualities that are nearly extinct in today's artifacts.

Following the 1994 conference at Dartington Hall, I visited the Pitt-Rivers ethnographic museum in Oxford. A Victorian creation, the museum houses many thousands of superb objects taken from traditional peoples everywhere in the world. These are exhibited in dense, comparative displays. The collections date from the time British explorers sailed the Seven Seas to expand the merchant empire. Some of the items showcased had been gathered by the naturalists on Cook's voyages. Instead of being arranged geographically, the artifacts were grouped by type. Thus there was a case containing medical implements from every continent, another with a wild variety of monies, and another showing baby carriers from tribes living everywhere from the Sonoran desert to Siberia. There were displays of forges, measuring devices, footgear for snow and ice, musical instruments, plows, and weapons, each version quite different yet akin to the others by virtue of its function. The museum comprised a phenomenal testament to the adaptive inventiveness of myriad "primitive" cultures. Each object was made of the materials that came to hand in the particular environments where their makers worked and dwelled—wood, bone, rushes, leather, stone, earthen pigments, and metal, very sparingly used. Glass for a sharp edge or sparkle. Shells and feathers for jewelry. Clay for containers and images of divinity. Cloth woven on dozens of different kinds of looms, countless patterns of fabrics.

It was a vivid array of articles that have for millennia been deemed fundamental to human life: children's toys; weapons, needless to say; masks for sacred drama; implements for tilling the soil, for cutting wood, for writing, for making music. The ways that different cultures devised the tools to meet those needs were endless, artful, and place specific. In that fabulous museum, technology—for once—made me hopeful and happy to be a member of such a clever species, with such widespread mastery of skillful means. It also made more poignant one conclusion of our conferences—that the time and memory and desire necessary to such vernacular "industry" is being blown away by mass production, mass communication, and mass markets.

The thousand languages that had the exact words for explaining the people's way of carving, basketry, sewing, and spinning have fewer and fewer speakers, and the silence they leave is deafening. Yet all those elegant "primitive" creations declared the innate human capacity to respond wisely, carefully, and beautifully to the demands of Nature and culture. That genius, our birthright, may yet be reclaimed.

Editor's Note

What follows is an extremely condensed version of the transcripts of these two historic conferences. There were, in all, nearly forty hours of discussion among a total of more than fifty participants.

Without the support of the Foundation for Deep Ecology, neither the conferences nor the preparation of this book would have been possible. Jerry Mander and Helena Norberg-Hodge were principal organizers of the 1993 conference. In organizing the 1994 conference they were joined by Satish Kumar and Teddy Goldsmith. The organizers were ably assisted throughout by the staff of the Foundation for Deep Ecology.

Transcribing is labor and intelligence intensive. Credit for turning speech into the text that was the basis of this book is due to Maria Gilardin, director of TUC Radio in San Francisco, who recorded and transcribed the 1993 conference, and Vicky Matthews, a colleague of Satish Kumar, who transcribed the 1994 conference. Their work amounted to 750 pages of dazzling conversation, which had to be abbreviated by half.

It grieved me to cut as much as I did. The participants kindly reviewed the edited versions of their remarks. Some simply signed off on them, others rewrote extensively.

When the final deadline came, it was necessary to cut even further, and this has resulted in a changed sequence of comments in some places. It also means that not every participant is represented in these pages. Now missing from these proceedings are sessions held at both conferences on the subjects of development, colonialism, and trade agreements. Happily, there is a superb book on these matters, with a number of Megatechnology conference participants among the contributors. It is *The Case Against the Global Economy and for a Turn Toward the Local*, edited by Jerry Mander and Edward (Teddy) Goldsmith and published by Sierra Club Books.

Finally, a note on the format of the conferences: Every session, save for the two concluding discussions, began with a series of statements or a briefing on a particular subject by two or more "panelists." An open colloquy among all the participants completed each session. People with comments were recognized by the chair and would take their place in line. When called on, they had just two minutes to make their points. This resulted not in direct dialogue so much as a mosaic of ideas prompted by the different topics and remarks of others.

The Participants

FRÉDÉRIQUE APFFEL-MARGLIN: Professor of Anthropology, Coordinator of the Centers for Mutual Learning, Smith College; activist; author; co-editor of and contributor to *Dominating Knowledge: Development, Culture and Resistance* and *Who Will Save the Forests?*

WENDELL BERRY: Farmer, poet, author, self-employed advisor to several agricultural economists. His many books include *The Unsettling of America, A Continuous Harmony: Essays Cultural and Agricultural, The Gift of Good Land,* and *What Are People For?*

PAUL BLAU: Scholar, editor, diplomat, union officer, scientist, activist; past president of ECOROPA; author of *The Destroyed Joy of Work.*

CHET BOWERS: Professor of education, Portland State University; author of numerous books, including *The Culture of Denial: Why the Environmental Movement Needs a Strategy for the Reform of Universities and Public Schools* and *Educating for an Ecologically Sustainable Culture: Rethinking Moral Education, Creativity, Intelligence, and Other Modern Orthodoxies.*

BETH BURROWS: President and director, Edmonds Institute; past president of the Washington Biotechnology Action Council; member, Biotechnology Working Group; organizer, writer, lecturer on trade and biotechnology issues; Master Gardener, Master Composter/Recycler.

FRITJOF CAPRA: Physicist, systems theorist; founder and president, Elmwood Institute; author of *The Turning Point, Uncommon Wisdom: Conversations with Remarkable People,* and *The Tao of Physics.*

CLIFFORD COBB: Senior Fellow, Redefining Progress; advocate of alternative indices of progress; co-developer of the Index of Sustainable Economic Welfare.

MARTHA CROUCH: Associate Professor of Biology at Indiana University; deprofessionalized biotechnologist; leading critic of the scientific method and of the new biotechnologies; author of "Biotechnology Is Not Compatible with Sustainable Agriculture," published in the *Journal of Agricultural and Environmental Ethics*.

JOHN DAVIS: Wilderness activist, writer, editor of *Wild Earth*; board member, The Wildlands Project; guardian, the Hemlock Rock Wildlife Sanctuary.

RICHARD DOUTHWAITE: Journalist, economist, manufacturer, author of *The Growth Illusion* and *Short Circuit: Strengthening Local Economies for Security in an Unstable World*.

GUSTAVO ESTEVA: Deprofessionalized intellectual; served in the Mexican ministry of planning; Chairman, ANADEGES (Analysis, Decentralism, and Gestion); advisor, Ejército Zapatisa de Liberación National; author of numerous books and articles.

PER GAHRTON: Activist; founding member of Sweden's Green Party; member, Parliament of the European Union; author, journalist, regular contributor to *Dagens Nyhetter*.

CHELLIS GLENDINNING: Psychologist and social thinker; author of "Notes Toward a Neo-Luddite Manifesto" and three books, including *My Name Is Chellis and I'm in Recovery from Western Civilization* and *When Technology Wounds*, a Pulitzer Prize nominee; board member, Earth Island Institute and Earth Trust Foundation.

EDWARD "TEDDY" GOLDSMITH: Campaigner, Green Party candidate; founding editor, *The Ecologist*; author of numerous books, including *The Way: An Ecological World View*; co-editor (with Jerry Mander) of *The Case Against the Global Economy*; winner of the 1991 Right Livelihood Award, Chevalier de la Légion d'Honneur.

SUSAN GRIFFIN: Teacher, playwright, poet, author; MacArthur Fellow; her books include *Woman and Nature: The Roaring Inside Her* and *A Chorus of Stones: The Private Life of War*.

ELISABET HERMODSSON: Writer, artist, songwriter; author of numerous books; recipient of the *Litteris et Artibus* Royal Medal.

SANDY IRVINE: Environmental Policy Officer and Lecturer in Media Studies, City of Sunderland College; author of *Beyond Green Consumerism*; co-author of *A Green Manifesto*; editor of *Real World*; associate editor of *The Ecologist*.

MARTIN KHOR: Political economist; author of numerous articles and books; activist; president of the Third World Network; director, Asia

Pacific People's Network; research director, Consumers Association of Penang; editor and contributor to *Third World Resurgence* and *Third World Economics* magazines.

ANDREW KIMBRELL: Public-interest attorney; founder, International Center for Technology Assessment, Jacques Ellul Society; former program director, Foundation on Economic Trends; author, *The Human Body Shop: The Engineering and Marketing of Life* and *The Masculine Mystique*.

DAVID KORTEN: Teacher, writer, consultant on development, management, and alternative development theory; founder and president of People-Centered Development Forum; author of *Getting to the 21st Century: Voluntary Action and the Global Agenda* and *When Corporations Rule the World*.

SATISH KUMAR: Editor, *Resurgence*; Director of Programmes, Schumacher College; founder of The Small School; author, *No Destination: An Autobiography*.

SIGMUND KVALOY: Farmer, philosopher, leader of the successful Norwegian campaign to stay out of the European Union; founder, Ecophilosophy Department, University of Oslo; founder and director, Setreng Institute of Ecophilosophy; author of *EcoCrisis, Nature, and Man*.

JOHN LANE: Trustee of the Dartington Hall Trust; painter; author of a number of books, including *The Living Tree: Art and the Sacred* and *A Snake's Tail Full of Ants: Art, Ecology, and Consciousness*.

KAIULANI LEE: Actress; author, *A Sense of Wonder: A Play Based on the Life and Works of Rachel Carson*; winner, OBIE Award for outstanding achievement off-Broadway.

JERRY MANDER: Senior Fellow at Public Media Center; program director, Foundation for Deep Ecology; acting chair, International Forum on Globalization; author, *Four Arguments for the Elimination of Television* and *In the Absence of the Sacred: The Failure of Technology and the Survival of the Indian Nations*; co-editor (with Edward Goldsmith), *The Case Against the Global Economy*.

ANDREW MCLAUGHLIN: Activist; professor of philosophy at Lehman College, City University of New York; board member, Orange County Land Trust, Sterling Forest Resources; author of *Regarding Nature: Industrialism and Deep Ecology*.

RALPH METZNER: Ecopsychologist; psychotherapist; professor of psychology, California Institute of Integral Studies; co-founder and president, Green Earth Foundation; author of several books, including *The Well of Remembrance*.

MARIA MIES: Sociologist, ecofeminist; professor of sociology (retired),

Fachhoch-Schule Köln; co-founder, feminist organizations and journals; lecturer; member, Feminist International Network of Resistance
to Reproductive and Genetic Engineering (FINRRAGE); author of
many articles and books, including *Ecofeminism* (with Vandana
Shiva); *Indian Women and Patriarchy*; *The Lace Makers of Narsapur*.

STEPHANIE MILLS: Writer, editor, lecturer; organizer, Great Lakes Bioregional Congress; author of *Whatever Happened to Ecology?* and *In Service of the Wild: Restoring and Reinhabiting Damaged Land*.

JOHN MOHAWK: Seneca Indian activist, philosopher; assistant professor
in American Studies at SUNY Buffalo; editor, *Daybreak*; former editor,
Akwesasne Notes; principal author, *A Basic Call to Consciousness: The
Iroquois Confederacy Statement to the Modern World*; editor, *Exile in the
Land of the Free: Democracy, Indian Nations, and the U.S. Constitution*.

ASHIS NANDY: Psychologist, social theorist; director, Centre for the
Study of Developing Societies; author of many books, including *Traditions, Tyranny and Utopias: Essays in the Politics of Awareness*.

HELENA NORBERG-HODGE: Philosopher, activist, teacher, linguist; director of the International Society for Ecology and Culture; co-director, International Forum on Globalization-Europe; author, *Ancient
Futures: Learning from Ladakh*; co-author, *The Future of Progress* and
From the Ground Up.

GODFREY REGGIO: President, Institute for Regional Education; filmmaker whose works include *Koyaanisqatsi (Life Out of Balance)* and
Powaqqatsi (Life in Transformation).

JEREMY RIFKIN: President, Foundation on Economic Trends; activist,
social critic; author of many books, including *Biosphere Politics* and
The End of Work.

KIRKPATRICK SALE: Co-director, E. F. Schumacher Society; founder, New
York Green Party; author of many books, including *Rebels Against the
Future: The Luddites, and Their War on the Industrial Revolution—Lessons
for the Computer Age*.

MICHIEL SCHWARZ: Researcher on cultural and political analysis of technology, technology assessment, and social debates on technology;
consultant to founding director of Foundation 567.

RICHARD SCLOVE: Director, Public Interest Technology Policy Project;
executive director, Loka Institute; author, *Democracy and Technology*.

GEORGE SESSIONS: Chairman, Philosophy Department, Sierra College;
ecophilosopher, mountaineer, activist; author, *Deep Ecology for the
21st Century*; co-author, *Deep Ecology: Living as if Nature Mattered*.

VANDANA SHIVA: Physicist, philosopher of science; activist, Chipko

Movement; founder and director, Research Foundation for Science, Technology and Resource Policy; author of several books, including *Monocultures of the Mind*; *Biotechnology and the Environment*; *Staying Alive: Women, Ecology, and Development*; winner of the 1993 Right Livelihood Award.

SULAK SIVARAKSA: Activist, social thinker, critic of the "religion of consumerism"; founder of the International Network for Engaged Buddhists; winner of the 1995 Right Livelihood Award; author of several books, including *Seeds of Peace*.

CHARLENE SPRETNAK: Ecofeminist philosopher; co-founder, Green Politics Movement (U.S.); California Green party activist; author of several books, including *States of Grace: The Recovery of Meaning in the Postmodern Age* and *The Resurgence of the Real: Body, Nature, and Place in a Hypermodern World*.

DAVID SUZUKI: Chairman, The David Suzuki Foundation; author (with Peter Knudtson) of *Wisdom of the Elders, Time to Change, The Japan You Never See*.

DOUG TOMPKINS: Mountaineer, kayaker, entrepreneur, environmental activist; founder and president, Foundation for Deep Ecology.

JAN VAN BOECKEL: Scholar, filmmaker, anthropologist; human-rights activist; staff member, Netherlands Centre for Indigenous Peoples; board member, Dutch Innu Support Group; co-producer, *The Earth Is Crying, Betrayal by Technology, It Is Killing the Clouds*, and *Reveal to Survive*; producer, *Questions on Europe*.

LANGDON WINNER: Professor of Political Science, Rensselaer Polytechnic Institute; past president, Society for Philosophy and Technology; author, *Autonomous Technology, The Whale and the Reactor: A Search for Limits in an Age of High Technology*; editor, *Democracy in a Technological Society*.

TRACEY WORCESTER: Leading activist for organic farming and sustainable agriculture in the United Kingdom; member, The Council of the Soil Association; trustee of Friends of the Earth, Transport 2000, E. F. Schumacher Society, and the Gaia Foundation.

Megatechnology and Development

⊘ San Francisco, 1993

As this part's title suggests, the concern of the 1993 meeting was mega-technology. "We are facing a condition of extreme technological excess," wrote Jerry Mander and Helena Norberg-Hodge in their invitation to the conference.

"The forms of technology that are upon us have evolved to a point where they are now of global scale and impact," they wrote. "They interlock with one another forming yet a more powerful global creature. We may call this megatechnology: computers, television, satellites, lasers, space technology, high-speed travel, agribusiness, combined with the institutional forms that are compatible with them—transnational corporations, trade agreements, dominant political powers, massive military technologies—also combined with the monolithic ideologies of growth, massification, exploitation of nature, superiority of the western world view, and superiority of human beings over all other life."

The coming together of all of these elements, material and ideological, into an inescapable system was described as the gravest threat, a "machine that exploits and kills cultures, nations, and nature."

Whether or not the participants were in entire agreement, they shared this sense of gravity, and devoted themselves, for the next two days, to describing this machine, its schema, its workings, and its effects.

Chapter 1

Opening Remarks

◉ DOUG TOMPKINS, *president of the Foundation for Deep Ecology, now living in a remote spot on the Chilean coast, welcomes the participants to the conference held May 22 and 23, 1993, in a residence atop Russian Hill in San Francisco. The room where we meet is open to the north, with its view of the Bay, Alcatraz Island, and the Marin shore opposite, and to the east, where there is a pleasant garden. Tompkins mentions his delight at witnessing the first encounters taking place at the meeting.* He says, "This meeting will have historical significance if it can raise the level of debate and create a voice of technology criticism," *and launches the beginning round of statements by the organizers and participants.*

Longtime San Franciscan JERRY MANDER *begins*: Many of you know that my book, *In the Absence of the Sacred*, argues that technological society has failed. The dream of a technotopian future of leisure, comfort, happiness, security, pleasure, abundance, wealth, prosperity, no work, all play, no death, and no disease has not materialized. It was an advertising fantasy meant to accelerate consumption and the proliferation of technology and to move us all more deeply into the commodity system. But instead of bringing a technotopia, technological society has brought alienation, frustration, distress, suicide, drug abuse, abusive relationships, and family breakup. In the death of the oceans, the pollution of air, water and soils; in the extinction of species, the loss of biodiversity, and the loss of forests; in global warming, ozone layer breakdown, and acid rain, we see that technological society has brought us to the brink of the breakdown of the natural world. It is now time to call technological society a failure and to begin trying something else.

⊘JERRY MANDER *talks about campaigns he's worked on at The Public Media Center, battling industrial forestry, the James Bay Hydro Projects in Quebec, the Narmada Dam in India, and various biotechnology issues:* Lately, I've been involved in battles against trade agreements which are, after all, only the international organizing mechanisms that work with technological society—its system of delivery and control. In fact all of the so-called environmental issues I've campaigned on as an activist over the years are truly consequences of technological excess. They are not identified as such. Yet megatechnology is a system with its own ideology. It's important to name the beast by its proper name and to argue and organize and work against it.

⊘HELENA NORBERG-HODGE, *a Swede with ties to several lands, begins by saying that she sees the system tightening down, with a dramatic shift toward reductionism. Nevertheless, she sees all of this as putting a group like ours on the side of the majority of humanity for the first time in history:* We are seeing an increasing polarization in society; the gap between government and industry—the institutions of power—and the rest of the population is widening. In virtually every country there's been a tightening up of the dominant view both in the media—all the major newspapers—and in academia. I see a dramatic shift toward ever greater reductionism and a marginalization of the broader holistic perspective which is a prerequisite for understanding the complex relationships between the economy, society, and ecology. At most universities, whether in Stockholm or Berkeley, biologists are increasingly being turned into biotechnologists; plant biology, agroforestry, and other such subjects are disappearing from the curriculum; the geography departments are being closed down.

With industry and government working closely together to further growth, the system is poised to take an enormous leap toward globalization that, if it succeeds, will lead to an enormous increase in unemployment, crime, racism, and environmental breakdown, and just about strangle everything that lives. We can also see that it has become so top-heavy that it may collapse under its own weight. An understanding that the breakdown of community and of natural systems today is the consequence of an interaction among Western science, technology, and economic growth is urgently needed.

People are so attached to science, the world view that gives rise to "megatechnologies." These technologies often masquerade as small, clean, and "decentralized" even though they are part of systems that are highly centralized and polluting. We need to look then at technology, but always also come back to look at its father, which is science.

It's vital that we also understand the economic paradigm, which, together with technological innovation, constitutes what we call "development" in the South and "progress" in the North. What's so frightening is that most people have a completely passive view of progress. There is a sense that you can't stop progress. It's seen as an evolutionary force. So we are dealing with a world view today which passively regards megatechnology and ever greater globalization as an inevitable evolution. People interpret the changes that have been wrought by technology as part of the cycles of change that are life. They don't distinguish between the changes that are the consequence of policy and funding and the changes that are the consequence of life processes.

When people in the North ask me, "Why on Earth is it that traditional peoples like the Ladakhis—if they were so healthy and had such a wonderful, happy society, and a balance with the land—are rushing for this modern culture?" It's seen as a sign of the frailty of such cultures, a sign that they must have been miserable after all since they seem to be looking for a new, innovative, free culture. People forget that in many, perhaps most, cases these cultures were subjected to forceful missionaries, to colonialists who literally held guns to their heads, and yet they didn't abandon their cultures. Missionaries came to Ladakh and worked for generations and had no impact on the mainstream culture. They managed to convert a couple of orphans.

What is rarely recognized is that modern technology is responsible for this breakdown. Of course the issue is more complex, but the seeming superiority and power of technology create a sense of insecurity and inadequacy that then produces the desire to associate with the modern world. This insecurity makes the young very vulnerable to the pressures of the global consumer—culture which exhorts them to leave rural communities in search of an urban, modern, consumer lifestyle. In addition, the incredible magic of modern technology, the speed of racing through the countryside on a motorcycle, appeals to the young, particularly to teenage boys. Around the world, the teenage boy is the link that breaks the culture.

The North-South divide is shifting very quickly. The transnational corporation is the institution that is promoting this development, which is leading to a technologization of the world. It's now a global system tightening its links. I'm shocked at how little corporations are discussed, seen, or noticed. Perhaps it's because we've almost all grown dependent on them. When we make visible the invisible hand of the corporation, we'll see that, as Teddy Goldsmith said, "For the first time in twenty-five years we're on the side of the majority." To that I would add, "The problem is that the majority doesn't yet know that." Yet we *are* on the side of the majority because right now in the North the corporations are dropping labor—people who are completely dependent on employment for survival and identity—to rush to the other side of the world where labor is cheaper to pull people into sweatshops. In the South, community, culture, and more sustainable, diversified local economic systems are destroyed. Of the thousands who leave these rural, local economies in search of employment in the global marketplace, only a tiny fraction get a job, so in the South unemployment rises, too.

⊘ Whereas others in the group have their qualms about doing so, Kentuckian WENDELL BERRY *unhesitatingly labels himself a Luddite. He differs with Helena on the notion that a perhaps unselfconscious-as-yet majority might be in agreement with this broad critique:* I'm a Luddite, not a Neo-Luddite. I've always been a Luddite. Where the issue is between the machine and the community, you choose the community. I think that to the extent you're able you have to get out of this larger industrial economy. You have to articulate and make the difference first of all between yourself and it, and then between your household and it, and then if possible between your community and it. If your community articulated and made the difference between itself and this other economy, if it made itself a local economy to some extent, then you'd have a real start.

As far as I can see the majority is not on our side. We're a small minority and we are losing. What we have to do may be impossible, and that makes no difference at all. Win or lose, our task is to work toward a less destructive economy.

⊘ WENDELL BERRY *observes that this meeting* "couldn't have taken place without the help of the thing we are against to start," *and finds intolerable, but possibly ineluctable, the implication that intellectual discussions like ours will be to the benefit of the other side.*

⊘ Austrian-Berkeleyite FRITJOF CAPRA *sees in the present condition a void of meaning, a state of "ecological illiteracy," and a delusion of mechanism:* What we need more than anything else in this fight against megatechnologies is imagination and creativity. The Elmwood Institute, which I founded, focused on ecological literacy, which we defined as consisting of three components: knowledge of the principles of ecology, understanding the language of nature, thus literacy; systemic, contextual, or ecological thinking; and the practice of ecological values. Ecological literacy thus defined is the antithesis to the megatechnological society. Deep Ecology, as Arne Naess has put it, urges us to ask deeper questions.

Megatechnology tries to prevent us from asking deeper questions. The megatechnology society believes that there is a technological solution to every problem. This would be correct only if the world were a machine.

Ecological thinking is contextual thinking, and context is meaning. If you can put things into a larger context then you give them meaning. The megatechnological society is devoid of meaning. There is an absence of the sacred. This is in antithesis to Deep Ecology, which provides content and meaning.

⊘MARTHA CROUCH, *who renounced a brilliant career in biotechnology, focuses in her remarks on the necessity to make alternatives to dependence on megatechnology more tangible; she speaks from her own experience of setting up a largely self-reliant Hoosier household:* These old Amish quilts remind me that there are people who have actively chosen what kinds of technologies to live with. You'll notice that the fabric in these quilts doesn't have any pattern in it. The idea was that patterns and buttons were showy, a kind of conceit. But look at the beauty they created with plain, colored fabric!

I'm a reformed genetic engineer. I was a success story of the post-Sputnik era. I grew up in the time when new math was coming into the schools, when the National Science Foundation was established to try and get young people, young women in particular, and other "diverse voices" into the scientific enterprise.

I was always interested in flowers. Through this post-Sputnik encouragement and direct training program I decided that the way to pursue my interest in flowers was to become a botanist. I ended up using molecular biology to study flowers, and doing genetic engineering on flowers.

In the last few years something happened that lifted the veil. I saw that through my inquiry I was contributing directly to the destruction of the things that I love. This had been obscured in my scientific profession. My original love of life, particularly of flowers, had been turned into the torture of flowers. When I recognized that, I had to give up my research career. I quit at a fortuitous time. I was at a point in my career where I was quite visible. I was on grant panels, running conferences, interacting at the levels of policymaking in plant molecular biology, and consulting for companies like Unilever and Calgene. So I was able to use this conversion experience, this reformation, as a standpoint for talking about the issues of technology to an audience that is pretty refractive. I have been invited into places like Purdue and Iowa State, and I can talk to agronomy and science students in a language familiar to them. Before I'm marginalized to the point where I'm not invited anymore I'm trying to use that position for all it's worth. I've been talking as a heretic to former colleagues and to students, hoping that they'll hear me and that some of the students will change course before they find themselves in a position similar to that I found myself in.

One of the things that I discovered in talking to people in the sciences and in ag schools is that although they can be brought to the point of seeing the problems with the enterprise they are involved in, they have no plausible basis for alternatives. They have never grown their own food. They may be botanists, but if they walked out in the forest many of them would not know the trees. People in general are so disconnected from any alternative vision of how to live, and so dependent on the industrial technologies, that the thought that there may be a severe problem with those technologies is genuinely terrifying. Until there is some way of making alternatives concrete, I don't think many people are going to be willing to see the depth of the problem.

In my own community I'm working on simple things like setting up our households so that they are as independent as possible from industrial processes and corporations. It's a powerful thing if people can come over to your house and see that you and several other people in the community are growing most of your own food and having fun doing it.

⊘JOHN DAVIS, *a denizen of the Adirondacks, observes that very few environmentalists as yet are questioning technology itself, or even acknowledging that certain technologies may not be reformable. He goes on to make a fairly stark statement about what we must do, if biodiversity is to be saved:* In my opinion wilderness is incompatible with industrial society. We need to dismantle industrial civilization if we are serious about saving biodiversity on a large scale. An effort to make most of the continent wild again necessitates radical fundamental changes in society.

⊘ *Then Davis alludes to the North American Wilderness Recovery Strategy (the Wildlands Project, for short), which, based on the axioms of conservation biology, would establish and link ecosystem reserves across the continent as absolutely essential to preserving its biodiversity.*

Shifting the topic to the politics of globalization, PER GAHRTON *speaks from his experience as a member of Sweden's parliament and a Green activist, speculating that the European Economic Community (EEC) is destined to become a superpower. He mentions that other Green members of other parliaments, and even broad majorities in some nations, such as Denmark, opposed entry into the EEC:* I'm mainly preoccupied with fighting the plans to create a big power in Western Europe, the European Union. The Danish referendum was a distressing show of the arrogance of power. The Danish people voted no last year. That was not accepted by the government. The proponents have been manipulating for one full year and finally succeeded in having a yes vote. The ideology behind this plan to create a Western European superpower with nuclear power and nuclear arms, et cetera, is to fight with the U.S. and Japan in order to dominate the world. Most people don't know that most Greens in the European community are against this project. In Belgium the Greens voted against the Maastricht Treaty in Parliament. The Green group in the European Parliament also voted against this project. It has nothing to do with nationalism; it's a very deeply ideological question.

As a sociologist I was never a Marxist, but I believe very much in the basic truth of dialectics. I returned to Parliament as a Green in 1988, and we proved correctly that there was no power to be found in Parliament. We were also thrown out by the voters in the next election.

I have been active in the European Greens; maybe something can still be found in political parties. There are now twenty-six Green parties that are members of the European Greens; there are ten new Eastern European parties. So it's a pretty big organization. There are parliamentarians in many countries—Brazil has one, as do Georgia, Azerbaijan, and Armenia in Eastern Europe. A planetary Green structure is now emerging. It's weak, of course. Although I have my doubts about parliamentary politics, I'm very active in this organization.

My latest book is called *Let Grandmother Decide the 21st Century*. I discuss the modern versions of the seven deadly sins: technologism and biologism and capitalism, urbanism, communism, colonialism, and militarism. Who is behind all these evils, not for the last 200 years but the last 10,000 years? Of course men are behind it, male men, 99.99 percent of the culprits are men. But I find it's not all men; not the family fathers probably, nor those who have a stable life, the men who stay on in their small societies, but probably the frustrated younger brothers, the ones who didn't inherit the farm, the bachelors who have to set out to find a new kingdom and marry the princess. They're the expansionists, creating new societies, new villages, inventing and developing things. Thus my hypothesis: If the bachelor is the type responsible for the mess we find ourselves in, who is the bachelor's opposite? Grandma. I haven't tested it thoroughly, but it might not be so bad to speculate about a society ruled by the values and visions of grandmothers.

⊘ *After summarizing a Swedish sociological study of power elites,* PER GAHRTON *remarks,* "Politicians nowadays mainly adapt to what scientists and business have created."

⊘ CHELLIS GLENDINNING, *who lives in the village of Chimayó in northern*

New Mexico, laments the lack of a language to bring to a systemic analysis of technology. As a psychologist, she diagnoses those of us in Western civilization as suffering from post-traumatic stress disorder. One symptom, she notes, is the widespread tendency toward dissociation expressed in bizarre attitudes like "you create your own reality": When my second book, *When Technology Wounds,* came out in 1990, I was asked to go on a radio program with Marvin Minsky of MIT, one of the primary founders of artificial intelligence. The people at National Public Radio assured me that Minsky was a very nice man, and that it would be a delightful conversation. "Neo-Luddism Is Sweeping North America" was the title of this whole show, which was about ten minutes long. When the program got underway, though, I quickly realized that I was the foil for what is called "good radio." In other words, they were making fun of me. Minsky was to be the serious interviewee with the reasonable ideas and the impeccable background; I was to be the questionable fringe thinker. I was disoriented, believe me! But I gathered myself and tried to deepen the conversation by bringing up questions of underlying values and making a systemic analysis. I don't think that Marvin Minsky or the radio guy got it.

At one point, the commentator asked me if I had any complaints about computers. I reeled off about six—from computerization's effects on society at large to the question of its primary beneficiaries. One of these complaints had to do with health effects. I had interviewed a group of workers from a GTE computer-manufacturing plant in Albuquerque. They were all sick, and one of their co-workers had died of cancer. Minsky's response to this problem was, "It doesn't matter." This was a sobering moment for technology analysis! It turns out that Minsky is one of these scientists who favors downloading all our minds' information onto computers so that human life will no longer be necessary.

I'm a psychologist. One of the great influences in my life has been Lewis Mumford, whose work taught me how to think in a systemic way. For years now, I have grappled with the predicament we face because we lack a language to further a systemic analysis of technology. Meanwhile, I am observing that if anything is "sweeping North America," it is confusion—confusion about what is happening to the human community, confusion that is manifesting itself in what we might call postmodern attitudes, what used to be called solipsism, that paltry little you-create-your-own-reality philosophy. I encounter this attempt to make sense of things a great deal these days. People just seem to be flailing about, trying to figure out what's real, and I think that what's missing for them is a full-bodied, big-view analysis of the technological world.

In my latest book, *My Name Is Chellis and I'm in Recovery from Western*

Civilization, I present the idea that we in the technological world are suffering from post-traumatic stress disorder (PTSD)—in both the readily identifiable personal ways, but also in collective ways. I believe that behind all the painful and widespread forms of PTSD rampant in society today lies an "original trauma": *our alienation from the natural world*. The symptoms of PTSD are so much a part of everyday life in the techno-world: hyperreaction, thinking disorders, psychic numbing, flashbacks, arrested development, denial, addiction. They're everywhere. Can you see it? The psychological construct of this affliction fits modern civilization to a T. It's not just that individuals are suffering, it's that the very structure of society and its institutions are manifesting these symptoms—and then passing on the inherent trauma of civilization to the next generations.

The baseline symptom that lies behind all the others is *dissociation*: psychic alienation, splitting and shutting down, freezing our awareness into an unassimilated state. This is what the individual psyche does when it faces an untenable situation—abuse, violence, social chaos, combat—that it cannot handle. Another of my heroes, Paul Shepard, points out the similarity between this process and what happened to humans in the West 10,000 years ago when we began to dissociate ourselves from our place in the natural world through domestication. According to Shepard, "wild things" became "enemies" of the new human-managed reality which was the "tame." Because survival was coming to be based less and less on a psychic openness to the natural world—more and more on control and rationality—fears, impulses, and dreams had no place for survival. They were driven deeper and deeper into the unconscious, and *voilà!* You get the same dissociation that occurs in individual trauma, only now widespread and collective.

My favorite encapsulation of this state of mind comes from Choctaw-Cree writer Gerald Haslam. He tells a story about a young Indian who has witnessed American soldiers wipe out his entire village and is about to be murdered himself. He has never seen such brutality in his life. Haslam writes about these final moments of realization: "Hawk found himself feeling a strange kind of pity for these hopeless creatures who possessed no magic at all, no union with Earth or sky, only the ability to hurt and kill. . . . They were sad and dangerous like a broken rattlesnake." This sadness, this brokenness—this is how I see people who have come up through the dominant society, who live in and believe in technological civilization.

I have tried to apply the insights of individual trauma recovery to our collective healing. The task is to knit our shattered selves and broken world back into the Whole. This certainly involves political protest, challenging corporations and government—but it is more complex. It involves remembering who we are; facing the trauma and our myriad losses; bringing to consciousness the story of our humanity, of our shattering, of how we have survived despite the worst of conditions; the story of our irrepressible strength and potential; the remembrance of sustainable, spiritual community.

ⵔ Swedish bard ELISABET HERMODSSON *talks about the Big Bang theory as being a technocratic creation myth and describes her lifelong resistance to, and protest against, positivistic science:* I am a writer and an artist and also a songwriter. As a writer I published about twenty books, most of them poetry, but also critical essays against the positivistic science, big science, also against new physics. I'm protesting against that big technological society and have been since the beginning of 1950. May I read the English translation of a poem that I wrote in the beginning of 1960?

> once upon a time
> we were to be pitied
> we were in mortal fear
> we believed in spirits, gnomes
> god and other kinds of superstition
> now we feel safe
> for we know everything
> control everything
> we have rational explanations
> for everything
> we make use of matter's minutest particle
> for our purposes
> and we are much to be pitied
> more than ever before
> never has space been closer
> never has responsibility been greater
> never have we known more fear
> and we do not believe in good or evil powers
> nor in gods and other superstitions
> we believe in ourselves
> and never has space been wider
> and never have we had greater power
> and never have we been more powerless
> we believe in progress
> and never has catastrophe been so close.

Herewith a short excerpt from ELISABET HERMODSSON's *paper "Man in the Modern Image of the World," which she wrote for the conference:* The progress of technology is proceeding with a furious speed and at the same pace nature is destroyed. Our knowledge of the dangers, our knowledge about everything, is increasing. But nothing happens that would radically change the course of events. Progress advances with a furious speed but is still on the same old spot.

The image of the world, as today pictured by all of humanity—if one were to map it out, maybe not even the smallest common denominator would resemble the one that is known as "the modern image of the world." Because on one hand there are still primitive societies left in the world which have a completely different view of the universe, and on the other hand there still exist even in our civilized societies a lot of people for whom modern science with quantum fluctuations, quarks, and fleeing galaxies simply is not a reality. Thus, you do have to ask yourself who has the right to decide about the formulation of the image of the world? Is it a question of education? Whose image of the world is the genuinely correct, whose image of the world is the most functional in the real needs of the world?

We still have different societies on this Earth which possess other images of the world than the scientific one, but our civilization is in the process of conquering all other societies and their image of the world. Is it because our image of the world is more accurate than all others, or is it because it got more money and political power to back it up?

In my critique against science I have concentrated on the leading principles. For example the idea of freedom from values, a smart idea that liberates scientists from responsibility, a nonethical attitude that makes it possible for scientists to do whatever they want without thinking about the consequences. Other ideas that I have criticized are the so-called objectivity: Science is objective when it says, for example, that nature's primary characteristics are only the measurable characteristics and not the qualities. The consequence is that science has demystified nature and taken the spirit away from the forest, from the lakes, from the mountains, changing all the poetical visions, all the poetical views of nature that other cultures have, and changing all the words into technical terms.

That scientific principle about finding the uttermost particle is also a very destructive idea that originates from the idea that the whole is the sum of the parts.

The Big Bang is a cosmological theory about the universe and says that all that exists has been born in an explosion twenty billion years ago. This theory has been accepted and is taught just as if it is the truth and proved. Of course it is not possible to prove it; it is used as a common language in scientist circles. Yet this Big Bang is the technocratic myth; it is the creation myth of the technocratic society.

⊚ELISABET HERMODSSON indicts the whole scientific enterprise, with its attendant supertechnology, that regards the Big Bang as axiomatic; she mentions the gigantism and destructiveness to surroundings of observatories and linear accelerators.

⊚Malaysian economist MARTIN KHOR addresses the socioeconomic forces abetting technological change. From his experience as a founder of the Third World Network, he stresses the value of linking struggles across national boundaries: Each socioeconomic system has its own laws and mechanisms that either stabilize it or drive it forward. Socioeconomic systems can interact with one another, penetrate each other, and either destroy each other or influence one another in particular ways. The study of the complex of relationships between the laws of socioeconomic systems and their results in terms of relations between people in terms of equity, marginalization, power, and domination led me to an understanding of the historical background and the geographical nature of the present world in which we live.

Particularly important are the relations between the colonized and colonizing countries, or what we now call the North-South relations, and also within particular societies in the South: the link between the modern economy and the local communities or the indigenous socioeconomic systems which are being reshaped and influenced by the modern economies within our societies. In our work with the nongovernmental organizations we found that many local communities are being affected by the destructive nature of imported technology. Fishing villages are being destroyed by trawler boats and by industrial pollution; indigenous people's forests are being taken away from them; and farmers are being evicted to make way for the urban industrial complex. These are two aspects of the same thing: the forces that have led into the world social crisis with increasing marginalization, poverty, and inequities on a North-South level as well as within our societies, and the destruction of the environment. Technology plays a role in these two different phenomena.

The Consumers Association of Penang, where I worked after teaching political economy at the university, was pioneering within the Third World in trying to link the issues of basic needs, consumer rights, and national social structures. In linking up with similar groups, particularly in the Third World, we realized that not only did we have to bring the level of our struggle from local communities to national macro policy, but that this national level was also parochial, in a sense, and we tackled the international structures and institutions which continue to be so much part of the problem.

At a meeting in 1984 of many groups, mainly from the developing countries, we founded the Third World Network, to act as a communication point between community-level groups in different Third World countries that were struggling against environmental pollution, against the destruction of natural resources, against poverty and inequities, and to bring the concerns of the grassroots into the national arena so that we could, for instance, examine the role of the World Bank in destroying the forests in so many different countries; could pinpoint the companies and the World Bank transferring industrial agriculture to the Third World through the Green Revolution; could look at how megadams are promoted throughout the Third World, and how toxic industries and pollution are being exported to the Third World by transnational corporations. There are only so many communities one can work in and only so much that one can do in relation to national policies. Unless we look at the international roots of the problem and tackle it at that level, go and look at World Bank policies, look at what's happening in relation to GATT and Free Trade, look at the transnational corporations and what drives them forward and what it is that can restrict them or not, unless we tackle the system as a whole, we will forever be trying to wipe up the mess at the margins. The Third World Network was created to take on the international forces where they are and to empower the majority whose voices usually are not projected in the media and whose problems are not seen on the international level.

There are two battlefields at least. One is a battlefield of knowledge: the university, the book, the media, and so on. The other is the battlefield of social activism. It is very important to link these two battlefields together, so that those who are struggling at the rim of knowledge, in universities and academia, and those who are in the political struggles, in UNCED, in GATT, fighting the World Bank, and the transnationals, can help one another, so that the knowledge that we have can inform the struggle and the struggles can direct those of us who are doing research.

⌨ ANDREW KIMBRELL, *who labors in Washington, D.C., notes that Marxism's failure to adequately explain the crisis of our time leaves the politics of the means of production themselves as the salient issue:* Looking back, it's clear that the major political struggles of this century have primarily been about creating a more economically just society, and a fairer distribution of the ownership of the means of production. This was certainly true for those of us who devoted our youthful years to the Civil Rights and Anti-war Movements; our passion was social justice and a more equitable distribution of society's wealth. Anything that distracted from this great struggle of working people and the oppressed was viewed with suspicion. I remember passing Earth Day in 1970 in Central Park and thinking it was nothing but a large collection of bourgeois kids defending their summer homes.

Fortunately, I was omnivorous in my reading. I began discovering a whole tradition of radical thinkers who saw oppression based not solely on economics but on the technologies society used. I can still recall the excitement of reading Friedrich Jünger, Lewis Mumford, Jacques Ellul, André Gorz, Theodore Roszak, and later Jeremy Rifkin and Wendell Berry. Through these mentors I began to realize that the central issue was not the ownership of the means of production but the politics of the means of production themselves. This century's revolutionaries had fought valiantly for a more just and humane society, but they had not realized that their dreams could not be realized in a technological milieu which is inherently totalitarian and dehumanizing. My revelation led me to go to law school in my late twenties in order to devote my life to challenging the current technological system.

We are now at a remarkable historical moment, one that provides real possibilities for a new movement on technology. We have recently seen the end of Marxism as an effective alternative vision for society. This has left a large lacuna in our politics. This vacuum can be filled by a new radical visionary movement which goes well beyond Marxism in understanding the need for replacing our current technologies and technocracies with democratic and sustainable technologies. We are therefore in urgent need of a new revolutionary movement, one that finally addresses the politics of the means of production themselves and provides a blueprint for overturning the current totalitarian technological system.

 Like Per Gahrton, SIGMUND KVALOY *speaks of his engagement in struggles against his country's entry to the EEC. Then he raises one of his basic precepts: the distinction between the complexity characteristic of natural systems and the complication typical of megatechnology:* For over thirty-two years since the increasingly technocratic Norwegian government first tried to maneuver my country into the European Community (EC)—later the European Union—the major engagement of my life has been to keep Norway out of it, not least to demonstrate to other nations how independence is a key factor for democracy, welfare, and a meaningful life. After two referendums—1972 and 1994—that both flung a "no" in the face of "our" government, our point has really been floodlighted. Norwegian employment is the highest in Europe. A vast majority—65 percent—of our neighbors, the Swedes, regret bitterly that they joined, saying, "We never got a chance to discuss this matter like the Norwegians did." Austria says the same.

Sigmund Kvaloy traces the development of his understanding from being an electrical systems specialist in the Norwegian Air Force through his philosophical studies at the university, to a study at Columbia University of the aesthetic problems of computer-generated music, to an epiphany on hearing Thelonious Monk's improvisations: One evening in New York in 1967 I found myself in the Five Spot Cafe listening to Thelonious Monk and his group improvising. That turned my life around. Suddenly I understood the difference between *complication* and *complexity*, between mechanic and organic.

In the middle of the second phase of the fight against the EC, around 1971, 1972, some of us from the Norwegian ecopolitical-philosophical group decided that these are very useful concepts for analyzing the European Common Market—including free market competition—how it is forced by its own axioms to try to build a union. A politico-technocratic union is needed to stem and order the market forces that would otherwise produce a chaotic situation, however tuning that ordering so finely that the motor of competition can still have sufficient effect against the U.S. and Japan. It was very much a case of trying to analyze the ways these competitive powers win over each other by using high technology and how this inevitably creates not only unemployment but, more seriously, the total eradication of meaningful work, which we think is the basis of any viable society.

In Norway, teachers are nowadays obliged to introduce environmental subjects at all levels in the schools inside all their different disciplines. Our ecophilosophy group has involved itself in this, saying it's now extremely important to teach to the student the difference between the organic and the mechanical or the complex and the complicated. And to give concrete demonstrations of the difference by bringing them out of the schoolroom into the different workplaces up in the mountains, out in the fishing hamlets, into the factories and offices, and to do this systematically. One of the main reasons why we have an accelerating and seemingly unstoppable global ecosocial crisis is that we confuse the complex with the complicated. We think that the modern world view, including nature and human society, is a complicated structure, an intricate machine structure, and we do things on the basis of this misunderstanding.

A California-to-Michigan transplant, STEPHANIE MILLS, *by way of invoking the practice of ecological restoration, speaks a word for nature:* I've been thinking about this problem we have of perceiving the degree of change. The metaphor that keeps coming to mind is the idea that you can immerse a frog in room temperature water and slowly raise the heat and it will suffer itself to be boiled to death; but if you plunge a frog immediately into boiling water it's shocked enough to get out. So the gradualness of this technological and economic globalization makes it difficult to work against. So much of it has been flying under the banner of practicality. It's become impractical to cleave to the kinds of ideals that were very clearly expressed years ago.

It's worth articulating these truths very clearly and intransigently because truth is becoming so narrow.

In watching what's been going on in the national scene in the U.S., I've been horrified by the encroachment of what Bertram Gross termed "friendly fascism." The fact that it's been possible to engineer a consent to these changes is frightening to me. One part of the antidote might be called ecological literacy or simply knowing natural history, that there is a considerable gap between the principles and the actuality. It's possible to have a whole philosophy based on ecological principles that doesn't translate to the actual ground you are living on. Getting out and looking at the land community and paying attention to it is very important.

Ecological restoration offers a range of possibilities. One of them is that landscapes can be restored to a degree of health, and in the process of doing that you learn a great deal about what *was* there. You investigate the processes that destroyed the biodiversity in the first place. You also learn how so many of the elusive and enigmatic parts of ecosystems vanished under industrial civilization. The question of whether or not *they* can be restored is open. It could be that the enigmatic microflora, the ultimate ground of our being, can't be replaced. Any person can grasp the implications of that, given the opportunity, so restoration endeavor is a factual ground for Luddite ideas and their implications.

To abandon the elite position of the scholar and philosopher and to get into a situation where you really court and follow the common wisdom is a big leap. I recently spoke with a landscape architect who is doing some forest restoration in Central Park—with a group that generally makes its decisions by consensus. She says that the decisions that they make without thoroughly consulting everyone in the group have tended to be the most fallible ones. The information you are getting is not just my opinion or anybody else's opinion, it's what people have observed of the places where they are working. So it's not mere ideas— it's natural history.

 ℘ *Seneca activist* JOHN MOHAWK *speaks of indigenous peoples' struggles for cultural survival as being identical with the struggle to preserve as-yet- undestroyed parts of ecoregions, and megatechnology wielded by transnational corporations as being the force they're up against:* Indigenous peoples are in fact the first line of defense of the extensive and as yet undestroyed rainforest, forest areas, and other ecoregions of the world. Indigenous peoples are under pressures. They and their languages are disappearing. People need to know about this. Indigenous use has in fact shaped the rainforest in the Amazon. Indigenous peoples are struggling to save their culture. Their culture is inextricable from biological regionality. They are one of the major political forces in the world organized in defense of wilderness—if you want to call it that, although this is of course a Westernized way of thinking about it.

I teach a world history graduate course in the American Studies Department at the State University of New York at Buffalo. American Studies begins with the European Diaspora and the invasion of America and how that affected the indigenous American populations. In the same centuries we observe the rise of racism and slavery and how the modern era is born. It runs its course through the enclosures in Europe and the rise of the Industrial Revolution and on through the era of women's struggles, specifically in the United States but eventually worldwide.

Each year we go through all this and a unit on Puerto Rico, on the slave communities, on the post–Civil War period, the Harlem Renaissance, and the Civil Rights Movement. There are units touching on all the big topics that politically correct people who go to the universities think they want to study. Toward the end we get to world survival, indigenous survival. Indigenous survival really looks at modern megadevelopment.

I have to report that the students are much more enthusiastic earlier in the course: The women want to study women; the blacks want to study black history; the Indians want to study Indian history. When we

get to these real concrete problems that people feel, out of politeness the
students read it but there is a general feeling of uneasiness. The black
people have trouble connecting how the issues of industrialization and
of world domination through centralization of economic power affect
them. White middle-class women want to talk about issues that affect
white middle-class women. Black women want to talk about issues that
affect black women. Everybody is into their own struggle.

Megatechnology is probably the major cause of human displacement in the world today. In wars all over the world most of the soldiers
are fighting indigenous peoples over territory, resources, or minerals.
These conflicts are driven by a world network of multinationals that are
based in North America, with surrogates in Indonesia, in Burma, all over
the world. The Japanese are part of that. The rainforests ultimately are
threatened by people who want chopsticks and furniture. We are connected to that; history is connected to that. If we are not aware of how
it all connects, then we are part of the problem, not part of the solution.
Everybody is aghast at slavery. Everybody is against killing Indians. But
when we get down to how we are now participants in and particles of an
industrial society which is perpetrating all of that, it becomes harder for
people to acknowledge the connections.

The West has defamed indigenous peoples. Indigenous peoples are as
distant from the ideological and economic centers of Western culture as
it is possible to be. They perceive reality in ways diametrically opposite
to the way of the West. There are many different indigenous realities,
but they all have that distance.

Maybe the West hasn't encompassed all of the knowledge and experience of the world. In postmodernism Foucault and others argue that
not only does language construct reality but language creates reality's
limits. If your language lacks words that express a certain idea you can't
construct it. In other languages all around the world there are ideas that
are not only untranslatable into English but that would need a whole
book for their expression. Postmodernism is barren of the ability to
translate humankind's broadest imagination about reality. Indigenous
autochthonous peoples can provide us with some of those ideas.

⌐Ashis Nandy, *with subtlety, discusses the politics of knowledge and
foresees the vanishing of "science as we know it" before the overwhelming
demand for technological application. He also describes the institutional capture and neutralization of environmentalist dissent:* I come from India, a
part of the world where something, to be truly human, has to be old.
Some decades ago a group of scholars in western India worked for years

on the *Mahabharata* and examined it for interpolations. Ultimately they discovered that out of a hundred thousand couplets in the epic, nine-tenths were probably interpolations or later additions. If you take these scholars seriously and eliminate the interpolations to restore the purity of the epic you are left only with a truncated version with which Indians have lived for only a very small part of their history. That something is old does not necessarily mean that it cannot be new. However, that newness can be introduced into the old in different ways by different societies.

This century's mad rush always to find something new and use a language of disjunction as opposed to a language of continuity is part of the very problem we are discussing.

Thirty years ago when poor countries were called poor countries and savages were called savages, those were the golden days. In front of my eyes things have changed. First, "poor countries" got promoted to "backward countries"; the language of progress took over even poverty. Then they became "underdeveloped" societies, and now they are, of course, "developing societies." Someone has said that the next century is going to belong to China and Japan. So the "developing" countries are now doing well.

So is the estate of science and technology, which has been subjected to a lot of criticism by some of us. It also is doing well. One of my favorite sets of data was the one that was submitted to UNESCO in the mid-eighties as part of a report. It showed that if the present growth rate of science and technology continues over the next thirty-five to forty years the total number of scientists and technologists will overtake the total world population. Things are also taking care of themselves in other ways, too. Over the last few decades the proportion of pure scientists in this estate of science and technology has been declining. In the last fifty years while we were criticizing science the percentage of scientists in the realm of science and technology had already declined to less than five, and it is still declining. It is now, according to some estimates, about 3½ percent. So we can imagine that science in the future will probably survive only in the guise of technology.

Many years ago a friend of mine told me—I was a young political psychologist—that if you reverse what you study, it will always reach more interesting conclusions. That is, if you are studying the psychology of politics and take a break from it and look at the politics of psychology, you can bring a different kind of insight to your studies. I took him seriously; I have never looked back since then. I have been studying the psychology of politics with an awareness of the politics of psychology as a way of looking at problems that can be adapted to many situations. It certainly informs what I am going to say.

Usually we love to talk about the Establishment in normative terms: what should be done about it. Somebody said this morning that industrial civilization should be dismantled. The Establishment, too, loves that kind of radicalism, because the more you talk in purely normative terms—what should be done, what ought to be done, what could be done—the better off they are. The people who really wield power—in the absence of a better word we are calling them the Establishment—always have a better political theory of us than we have of them. This asymmetry shapes the nature of the world in which we, with an exaggerated sense of urgency, try to intervene. In this process, we become willing objects of political management. Let me give you an example from India. Over the last two decades, as the Environmental Movement has gained in strength, the Indian state has established a parallel system of environmental initiatives. So we have within the government, in international bodies and within the university system, an entire new structure of environmentalists. They are the "official" environmentalists. What was originally a voice of dissent, a debate between the Establishment and dissenting voices, has increasingly become a debate between two sets of environmentalists; the government and the political elite now enter the scene as dispassionate, distant arbiters between two sets of environmental experts, one of them supposedly using the language of sanity and the other the language of the lunatic fringe. The aim is to relocate the dissent in such a way that dissent begins increasingly to articulate itself according to Establishment rules. It even has to claim that it is as "rational," "sane," and "scientific" as the Establishment environmentalists to become audible.

The obverse of this process is the systematic effort to pre-empt the voice of the victims. There are hundreds of communities in the world where today the anthropologists' understanding of that culture has superseded the local understanding of culture. Even dissenting movements trying to articulate the interests and problems of those communities have to talk in the jargon of, address themselves to, or use the knowledge of, specialist professionals from outside the community.

⊚ With a passion strangely lyrical, GODFREY REGGIO *urges us to see how utterly technology has transmogrified earthly life. He voices the notion, later to be disputed, that we don't use technology, we live it:* I don't trust the language that I possess and use. I say that not for any lack of love of the

word. Language is being subtly taken from us; metaphor is giving way to technological metamorphosis. During the last quarter of this century the new global media of mass communications have astoundingly begun a transformation of image as the global mass language. This scenario reflects an ontological shift that blasts the human mooring from its center of gravity into an unimaginable postnatural and posthuman orbit—a sure turning point where reality and the image of reality meet, a moment of total consequence. The globalized world is a new world coming, a new world here, the future present. It is a world engulfed in the shadow of the mass, entering the awesome domain of the digital—a world of new definitions, new functions, new needs, new classes, a world in shock. What I'm struggling to say is that we don't *use* technology, we *live* it. Technology is a way of living. In saying this, I'm trying stretch my own boundaries. I have been forced to confront these feelings by being human and alive and feeling my suffering and that of others. But the very words that I use to describe myself and the things that I feel are inadequate to describe this phenomenon.

I came to the feelings and thoughts I have not from an academic background but from working as an organizer with street gangs in the barrios of northern New Mexico for nine and a half years. I experienced suffering and injustice in a way that I hadn't realized was possible coming, as I did, from a middle-class background. I got to understand that most of the people that I had the opportunity to work with were quite fine. It was the world we lived in that was really upside down.

I am astounded when people actually feel that they are within reach of solutions. I'm astounded that we don't see the enormous complexity and omnipresence of the technological dimension—how the world is being remade in the image and likeness of technique. Perhaps the most important thing we could do would be to celebrate this tragedy, to celebrate the end of the global world. I don't believe that there is any putting this world back together. This new world, these new necessities, are inherently unsafe for humans and all living entities, for nature herself. This world cannot be made safe, equitable, just, or honorable! That's not to say that there is nothing to do. (I am saddened when I hear about *global* environmental movements. The very concept is a contradiction. Anything global eliminates the unique, the different, that makes up the complexity of the web of life, that mystery that holds its unity in diversity. The Catch-22 is that our way of living has created a global residue, a new index of global problems, that now quite "naturally" appeal to global responses.) Quite the contrary. Our covenant with the human will, with freedom, is more pressing than ever as we approach an unknowable watershed of technological primacy. Now is the time to act—urgently.

What we are looking at is of a scale and a scope that is incomprehensible. It's something that defies the language that we possess. Our language is at once powerful and humble, it has limits, it's human. What we face is tragically not of a human dimension.

That's not to say that we shouldn't make the effort, especially through language, to understand, but it's time to reclaim a language that begins to give access to what it is that we are dealing with. In a real sense we must begin to rename the world in which we live. Human language has an heroic role to play. For it is in language that we struggle to name the truth; it is through language that we can re-create the world. In language rediscovered is the womb for a free and direct act.

How does one become a Luddite when the whole world in which you live is itself technology? Luddite as a term, an idea, has perhaps receded into waves of history where a thousand years ago is, astonishingly, but a score of yesterdays. Immersion in the medium is approaching total, as global momentum builds off a billion times a billion unquestioned technological routines. I would urge us to stretch our imaginations as to the technological world in which we live. This world is so complex and so far beyond the narrow confines of our rationality, our analysis, our books, and our films. We all have to begin to discover the unknowable consequences of what it means to live in a technological universe. We live in a new world, the laws of which we have not even begun to understand. We don't question the world in which we live: We are remarkably becoming an alien species facing the loss of our identity as human. So we have to begin again to try to feel, and through that feeling bring about some appropriate utterance and action. In this journey or odyssey we might consider negation to be of more positive value than making political responses. In being able to say no to those things that tie us into this world, the technological umbilical cords, we can begin to say yes to a freedom, to an imagination that indicates our existence as human beings.

⊘ JEREMY RIFKIN, *a tireless iconoclast from Washington, D.C., pronounces this moment to be the dawn of "the Age of Biology," declaring that biotechnology can be expected to revolutionize production—and displace workers—far more dramatically than industrial technology, or* pyrotechnology, *ever did. He urges us to seize the moment to organize around food and jobs*: Over the next decades, we will be moving out of 5,000 years of fiber-based and metallurgical technology and into a biology- and electricity-based technology. In its impact on the world and on future generations this irreversible transition goes beyond the Industrial Revolution. We are moving away from fossil fuel use into genes. The question is, How we are going to organize the next half-millennium of our history, the age of biology?

There are two broad philosophical currents to choose from. One is the corporate paradigm: a global marketplace prompted by information technologies and genetic technologies. We now have to face the nexus of information technologies, biotechnology, gene splicing technologies, the globalization of politics, corporations, and the marketplace. We are not moving into an "information society." Information is just the management mode for the age of biology. The industrial age wasn't called the print revolution, nor was the agricultural age called the oral revolution.

People here have been articulating the other philosophical position for the last thirty years. It is an ecological vision for the age of biology, a sustainable, deep-ecological approach to reparticipation from the local biome to the biosphere. Ultimately it's a philosophical battle for world views. And it's very much a political battle around the new institutional relationships. The current rapidity of change makes it a much more dramatic transition than the transition from medieval agriculture to the Industrial Revolution.

Will the corporations be allowed to enclose and commodify the last remaining commons on the planet—biology? Or can we muster up enough philosophical and political will to keep that commons open and to develop a new ethic of reparticipation? We need to concentrate on the food chain and jobs. These are the two battlegrounds that will determine whether we succeed or fail. The food chain brings together North and South; it relates the whole means of production from the field to the consumer and ties together health, environment, and justice.

Just now emerging in the 1990s is the question of jobs. We are going to see the final triumph of technology in this decade. The kinds of prophecies first heard in the Keynesian 1930s are now coming to pass. By the end of this decade tens of millions of workers in the industrial world will be marginalized. In the past victimization was perpetuated by one group enslaving another. Now victimization is by obsolescence. In every sector of work, from agriculture to manufacturing, to white collar and service, first tens then hundreds of millions of people are going to be unemployed. This is going to create a tremendous crisis. We need to organize around the food chain and to seize the high ground on unemployment and jobs. We need to develop a critique of the technological world view and to be able to say to the next generation that the alternative is meaningful employment in a sustainable framework.

⊘ New Yorker KIRKPATRICK SALE *shares with us the lessons of the original Luddites' rout and urges on us coherence in ideology, goal, strategy, and commitment. Even at that, Sale thinks, the modern-day equivalent of a necktie party may still attend this rebellion:* If there is an exhaustion of the Environmental Movement I think it's because we have come to the realization of how this society is destroying the Earth despite all we have done. We have accomplished wonderful things in the last thirty years. Trees have been saved, water has been saved, people's relations have been changed: It's the most successful social change movement that the country or the world has ever seen. Yet we are losing this battle.

Because of all this my thoughts turned to the Luddites. I saw there a movement of heroes who went up against an unconquerable force and were destroyed. I thought it was about time that we talked about it and thought about and saw ourselves in those terms. It's not a happy lesson to look at. In my book on the Luddites I call them "rebels against the future" to suggest some of the futility of all that. And it is a futility that I am conscious of daily in doing what we do. It's not quite the same as hopelessness, though hope seems to me to be one of those Christian Progressive ideas that we might just as well disabuse ourselves of, and work from there if we must, understanding the darkness of all this. The Luddites failed, and there is no reason to think that we won't fail.

Nonetheless here is the subtitle of my book: "Lessons from the First Industrial Revolution." As we go through our second industrial revolution those lessons could be the ones that we need. The first is the need to share a common ideology. The ideology is already there—I don't think we need to create it. Mumford and others have given us that ideology—what we have to do is agree upon it and out of that come up with a goal, an agreed-upon strategy and an agreed-upon commitment. These are things that the original Luddites never had, but these are things that the Neo-Luddites might be able to create: an ideology, a goal, a strategy, and a commitment.

We have to be very serious because the Neo-Luddites, like the Luddites, are revolutionaries, and they are perceived as revolutionaries by the Establishment. When the first Luddites began their uprising, they called the Establishment "the thing"—that's what we still can call it— and it came down upon those people with great vengeance, with great repression. We, too, face exactly the same fate. We will all hang together or we will all hang separately.

That is the depth of the seriousness of what we will have to do, of the commitment that we will have to make. I'm not sure if we are prepared to do that. But it is worth doing and worth calling ourselves Luddites, because we are indeed going to be called Luddites no matter what other name we choose for ourselves. We might as well, like the Quakers, embrace the name that they use against us.

Californian GEORGE SESSIONS *characterizes megatechnology as moving toward the total domestication of the planet and asserts the grave seriousness of the extinction crisis. Time is running out for the world's wilderness, and Sessions wants us to get cracking to protect it:* I appreciate Jeremy Rifkin's analysis of the future alternatives humans face—an ecological world versus a domesticated artificial world of consumerism dominated by transnational corporations. But the most crucial aspect of the ecological vision, which I haven't yet heard coming through at this conference, is the necessity of protecting what is left of the Earth's wildness and biodiversity. The world's leading ecologists and conservation biologists, such as Paul Ehrlich and E. O. Wilson, claim that biodiversity loss is the single most important aspect of the global ecological crisis. I am coming more and more to the realization that Thoreau's 1851 statement, "In wildness is the preservation of the world," is probably the single most important claim that has been made in the last 150 years. Thoughtful environmentalism in the twentieth century consists of exploring and putting into practice the implications of that claim. The vision of the transnational corporate global economy consists largely of nullifying that statement: of bringing the entire Earth under the domination, management, and control of humans, of treating the Earth as commodities for exploitation. And we are talking not only about the wild ecosystems, plants, and animals; we are also talking about the commodification, exploitation, and domestication—the dehumanization—of people, as Huxley and Orwell foresaw. The ten-year period Rifkin is talking about is also absolutely crucial for protecting what's left of wildness on the Earth. At present, we're doing a miserable job of protecting wildness all over the globe. If we don't get immediately serious about rolling back the corporate megatechnological global economy vision and protecting what's left of wildness, I'm afraid that in the near future we're going to find ourselves domesticated in an Orwellian cage from which there will be no escape.

⊘ VANDANA SHIVA *raises the specter of the enclosure of the biological commons through the instrument of intellectual property rights. She also tells of the denigration of vernacular science and technology through the "doublespeak" of development:* My critical perspectives on technology really started with thinking of technology as the thing the Third World *lacked* as the reason for its underdevelopment and poverty. As a result of science and technology training, that's what you feel. You want to bring technology to the rural people, to the poor. Then you realize you are taking the wrong technology and they have the right one. The reason they are getting poorer is because the systems that thrive on a certain kind of technology are systems that simultaneously take over power over resources, knowledge, people, and institutions. It's not so much technology that's a problem but a certain technology taking a stance as being the only one that's scientific. Other technologies that fit into sustainable systems are being denied that status as if people don't have minds, tools, or hands and can't create. These two different worlds of science and technology have coexisted in my mind and in my experience.

My background is in physics and philosophy of science. However, I choose to work on things that affect nature and the largest number of lives on this planet—thus my work on agriculture. Inappropriate systems of science and technology are always introduced as "development," as "progress." The reading of the environmental crisis in India has always been a critique of technology.

I focused my technology analysis on agriculture because in our country it is the lifeway of 80 percent of the people and it provides everyone food. My colleagues would say, "In agriculture, you are not critiquing science and technology." But by the time the ideology of science and technology transfers into the real world, it operates through forestry and agriculture and fisheries. Now in the notion of intellectual property rights the whole system is combining to take away rights from people long before the technology has displayed its success. What is the biotechnology that indigenous communities don't have and the gene splicer has? It's the power to torture. Yet that part of technology is treated as the power to create, a system that should be rewarded and protected through intellectual property rights. Somehow we have to show that biotechnology is not creation but destruction. Because the system is jumping so fast and making so many claims that have absolutely no basis, it is vulnerable. That is where we get our openings.

I don't feel pessimistic—I probably would if I only dealt with academics. Talking half an hour to 200,000 farmers who are willing to do something is a wonderful tonic against pessimism. Gandhi gave us the word *satyagraha*. The term means "fighting for the truth." We can say that any system that violates or destroys life is a system worth violating. It doesn't matter what our chances of success are. You don't see success as linked with truth. Truth is truth. You live it.

Because technology is now turning living systems into raw material, for the first time everyone is a potential Luddite. The same technologies that throw out millions of farmers in the South will throw out millions of workers in the North. We just have to be creative enough and responsible enough to keep articulating the connections. People themselves will find ways to act as long as we can show them that the lack of jobs is related to this emergence of technology and not the Mexican or the Chinese migrant. If we can just do that we can avert a lot of violence. Otherwise, misunderstanding where the threats to jobs are coming from is going to make people kill each other and destroy themselves, long before the system destroys itself and it destroys the world. Technology is used very ideologically. And we have a major responsibility in naming a certain kind of technology, created by a certain kind of interest group, as being at the heart of the matter.

⊘CHARLENE SPRETNAK, *a Northern Californian, begins by mentioning the universality of the need for community-based economics and gently reminds us that the scores of Green parties worldwide have been articulating such economics in their platforms. She also raises the vast subject of modern meaninglessness and urges renewed respect for the great spiritual traditions as the remedy:* Much of what has been said here thus far can be found in the platforms of the more than sixty Green parties worldwide. The Green economic program is a counterforce against the global market: community-based economics that would keep money circulating largely within a community and a region. The mix would include nonprofit community-development corporations, businesses with profit sharing or employee ownership, credit unions, cooperatives, farmers' markets, and the availability of microloans for very small businesses (which are usually run by women with small children). The idea is to spread ownership and wealth as broadly as possible, providing far more economic security to a region than would be gained by betting its future on the export model. There is nothing wrong with trade, but the ideology of the global market is extreme—and extremely insecure.

It's really come down to the fact that what's good for Oakland, California, now is good for Calcutta: All communities need to rescue themselves to a large extent from the grip of the global market and from the

New World Order instituted by GATT, which is a transnational corporate oligarchy. For Greens, however, community-based economics is not a goal in itself, enjoying that hallowed centrality of economics in other political orientations such as classical Liberalism and Marxism. Community-based economics is encouraged *in service to community*. It is seen as a way to repair and re-create the bonds that have been destroyed by modernity.

During my years of research for my book *States of Grace* I focused on the losses inherent in modernity and on the necessity for a recovery of meaning, which becomes fragmented and destroyed. I was exploring the meaninglessness so common to modern life. I had to engage with the contemporary "denial of meaning" asserted by deconstructive postmodernists. Like feminists and other activist movements, the deconstructionists examine the ways in which concepts and hierarchical relationships are socially constructed. As an alternative to that reductionism, which focuses only on the *forms* of power relations rather than the *content* of the modern belief system, I proposed *ecological* postmodernism. Social construction of concepts requires scrutiny, of course, but so does the recovery of essential realizations denied by modernity, such as the profound interrelatedness of all life and the unitive dimensions of being. In *States of Grace* I suggested a cosmological reframing of comparative religion that understands the great spiritual traditions as counterforces to the existential denials of the modern, mechanistic world view.

⊘DAVID SUZUKI *recalls his shock, as a science undergraduate, at learning that the Holocaust was, in a sense, the product of scientific enthusiasm. Heroic myths still condition science education, he says, and the malevolent outcomes are still discounted. He also talks about his disillusionment with television as a medium for the ecological message:* I'm a third-generation Canadian. The consequences of the Japanese attack on Pearl Harbor in 1941 really shaped my development and outlook. My country then classified all Japanese-Canadians as enemy agents and imprisoned us for three years. In 1958, a year after Sputnik, I graduated from Amherst College. It was a time of great fear of the Soviet juggernaut, yet paradoxically there was tremendous exuberance about the possibility of science. I was one of the beneficiaries of the American effort to become competitive in science. I grew up believing that nothing lay beyond inquiry by science and answers could be provided to the deepest secrets of nature if scientists were given enough money. Science was a way to push back the frontiers of ignorance and superstition.

It was only when I became a teacher and students began to ask me about the history of genetics that I discovered what had *not* been taught to me in all the years of my education as a scientist: that it had been the exuberant claims of geneticists that had created the social climate leading to the incarceration of Japanese-Canadians. I learned that the Holocaust was in a real sense a product of one of the leading genetics communities in the world, in Germany. It didn't spring from the mind of a few nuts who happened to be racist. It had been fostered by the tremendous enthusiasm of geneticists about what they were discovering early in the century. I hadn't been taught that Joseph Mengele was a geneticist who was doing his studies at Auschwitz while supported by peer-reviewed grants.

So I learned that the history of science has been manufactured by the scientific community, so that geneticists appear as heroic warriors in the service of humanity: men and women out to improve the lot of humankind.

In part because of this realization that science has such an enormous impact on people, back in 1962 I began a career in television to try to inform people about science through this powerful medium. Again my naïveté is indicated. Although I knew the television schedule was like a great cesspool, I thought my programs were going to glisten like jewels that people would seize. I only realized much later that when you're in a cesspool, you look like a turd like everybody else. Originally, I thought people would turn on "The Nature of Things," watch it intently for an hour, then turn it off and say, "Wow! Wasn't that interesting! What do you think?" Of course people don't watch television that way at all. At the end of a six- or seven-hour period of watching television people can't remember whether something they recall was on "The Nature of Things" or the "X-Files"! The challenge is to think holistically; to think in terms of geological time; to think conservatively. But television teaches us exactly the opposite: It fragments; it has no connection with history or duration; and its overriding message is "consume."

In 1979 we were preparing a program on a battle to stop logging in a watershed on the Queen Charlotte Islands, which are often referred to as Canada's Galapagos. The opposition to logging had been led by a Haida artist. When I interviewed him, I asked, "Why are you fighting so hard to stop the logging? After all, most of the loggers are Haida and even if the trees are cut down, you'll still have your home and work. Logging is bringing money into your community. So why are you struggling so hard against this?" He replied, "Of course, if they cut the trees down I'll still have my job and my home, but then *we'll be like everybody else.*" That simple statement opened my eyes to the fact that there are people whose identity doesn't end at their skin but in the community of organisms that define who they are and why they are.

⊘ Entrepreneur-turned philanthropist, longtime mountaineer, and kayaker Doug Tompkins *talks about leaving commercial activity, which he now regards as being one of the driving forces of ecological destruction. He praises the group for representing a spectrum of concern that includes far more than technology criticism. Finally, he lists some of the authors who changed his life:* My background has been business; I very enthusiastically got into business when I was about 21. My adult life has been occupied with the building of a successful business. In the last six or seven years, though, it turned against me. I started coming to work realizing that I was more concerned with the reasons that the natural world was falling apart than attending to managing my business. I am a mountain climber and wilderness person. I began to see my favorite wild places being intruded on by industrial society, especially tourism and industrial forestry. I faced a lot of the same frustrations many of us have in terms of seeing how one could personally take up the fight and resist this onslaught. Eventually, of course, I started to understand that commercial activity, the promotion of consumption itself, is one of the driving forces of the ecosocial crisis. So I started to extricate myself over a period of years from business (in my case a business promoting needless consumption —fashion!) and to devote myself full time to activism on the other side of the line. And through this process I found that many of my friends were also experiencing the frustration of understanding what was driving the crisis and yet feeling helpless to do much about it.

Scholarship has helped inform my activism—and trying to come to an intellectual and, if possible, an emotional understanding of this crisis. I recommend to anyone who will listen to read as much as one can, especially of the circle of thinkers and writers either in this group of technology critics or the Deep Ecology/nature tradition thinker/activists such as Naess, Leopold, Muir, and Thoreau, to name some of the bigger names. I should point out the obvious, nonetheless, that this incredible group gathered here today could hardly be simply described as technology critics because their thinking, writing, and activism is so comprehensive it covers virtually all realms of social, peace, gender, and environmental concerns.

⊘ A resident of New York State, Langdon Winner *speaks of his long-term study of the political forms that are packaged as technological systems and*

worries about the apathy and passivity of so many people as these forms are
imposed. Can ecologically inspired alternatives to galloping autonomous tech-
nology be envisioned, he wonders? And couldn't they be attractive enough to
enjoy popular preference? What often seem to be totally overwhelming
technologically embodied forces are, from another point of view, tendencies of a fragile, vulnerable beast. If we look today at the systems of
oppression Lewis Mumford described in *The Pentagon of Power*, some of
them have already crumbled, the military and political structures of the
Soviet Union, for example. The American Cold War apparatus, another
prime manifestation of the "megamachine," has also suffered some set-
backs and now struggles to justify its existence in the post-Cold War era.
The idea that young people can find an easy living by working in the
military-industrial complex is no longer a plausible strategy. Even more
important, it's clear to a great many people that the ideology that supported the building of systems like these—the ideology of progress—just
isn't working. For two hundred years the formula was science advances,
technology develops, and the human condition improves. It's clear that
we can have the first two of these steps, but their connection to human
well-being is now widely recognized as highly problematic at best. Evidence of the breakdown in the old-fashioned model of progress is everywhere to be seen in decaying cities, environmental decay, and burgeon-
ing populations around the world left high and dry by computerization
and other technological revolutions.

As a student of political philosophy, I pay attention to the ways in
which political forms are packaged as technological systems. Much of
our moral, social, and political life is deeply involved in technological
regimes of one kind or another. For those who care about human freedom, the complexion of these regimes is often worrisome. Most people
in our society see themselves not as free citizens able to take action, but
rather as subjects of an entity beyond their control. They may call it the
"economy" or "technology," but they recognize that whatever "it" is
does not give them much choice; they must simply respond to what "it"
requires of them. In workplaces, homes, and local communities people
find themselves driven by developments that seem to spew out of a vol-
cano and alter the social landscape. Looked at more closely, of course,
these developments always involve deliberate planning and strenuous
endeavor—building and imposing a number of new, interconnected
regimes. The worldwide regime of "lean production" is one such example: a way of organizing machines and people for production that begins
in the Japanese automobile industry and is now being installed in every

corner of working life, replacing earlier models of craftsmanship and mass production. Another regime of this kind involves the merger of previously separate electronic technologies—telephone, television, and computing—into integrated networks scheduled to be the focus of social activity in every home in every country in the world.

We need to study, analyze, debate, and often resist such regimes as they are being assembled. But that is not enough. If there is no living sense of alternatives, our descriptions and criticisms will have little lasting effect. Much of my own time is spent teaching science and engineering students, the very people slated for important positions in the megamachines of tomorrow. When I present them with a critique of the knowledge forms of Western rationality or point out the ecological or cultural pathologies associated with major technological regimes in our time, they often ask, "So what do you suggest we do?" That's a very difficult question to answer. Where are the plausible, working models of alternative ways of practice? Can we make alternatives to technologically embodied authoritarianism so clear and appealing that people will freely choose them? I believe it is possible to imagine varieties of material culture based upon a sophisticated understanding of the principles of ecology and social justice. If enough people were to devote themselves to creating working models of this kind, it is possible that the populace as a whole and the next generation of technical professionals in particular would flock toward that promise. Change of this magnitude often seems beyond reach, but it can happen rapidly. During a relatively short period in the eighteenth century, restless American colonists completely dismantled a deeply entrenched system of relationships and dependencies associated with monarchy, not just their ties to the king but a whole social system of hierarchical arrangements. The old structure, one that seemed permanent, suddenly lost its rationale, went liquid, and collapsed as new forms of social and political life were created for a reconstituted nation, a process Americans remember as "The Revolution." Changes of that magnitude are definitely possible at present and just as necessary, in my view. A crucial step is to disconnect from a host of lethal habits that define our present relationship to technology and to reconnect our lives to social and technical patterns that are sane, humane, and workable. An example of what I am talking about is the movement to disconnect from the technological regime that links the mechanical-chemical regime of agribusiness to supermarket shopping, replacing it with networks of community-supported, biodynamic farms. The political thrust of a sensible Luddite approach involves concerted efforts to build feasible alternatives, working at the same time to persuade large numbers of people why they ought to abandon their current sociotechnical dependencies and join the search for more healthy technological cultures.

As I've struggled with these kinds of questions over the years as a scholar, teacher, and academic, I've often been interested in defining differences, what separates my own views from others in the same range of concerns. Right now I'm much more interested in finding areas of commonality, and ways to connect my work to others. Looking back on my life now, I've noticed—and I think this is true of intellectuals generally—that I've often been wrong, but seldom in doubt.

⊚ In support of the spirit of consensus guiding the discussion, LANGDON WINNER *recalls his reaction, a few years earlier, to Chellis Glendinning's "Notes Toward a Neo-Luddite Manifesto," which was to differ on any number of points large and small. Winner announces that he's prepared to put aside those differences in favor of working together to define common grounds.*

Berkeley resident SUSAN GRIFFIN *also speaks of the unacknowledged biases inherent in a science influenced by a Judeo-Christian theology that derogates matter. She relates this to the great theme of all her writing, the attempt to articulate the form and consequence of the various cultural, psychological, and gender-based understandings of self and other:* Over the past twenty years or so my work has centered on self and other and how we define or think of that. I started to write *Woman and Nature* when I was a much younger woman. In that book I was connecting the oppression of women with the oppression of nature, and I started out somewhat naïvely. I noticed that many women writers, Emily Brontë among them, identified with nature in a way that men didn't. Male writers appreciate nature and feel with nature but experience themselves as other, whereas women feel themselves to be the same as nature. That intrigued me. In the Romantic Movement, which is so important to our thought, Wordsworth in *Intimations of Mortality* gets close to realizing that he *is* nature. Most of the time, though, nature is something very lovely, but it's out there and different. I began to follow that path and I followed it very much as a poet. My intellectual history has been not a fight but a wedding between the inchoate and the clear, the poetry being part of the inchoate. So I wrote *Woman and Nature*. It's an attempt to give voice to that which is not given voice within this culture, to the feminine and nature, which is usually presumed not to have anything much worth saying. So no one bothers to worry about that voice. I began to understand that to get at the core of this different relationship that men have with nature I would have to look at the history of science. That's when my naïveté stopped.

⊘ *A theme that gathers intensity throughout the meeting is questioning the character of scientific knowledge.* SUSAN GRIFFIN *continues:* When I say naïve, I mean I also thought that scientists knew something. I only understood scientific knowledge in a very naïve way. When I was younger one of my heroes was J. Robert Oppenheimer. I just loved the quality of his mind. When I educated myself in the history of science, I found in that history an enormous bias. For one thing that science came from the Judeo-Christian theology, which derogates the material world and presumes that spirit and matter are at war with one another. That separation is fundamental not only to Western culture but to this global technological corporate culture. That separation allows a relation to nature as other, an object without soul or spirit, without center, so that you don't have to have an I-Thou relationship but an I-It relationship.

During that period of history when America—which was already here —was "discovered," the modern scientific point of view also was launched. The massacre of native peoples all over the world, slavery, witch burnings, the Inquisition, and a wave of anti-Semitism, too, were all going on in the same period.

My latest book, *A Chorus of Stones*, moves from there. I wanted to find out for myself why it was that we turned scientific brilliance and our major weaponry toward a military strategy that focused on the bombing of civilians. This happened without much comment in the twentieth century. People talk about how terrible it is that we are going to destroy the Earth with nuclear weapons and not why that technology should be aimed at civilians. This gets back to the self and other.

While writing *Woman and Nature* and the book that followed it, *Pornography and Silence*, I began to understand that all those qualities that we try to domesticate in women really are qualities which are human. What inquisitors are trying to burn in a witch is a quality that is human. It is the part that is nature, the wildness, and that which is mortal. We understand mortality from the moment we are born; it is in our bodies. Understanding what's happening emotionally is of primary importance, because one of the errors this civilization has made is to disregard emotions. Of course they can't be: The emotionality that is disregarded comes back, you know; it never can go away. It's like an ecological system; people say you burn waste, but we know that it enters the atmosphere in a very toxic form. One of the major emotions driving Western civilization is the fear of mortality, and of death and loss of control, which became enormously accelerated in the twentieth century. Hence the desire to dominate those who are perceived as other, particularly when those who are perceived as other are associated with, and become the symbols for, nature.

Sir Hugh Trenchard, the father of the Royal Air Force, was important in developing the military strategy of "strategic" bombing, the bombing of civilians. This man earned his military spurs both in India and in Africa. In Africa one of the things he did in order for the British Empire to subdue the people was to set fire to their villages. Twenty years later he was doing this in Europe. And that was the precursor of the fires in Hiroshima and Dresden.

I'm now working on a book called *Sustenance*, using my own experience with chronic fatigue immune dysfunctional syndrome. This illness, AIDS, and the rise in lupus and multiple sclerosis really show the deterioration of the environment and its increasing inability to support human life. I want to connect that and my own experience with illness to the social order that lacks compassion for people who are ill, and to the fact that within this civilization we reject subjective experience. For example, doctors are hardly interested at all in what you experience in your body, which is absurd. You become so sophisticated in your knowledge about the body when you are ill. So to come back to where I started, it seems to me that the self and other are one. When we destroy our own experience, then it makes us completely unable to understand or relate to the experience of another.

Chapter 2

Open Dialogue

☙ *After each member of the group present makes an initial statement, a general discussion begins. The format is such that people make their comments in the order in which they raise their hands, which does not allow for direct dialogue but for a general synthesis.*

☙ FRITJOF CAPRA *opens:* As we were going around there was an implication that we were categorically against technology. This statement is either a sloppy way of speaking or it is hypocritical. I don't think we can maintain that we are against technology.

We can and must say that we are critical of all technology today, but we are not against technology categorically. Some technologies may not be saved; we can say we are against them and then articulate our criticisms of the totalitarian aspect, the industrial aspect, and so on.

☙ KIRKPATRICK SALE: The Luddites used the phrase "machinery hurtful."

☙ ANDREW KIMBRELL: It's terribly important to remember that technology is legislation, that technologies that any society uses will, to a large extent, determine what kind of society it becomes. Some technologies will allow for democracy, sustainability, community, and individual control of resources; some will favor elites, bureaucracies, and the destruction of the natural world. We need to define those technologies that give us one future versus those that give us another.

☙ VANDANA SHIVA: You can't live without technology on this planet. It is monopolizing power and embodying political privilege technologically that is so anti-life. That is what one has to be critical of.

☙ WENDELL BERRY: To say that you are going to be critical of technology isn't enough. That's like saying you want to use it very carefully or like saying that you only want to use atomic energy for peace.

⊘JERRY MANDER: First look at what is intrinsic to the technology. Where does a specific technology go, what does it produce, what is the totality of values that it embodies and imposes? Who benefits and who is harmed? Then it is possible to make a decision about it.

⊘WENDELL BERRY: What do you have to choose *against* in order to choose *it*?

⊘SUSAN GRIFFIN: If we just say we're against technology, that mystifies it and gives it a glitzy feeling as if it has more power than we do. If we see that it is a tool, then choice enters into it.

⊘PER GAHRTON: I don't think it's possible to be against technology without reservations. There are many kinds of technology that we want, such as windmills and the like. The major difference between us and the Establishment may be that we believe that there are always disadvantages to technology. We have a skeptical attitude toward technology. Another aspect is that technology always creates a new social situation. That brings me to the question of hypocrisy. Is it hypocritical to use computers, for instance, and faxes?

A new fact has been created by the invention of this technology. Of my twenty-five books, I wrote twenty on an old-fashioned typewriter. Now I write with computers, because everybody else does, because publishers demand that I write on computer. They want a diskette with my manuscript. A new social reality has been created. I have delivered thousands of articles by ordinary mail. But today I must deliver an article to the newspapers by fax because it would be too late otherwise and they are used to this.

You cannot live completely outside the society you are going to change. That's not hypocrisy, it's a kind of realism. Otherwise you need to be a secessionist, to leave and create an island outside. Maybe that was possible a hundred years ago, but now we cannot find any place on Earth that is unaffected by what's going on. Also it's not responsible just to get away and take care of yourself and not to bother about the rest. In the Green Movement we say that we have one foot in the society we want, and the other in the society that is there.

⊘GODFREY REGGIO: I don't see technology as this tool or that tool, good tools and bad tools. The larger consideration is that technology today is the environment in which life takes place. Technology has become the host of life. Technology as environment, as context, technology as postnatural nature, technology as a way of life is causing us to transit from the human, from history, into a hybrid species that I shall call "massman." Massman is beyond our conception of human, is a condition that eliminates the possibility of a free, creative, convivial existence. Massman as an entity is the price we pay for the pursuit of our technological happiness! The critical distinction between *technologies* and technology as a way of life should be recognized. We don't use technology, we live it!

In summary the crisis today is the crisis of way of life. Following the thoughts of Jacques Ellul, there are six quintessential aspects to that crisis: The first is a crisis of vision; the second is a crisis of humans separated from the source; the third is a crisis of scale and magnitude; the fourth is a crisis of acceleration, density, and mobility; the fifth is the crisis of human addiction to the technological order; the sixth is the interrelatedness of all crises. All things are related in the technological world. It's not the effect of technology on society, it is rather that everything is situated *in* technique—the environment, politics, the economy, culture, community, the individual.

🖎ASHIS NANDY: Per Gahrton seems to suggest that we have to live with modern technology, not by choice but almost by default, to survive. Perhaps one can give a better reason for people like us guiltily using modern technology. Broadly, there have been two kinds of critiques of technology. The first kind concerns size. E. F. Schumacher is a good example. The argument takes a position against large, or mega-, technologies. The other kind of argument has to do with the content of technology. Gandhi said any technology which was labor displacing had to be rejected. Implicit in Gandhi's position is the precept that all technologies which displace the distinctive human qualities of human beings must be rejected. In other words, the transportation technology which displaces your ability to walk is less dangerous than an electronic technology which makes certain kinds of thought processes unnecessary. This is exactly the reverse of the hierarchy of modern technology whereby a technology which displaces the higher functions of human beings is by definition superior to the technology that displaces simple human functions. Another way in which Gandhi attacked the problem was by talking about the conceptual grid within which the technology was embedded. He seemed to suggest that the grid of modern technology, the grid produced by Enlightenment Europe, was itself faulty, irrespective of the technology's content.

🖎ASHIS NANDY *goes on to discuss Gandhi's commendation of the bicycle, the lathe, and the sewing machine as fitting technologies.*

Next, WENDELL BERRY *frames an understanding of the errancy of our time, and of the work of correcting it, in terms of divorce and of connection:* I wanted to say something about stories. I have tried for a long time to explain to myself why I spend so much time writing essays instead of stories. It finally occurred to me that the dominant story of our age is the story of divorce. It is a story of separation, of blowing apart, as if our whole life were a logical deduction from the Big Bang.

There is another story: the story of how our life hangs together. And we've lost that story by permitting the media to sentimentalize it out of existence. When I was a young fellow there used to be a song that said, "I love those dear hearts and gentle people who live and love in my home town." That was not written by somebody in the home town, that was written by some songwriter who had gone to L.A. or New York, who never had a home again, even for Christmas. That's not a story, just as the "tea for two" version of marriage is not a story. For it to be a story there has to be a history of the pain involved. You might say that one of the dominant stories of our time is the individual success story, but that is the story of divorce, just as the career is a story of divorce.

The story of how life hangs together is the story of how it hangs together in spite of the pain. Because of the sentimentalization of community and family life, we've been reluctant to speak honestly about relationships and admit that relationships are imperfect. But they are. They are full of pain. It is inevitable. When you make up your mind to be faithful to one woman, that simply means that the next thing you will have to do is meet Calypso and you better have an answer. It's tough to keep making these choices. If you make up your mind to devote yourself to community, you don't want to say your life with your community is difficult because you feel that your community doesn't deserve to have that said. But it *is* difficult. And that means it is a story.

Every traveler nowadays is divorced, every traveler is undergoing that experience of separation from everything. Technology separated us, and every time it separated us it set up a little shop to sell us whatever we would have got free from whatever it was we were separated from: our places, our families, our loved ones, our communities.

We are proposing now to get involved in the opposite story, the story of connection, and that is a hard story to get involved in because there still are going to be things that you can't do without help from the corporations. I do think it is hypocritical to speak as we are speaking here and yet be dependent on the economy we oppose. It doesn't excuse us to say it is realistic; a hypocrite is a realist by definition. I think what you have to do when you think about these problems is accept the hypocrisy and feel it as uncomfortable enough that you will do something about it.

Every time you grow food for yourself without the intervention of the industrial economy, every time you have pleasure with a child without recourse to the pleasure industry, you are in the story of connection. And this is an humbling story. There is no way to be a hero in this story.

To be in this story you have to accept forgiveness. This is true of community life, family life, any kind of life that involves relationships that last more than a few weeks. Over and over again you are going to come to the place where you have to accept forgiveness in place of admiration, this thing that you wanted so much. But the choice is not, as all our propagandists have led us to think, between perfect and imperfect relationships; the choice is between imperfect relationships and no relationships. Because this industrial, technological, economic juggernaut doesn't lead to paradise, it leads to the nursing home where people die alone, with a game show on the television.

⚘ HELENA NORBERG-HODGE: I agree that there are no global solutions. However, there are very severe global problems and we need to raise awareness about these problems worldwide.

For the last twenty years I have spent three-quarters of the year with the Ladakhis who are living a way of life that is based on connection, on relationship, on an intimacy with the land, and they are living in such a decentralized way that they are almost completely powerless when the juggernaut strikes. Their world view and language is so in tune with specific natural environments and contexts that it does not allow them to understand what the juggernaut is all about. In order to stand a chance against the megatrends we need to centralize our opposition.

We also need to use technology to oppose further technologization. For instance, we have to think of strategies that make it possible to have your voice, Wendell, heard by more people. That might mean using the media, even having you on television or radio.

⚘ WENDELL BERRY *responds:* If you let the issue of need determine what you do, you don't have any protection. You are surrounded by need all the time, so there is no limit to what you have to get involved in. You have to let your own sense of obligation and your own integrity determine what you do. Maybe some of you know circumstances in which television is not reductive, but it reduces me. Every time I've ever been interviewed on television, I've felt reduced. If I'm going to engage people, I want to speak as carefully as I can. Which is to say that I'm a writer, not a television actor. I'm not going to permit myself to be reduced if I can help it.

⌖ KIRKPATRICK SALE *returns us to the problems of definitions and of making judgments:* Three short points about the question of technology. The first is by way of definition. Speech is a technology, probably our first technology, perhaps preceding fire, and is an intimate part of the thing we are as a species. Like all technologies, speech is problematic. The very moment that we learned to say, "Look out for the saber-toothed tiger about to pounce upon you," we also said, "We don't want anybody who has red hair in our village."

The second point is that there are kinds of technology which we *know* are not good. We could use the term "megatechnology" as long as it allows us to encompass microtechnologies and nanotechnologies. E. F. Schumacher defined appropriate technology as being smaller, safer, cheaper, and simpler. We know that when a technology is large and unsafe and expensive and complicated and at the same time massifying and uncontrollable, this technology is wrong. So we can define certain technologies as wrong as well as categorize the wrong uses of inevitable technologies.

The third point is that technology is separate from nature and from our soul. Nature does not have any technologies, nor does our soul. Technology is that which is the rationalizing, the objectifying process. We have to identify technology as something separate from the natural: different and problematical if not outright dangerous. And to be skeptical of it is not enough: We have to be deeply resistant to it. You used to see a bumper sticker that read, "Question Authority"—it should have said, "Resist Authority." Questioning authority and questioning technology is not enough. Our position has to be absolutely *against* technology. That is what our soul as well as nature herself is telling us.

⌖ JEREMY RIFKIN *declares that it's the power relationships which different technologies determine that should concern us and inform our judgment:* Of the two great cop-outs in this century, one is institutional: "I was only following orders," and the other is technological: "If it can be done, it will be done." The belief that tools are neutral is the great myth of the modern age. Every single tool is power. All technologies are extensions of our being. They allow us to expropriate space and compress time. Perhaps the most appropriate question should be, "How much power is expropriated by a given technology?" Are there technologies so inherently powerful that in utilizing them we undo our relationship to the scale of things, to our needs, the needs of the biosphere and of future generations? Modern technology is based on maximizing efficiency, the bedrock of our temporal orientation. Efficiency means to maximize your output in the minimum time, expending minimum labor, energy, and capital in the process. Efficient technology can never be sustainable —because maximizing output in minimum time means an expedient use of expropriating tools. American agriculture might be efficient, but it is not sustainable.

Efficiency is always at the expense of relationships. If this civilization thought that tools should be sufficient to the task, rather than efficient to the goal, we could be developing technologies that create intimate participation, rather than distancing us—developing technologies that sustain, rather than drain, the environment.

Homo faber exists; we are toolmakers, and we can never anticipate all the consequences of our actions when we use a tool to expropriate space and to compress time. The rule should be always to intervene on the side of elegance, constraint, and conservatism. We could begin to explain to our fellow citizens and especially the young people that we are not afraid of technology, but that our job as responsible human beings is to define the limits of power.

⊘ Elisabet Hermodsson *refines the power question and shifts the terminology:* The word "technology" originally meant knowledge of technique. That is a good thing. But I would rather use the term "technocracy." Megatechnology is the paradigm for everything, for thinking, for living, for business, and for war. You speak of language as a technology. But if we compare language with megatechnology or supertechnique, and consider that language is different from country to country, we see that this ruling supertechnique is making the whole world not equal but similar. I desire a technique that is different from country to country, that is just like culture and language and is everybody's knowledge.

Every technique has power, but different techniques represent very different sorts of power. And that technique which is taking the whole world in its government, that is the terrible technique that makes most of us into slaves.

⊘ Andrew Kimbrell *suggests that an image of a just and desirable society should be the point of beginning for evaluating technology, that technologies have implicit purposes as well as explicit uses that must be discriminated:* For most of this century "progress through technology" has been a kind of religion. And society is still entranced with the idea that technology is going to be our salvation and somehow create a heaven on Earth. A major concept which bolsters a benign view of technology is that technology is neutral, that it can be used for great good or evil, and that its consequences depend on the morals of those who use it. This is a myth. Technology is never neutral. From the wheel to the hammer to the nuclear bomb it represents power, power over people or nature. Once we have established that technology is not neutral, the next questions are, "If it's not neutral, what kind of power does it wield? Is the power appropriate or inappropriate? Further, what does a technology's power legislate about a society that uses it?" Just contrast the "politics" of two different forms of energy technology. Solar energy, for example, permits individual and community control, requires no scientific elite, no military elite, no major capital accumulation. This means that the energy source isn't centralized and therefore there's no centralized control, whereas nuclear power, regardless of how widespread its ownership, requires massive capital, centralized control of energy, large bureaucracies for safety, energy distribution, and waste disposal, and scientific and military elites. Solar energy is a democratic technology that can be responsive to the needs of individuals and communities, and for which they can take responsibility. Nuclear power is inherently totalitarian, and societies built around this type of technology become totalitarian regardless of their purported political beliefs.

Given that technology is not neutral, and in fact can determine the very political and economic structure of a society, the essential question then becomes, "Which technologies fit our future vision?" If we are looking for a more decentralized, more humane, more personal, community-based future we can only realize this vision by supporting those technologies that will allow for it. Attempting to create this future while ignoring the technology question—which has been the misguided history of much of the Progressive Movement—is politically incoherent.

⊘ ANDREW KIMBRELL *registers his comments on the hypocrisy question by saying it is unfair to ask those of us who spend our lives working long hours in opposition to the technological system to also be in absolute consistency about using only appropriate technology in our personal lives. That requires a kind of double heroism that few can realize.*

⊘ FRÉDÉRIQUE APFFEL-MARGLIN *offers the observation that for much of humanity, employing technology has been embedded in vital, respectful relationships with nature and one's community and that modernity initiated a great discontinuity in the human relationship with tools:* The antonym of rational efficient action, which is a way of describing modern technology, is ritual. In noncommoditized, nonmodern societies there is technology, but it is always ritualized. You build a house, you sacrifice to the deities. You hunt, you beg forgiveness of the animal, you revere your tool. It's universal. Modernity is unique in not having done that. What is rational efficient action as opposed to ritual? It is an issue of power. These three words—"rational," "efficient," "action"—mean that cognition is extracted from the body, from the world, from others, from nature. Yes, ritualized technology is transformative, but it gives a different kind of power because it is in relationship, making the relationship, maintaining it, regenerating a relationship with all the beings in the nonhuman world and with the others in one's own world. The power of modern technology is destructive because it has severed that connection. The severance of these connections is rooted in rationality that goes with efficiency, in which connections have no place. The first divorce is a divorce of rationality from the heart, from the spirit, and from the Earth.

We can't talk about technology in general. There is a watershed, and it's the watershed of modernity.

⊘ SIGMUND KVALOY *resorts to a tangible example to help us in distinguishing between good and bad—or sensitive and insensitive—technology:* I have two tractors on my farm. Selma is a very light 35-year-old little Volvo, named after the great landscape-loving Swedish author Selma Lagerlöf. When I plow and hit a big rock, she will spin her rear wheels and I'm sitting low so it is easy to climb down. I go behind and help Selma with an iron bar. While I'm down on the ground I may find something strange in the soil. Once I found a flint arrowhead that must have been there for several thousand years, suddenly revealing to me the enormous historical span of my foremothers and forefathers, forming and being formed by this landscape: how all that is the very basis of my existence.

The other tractor is a big modern thing. You have to climb a staircase to get into it. Once there, you are encased inside of a house with air conditioning and stereophonic music or telephone calls in your ears. This tractor has an extremely powerful four-wheel drive, so you can have a massive plow with many shares and use it to plow the fields very much faster than before. You go on down the field. In the middle you may feel a slight tug. When you get to the end, you look behind you and see that the plow has been torn off, caught behind a rock. The tractor is so strong, it just sheared the connection. You received no bodily warning. The human worker and his technological tool can be seen as a unit. Ideally the tool, like the little tractor, should increase, or at least preserve, the person's complex bodily involvement with nature and with her community. Selma, the little tractor, is still an extension of myself. Whereas I become a mere extension of the big, modern, enclosed tractor with all its power and all its microprocessors. I can't even repair it. It cuts me off from my local community and from my own development as well. I'm here on my field listening to something far away, caught up in a past distraction; my neighbor's over there inside of the same kind of moving cubicle. Neither of us can feel the ground through the wheels, or through our spirits. Yet *urbanized* workers are levels more "off the ground" than we! The latest forms of modern or even postmodern alienation border on collective insanity.

⊘ SIGMUND KVALOY *continues, mentioning that some Norwegian Greens envision telecommuting and networking globally from their mountain valleys, then points out the inherent liability in the system:* The computer will proliferate as long as the microprocessor becomes cheaper, or costs the same. But that presupposes the continuation of the present system of global trade and corporate industry and finance. If that fails, microprocessors will not be cheap anymore! If the present infrastructure has broken down, and you are sitting around with your cow and potatoes, and if then your own computer breaks, can you go to your local blacksmith to have it repaired? Of course not! The smithy is not even there any more. The microprocessor's replacement depends on the trade system, et cetera, which is inevitably breaking down due to its insane abstractness. This breakdown is our hope, and the hope is well-founded, since it is concrete versus abstract.

⊘ WENDELL BERRY *also distills a lesson from rural reality:* In my neighborhood in the hay harvest, not so long ago, we made hay. All the neighbors would come together, pick the hay bales up, and haul them into the barn. And there were certain inefficiencies involved in that. You don't haul hay both ways. There are times when you're just not doing anything. You're talking with the other people. When you're doing that kind of work and there's a lot of it and it's awfully hot, you quit at times and rest and talk. This is a necessary community occasion. You can't call the community together and say, "Now you folks talk to each other for a while," because then nobody would think of anything important to say. The important subjects come up accidentally because of patterns which remind people of things they remember or want. And so essential information gets passed along. I learned some of the most important things I know in such intervals.

Now the mechanization of haying has been stepped up. Those of you who don't know very much about farming have nevertheless driven through the countryside and seen these huge round bales scattered about in the fields. These weigh fifteen hundred pounds. Because they're round and contain a large volume of hay, some of which can be wasted, they can be left out in the weather. So now whoever rakes the hay may never speak to the person who bales it. No crew comes together to carry it in. So this is a hateful kind of technology. One could whole-heartedly say, "Well, let's just eliminate that." But the problem is that there aren't enough of us left to staff the hay crews. So the question is not whether we want the technology or not. The critical question is whether we want the hay or not. And if we want the hay, this is the way we've got to get it.

If we're going to be intelligent about this issue, we've got to acknowledge our dependency on hateful technology. In order to get around this dependency, I think we have to start talking about community economics. That appropriately complicates the issue. In some of his writing about the history of the West, Wallace Stegner talked about those things that once possessed—at one time the steel knife, the hunting rifle—later cannot be done without—the telephone, automobile, and so on. They're very difficult to get away from. But if we acknowledge the difficulty and, in doing so, give a just definition of each individual problem as we come to it, then we may be able to get a solution.

⊚ What next took place was a briefing on biotechnology which, along with a panel on the subject that was held at the 1994 conference, and the discussions that followed, constitute Chapter 4.

Resuming the more general discussion about the language that veils technology with confusion and mystique, FRITJOF CAPRA *begins:* There is a profound confusion in our culture between human progress and so-called technological progress. Every technological innovation is automatically identified with progress. We should rescue the term "progress" and reserve it for human progress and the betterment of human life.

⊚ JOHN MOHAWK *makes a trenchant observation about the lineage of the religion of progress:* There is a 2,000-year-long tradition of Utopianism in Western culture. Because people imagined that they could create that perfect society, they felt justified in putting down resistance against whatever needed to be done in order to create that perfect society.

Modernity was really the result of the implementation of a succession of Utopian views: the Promised Land, Manifest Destiny.

Modernity is ending with the browning of Europe and North America and with the end of the European Diaspora. To think thus ends the modern period is an extremely optimistic view. The Utopian visions that led to the domination of the world by Europe and set into motion the ecological crisis of the planet have just been supplanted by successive and as-yet-unidentified Utopian visions. One started around 1940, with the promotion of the ideology that the future is electricity, or chemistry, or some other thing. Despite the early signs of problems, this ideology created an almost religious acceptance of progress as irresistible, as inevitable. It disarmed society. However, we also have the examples of people who have resisted. We need to keep those examples in mind as defining what it is that we are looking at.

It is mass development. It is an ideological process. I don't believe it to be economic development at all. If I went to the bank to borrow for a business enterprise, I'd have to show that the enterprise wouldn't cost more than the amount of the loan. Time and again it has cost more to build a major dam than what we were told. The costs of displacing people and of ruining an area are never figured into the plan. The proponents don't tell us what it is going to cost to pay for the aftermath of development. While we are weighing whether the technology is good or bad I propose that we also judge the ideological framework through which the technology is presented, promoted, and ushered into society.

The Amish community's opinion about technology and mass development is always that it isn't a good idea. They've been the only ones who have been right so far. The Indian community actually perceived that the reproductive element of life, the forces that created the Earth, were on the side of the creator of life. And that the creator had an antagonistic twin who was trying to destroy the reproductive part. The Western mythology is that whatever you use that makes change makes for progressive, positive change. I might say that our mythology fits the construction, but yours doesn't.

⊘Ashis Nandy deftly explains technology's special position in the modern nation-state as above and apart from the democratic process, a segue from monarchism to technocracy: According to one estimate in India today 600 million people or roughly 65 percent of the population usually go to the traditional healers. So, in one sense, no patent law, however stringent, will affect this 600 million. Nevertheless, the voice of these 600 million Indians who go to the traditional medical systems will not outweigh the

voice of the small community of modern doctors who run the Indian health system. This is part of a larger story. One of the main functions of modern technology in societies throughout the world is to keep a large sector of the population effectively outside of politics. Technology has become a substitute for politics in country after country and it is meant to be. This game started in the early nineteenth century, when after the French Revolution the monarchies in Europe began to crumble and various forms of representational systems were introduced in Europe. These representational systems helped to distribute the charisma which was originally invested or concentrated in the monarch. The idea of the people or the masses began to acquire a new sanctity. Among the ruling elites in Europe, however, there also grew a fear of this democratization. The "mob" became the fearsome symbol of what unrestrained democracy might do. In reaction freedom was defined as a value that had to have priority over democracy.

Because this value of freedom was seen to be closely aligned to the scientific spirit and scientific rationality, and modern technology seemed, rightly or wrongly, to be a direct derivative of this spirit, any technological decision also had to have priority over democratic rights of the people. Thus, while it was not possible to depoliticize the people, one could depoliticize sectors of life in the name of expertise, professional knowledge, and the privileged access to scientific spirit in certain groups of people.

Technology has consistently served this purpose not only in Europe, but in all state systems modeled after it. This has become one of the primary identifying principles of the modern nation-state system. Unlike the traditional state systems in premodern Europe or in the older classical or medieval state systems in countries like India, the state today is not only supposed to provide security, individual or collective, to the people, the state is also supposed to do two other things: to interpret and promote the spirit of scientific rationality and to ensure some working out of the theory of progress, through development or in other forms. Technology has become a means of marking out a sector of life where democratic principles and the voice of the majority can be legitimately "superseded."

Deepening the contradictions, pointing to the irony and sometimes blind futility of technology-that-would-be-progress, JERRY MANDER *mentions an analysis of efficiency and time saving which appeared in Ivan Illich's* Energy and Equity *as follows:* "The typical American male devotes more than 1,600 hours a year to his car. He sits in it while it goes and while it stands idling. He parks it and searches for it. He earns the money to put down on it and to meet the monthly installments. He works to pay for petrol, insurance, taxes, and tickets. He spends four of his sixteen working hours on the road or gathering his resources for it. And the figure does not take into account the time consumed by other activities dictated by transport: time spent in hospitals, traffic courts, and garages; time spent watching automobile commercials or attending consumer education meetings to improve the quality of the next buy. The model American puts in 1,600 hours to get 7,500 miles: less than five miles per hour."*

⊘JERRY MANDER *continues:* That is an example of a systemic analysis of the *real* human relation to a machine; such analysis needs also to include social, political, and ecological dimensions. E. F. Schumacher said small is beautiful. Leopold Kohr said slow is beautiful. Computers, faxes, phones, jet travel, Walkmans, television, and mass communication are accelerating the speed at which society and commerce operate, and demanding an unnatural emotional speed in everyday life. The net effect: alienation from nature.

And years ago Langdon Winner's brilliant article, "Do Artifacts Have Politics?" made the case that all technologies have observable political consequences that are the inevitable result of their manufacture and application, that are intrinsic to their form, and therefore nonreformable. Nuclear power, for example, by reason of its complexity, cost, and scale is inherently centralizing; solar power is inherently decentralizing. Only through more systemic analysis can the politics of the complex of technologies be revealed so that we can begin to think about whether we actually want it in our society. After that, how to get rid of a given technology is an even more complicated question.

⊘JERRY MANDER *concludes:* In this meeting we are attempting to develop tools for the systemic or holistic analysis of technology and of given technologies. It's common to judge these technologies, computers for example, solely in terms of their personal benefits to us. From environmental or social points of view, though, this is insufficient. A technology may benefit you personally, but what else does it do?

For instance, computers have made possible an unprecedented degree of surveillance of office workers. For workers in insurance companies, and phone companies, the rate of all data-entry keystrokes can be monitored continually by other computers; people are fired on this basis.

*Ivan Illich, *Energy and Equity,* New York: Harper & Row, Publishers, 1974.

The Forest Service has completely converted to computer management. Rangers who used to know the quality and character of the forests firsthand are now deskbound. What is lost? Only the most essential aspects of a human connection to nature.

Computers are also being delivered to native groups as a benefit so they'll be able to "manage their resources" digitally rather than by getting on the land and observing the game. The entire system of resource management by direct observance is completely undermined by the technology.

❷MARTHA CROUCH observes that some technologies encode not only politics but a fundamental belligerence: Now that so much attention is being paid to former military technologies and the question of what to do with all the excess military capacity, I've been thinking a lot lately about the conversion of those technologies—using satellite imaging to look at environmental degradation instead of looking for submarines, for instance. Taking the technology of World War II and converting it to so-called peacetime use in agriculture was a failure.* There was an excess wartime capacity for making ammonium nitrate for explosives. In order to maintain that capacity ammonium nitrate was used and promoted as fertilizer. The attendant problems are now well known. Chemical defoliants were turned into herbicides for agriculture, airplanes were turned into sprayers. It was a very direct connection: Bring the war home, convert weaponry to peacetime use. Beating swords into plowshares is used to denote peace but was in fact a continuation of war—war against the land with the Earth ripped open by the plow. It would have been better to bury the sword and invent a new technology based on a different world view. The history of the intent and the world view of the maker is bound so tightly into such technology that I don't believe it's possible to convert it.

GODFREY REGGIO: An esoteric footnote—in theological thought something is said to have high magic when it is sacramental, that is, when it produces what it signifies, when it goes beyond symbol. It might be insightful to see the computer as precisely sacramental, a power capable of effecting a transubstantiation, something that produces what it signifies. If you take the idea of "as above so below" when you look at the microchip of a computer, it looks exactly like what a city

*The description of conversion of ordnance factories is from "Growing Peacefully: Ending Agribusiness's War on Creation," by Ron Kroese, in *Seed Savers 1992 Harvest Edition*, Decorah, IA: Seed Savers Exchange.

looks like from outer space. These tools are more powerful than their personal uses to us. They actually produce the world in which we live. We couldn't talk about the globalization of the planet without the computer. It's not that the computer is an addendum to that agenda; it is that which produces it. In that sense it has politics.

⊘ From the esoteric to the palpable, SIGMUND KVALOY *says that computers exact a cost in actual sensation:* With the computer and word processors and all these things that we are supposed to be creating on, with super-soft fingertip touch, we are losing this wonderful body. We are not even touching any more. The remaining challenges to use our body and our fingers and our muscles and our senses and our ability to intuit wholes are removed. Then the main problems in our life and the life of the globe are all supposed to be solved by sitting in front of this computer in bodiless abstract virtual space.

Biotechnology is very much involved in this removal. Through the computer and through the manipulation of life—which is biotechnology's rationale—humankind faces a most radical alienation. Combine those things and the end point is some kind of global supercomputer that will pose as the final solution to all these terrible problems, a self-propelling dynamic, heading blindly to transmogrify the living, self-regulatory system that is Gaia into a humanmade spaceship, a Servo-Globe. But as said before, that end point will never materialize, since concrete, nonvirtual reality, nature, says no. And nature is ourselves, no matter what the abstract models of the transnational corporations tell us.

⊘ MARTIN KHOR *helps fine tune an analytic tool:* We need to reconceptualize what we mean by efficiency. Whether something is efficient or not depends on our criteria and the objective. Normally efficiency is measured according to the quantity of x per unit of y. Usually it's the quantity of output per specified time unit. But if our aim is sustainability for the next 10,000 years, then we know now that maximum output per minimum unit of time can be very inefficient.

Also we need to ask, "Why do we measure output per unit of *time?*" Or, in agriculture, "Why is it output per unit of land?" If our goal is full employment, then efficiency would mean maximum quantity of labor per unit of capital investment. For that goal modern technology would be extremely inefficient. If what is important is the health content per unit of product, then in that case infant formula is extremely inefficient as compared to mother's milk. Or if what we are really after is happiness per unit of output, many modern products would be extremely inefficient.

⊘ PER GAHRTON, *a political man, begins the attempt to bridge the distance between reality as understood by Neo-Luddites and* realpolitik: Is the conclusion of Jerry's analysis on an individual level or on a social level? Is the conclusion that I, as a person who does not like television and computers, must set an example by not using them at all? If I do use them am I a hypocrite? On an individual basis I doubt that that is a good strategy. Of course, we need to make distinctions between different kinds of technology. Some technologies are so bad that we have to fight them on all levels and avoid them ourselves. Other technologies we might use although we wish that they didn't exist. Then there are technologies that are more or less good. The strategic conclusion or analysis is very important. Nuclear power should be abolished totally, and I think that it is quite realistic, but should computers be abolished? Or should we fight their bad effects?

As a politician, I ask myself, "How realistic is telling people that they shouldn't have any computers or television at all?" Could we gain support for that? Could we gain support fighting against biotechnology? We have to make some definition; we cannot just be a movement that is against all technology. Even Wendell had to make this deal with his conscience in order to get hay. This is the situation of most human beings. Strategy must be added to this discussion. A philosophical analysis should help the criticism, but it should draw a conclusion.

Slowness is beautiful and may be the clue to many of these problems. In a society where grandmothers were ruling, social change would be much slower. In the future we need slower change, if any at all. And as society, we need to take care of and make the best of what we have and abolish those things that we don't need. Need is a very ambiguous concept. When there were no cars at all you didn't need a car for transportation. When almost everybody has a car a new situation is created, a kind of social need. It is now much more difficult not to have a car. We must admit that technology creates a new society and thus a new reality in which people live.

⊘ *After a quick, sharp homily,* WENDELL BERRY *tells a story that teaches how some essential understanding is communicated through certain kinds of hard work and can be lost when labor's saved:* It seems to me that one motivating force of this program of technologizing everything is laziness. Another is our wicked impatience with mystery and complexity. And there is much to be said about mystery and complexity and their importance. But I'd like to speak just a minute about difficulty.

In 1961 and 1962 my wife Tanya and I spent several months in Florence, Italy. That was where my life began to change, because the peasant agriculture of Tuscany was a revelation to me. It had not occurred to me that land as steep and difficult as that could be so productively and beautifully and carefully used. Last fall we went back to Tuscany. The peasant agriculture of Tuscany now appears to be completely gone. Instead of the white cows that pulled the field implements, they use machines. The terraces are gone, which means that you see severe erosion. Apparently the Chianti country between Florence and Siena is now worked up and down the hill. While we were there a friend took me to his farm, which he had not permitted to be converted to machinery. He had invited a peasant farmer to come and farm there and this farm still was using the big white cows for field traction. It was a very rainy fall in Tuscany and the Arno was flooding. This peasant farmer said, "They wonder why there is water in their streets and they are plowing up and down the hills." Then he said, "If you work with animals you always work across the slope. This is because when you work with animals you work against physical difficulty." You can try this for yourself. If you have a hillside acre that you have to traverse on foot twenty times, would you cross it on the contour or would you go up and down the hill? When you eliminate that difficulty with the machine, you begin to work up and down the slope. With the wrong kind of technology you eliminate your physical connection with the landscape—and this has direct practical consequences. That country isn't going to last very long, I guess, if they don't invent a machine that will go back and forth across the slope.

If you eliminate difficulty you eliminate the quality of work, because you eliminate the body as a consideration in the way the work is done. If you hate difficulty so much that you are willing to eliminate the body from work, then you eliminate the physical sympathy between the work and the land.

   ⊘ LANGDON WINNER *returns to the swords-into-plowshares problem and the ineluctable necessity of working for such a transformation:* Military conversion remains an important problem. When you count in all the costs of the military economy in the U.S.A., it's still about $500 billion a year. Now that the Cold War is over, there is a great push to convert its people, organizations, and hardware to domestic purposes in much the same way that happened at the end of World War II. But the standard approach—taking military bases, plants, and employees and turning them from military to civilian production—does not seem to be working very well. The reason is that both Cold War technologies and the people trained to make and use them are very narrowly dedicated and difficult to adapt to broader purposes.

During the past two centuries the military approach to the world has produced much of modern technology, from interchangeable parts in industry to the jet airplane and the computer itself. This influence has given many of our technology-centered institutions a distinctive, hard-edged cast. If we don't find ways to convert the people and organizations of the Cold War to socially useful ends, they will, I believe, eventually seek to reproduce the conditions that seem to justify the existence of growing military power, a process I call "reverse adaptation." Looking for a new mission and public funding, they may begin to pressure society to define new enemies, begin a new arms race focused upon ingenious instruments of mass destruction. In that light what really needs to be converted are the people and communities—San Diego comes to mind—whose business has been lavishly supported preparations for war. We need to reeducate members of the military-industrial complex, using their defense paychecks to send them back to school to learn peace-oriented vocations.

CHARLENE SPRETNAK: With regard to defense conversion, it occurred to me several years ago that because defense workers do not put any useful products into the economy they're actually living off federal grants. I proposed, in *Green Politics*, that we continue the "grants" for three years, allowing workers—including the scientists and engineers—to study business and work with advisors to set up new businesses that would use appropriate technology, have profit sharing, have workplace democracy, be ecologically benign, and serve a regional market. This would create working models of a new kind of business instead of just throwing those people out of jobs. Of course, such a program is nearly impossible now since the federal government was bankrupted by the Reagan defense buildup, which channeled billions of dollars to the defense contractors while tripling the national debt.

⊘JEREMY RIFKIN *makes a dramatic claim about the degree to which technology is idolized, and to which some are willing to offer themselves up:* Technology has become our God. Interestingly enough, modern technology has the two defining characteristics of theology: One, we create ourselves in its image, and two, we imbue it with immortality. Before the modern age we would use organic metaphors to describe ourselves and our relationships. Today the highest compliment we pay a ruling technology is to redefine our language, our metaphors, our relationships, and our reality in its image. Once we explain all of nature, our own cognition, and our sense of our body in the language of the ruling technology, we are stuck. We can convince ourselves that the natural order of things is consistent with that technology. That's how we make our cosmologies.

In the modern age we have really imbued these technologies with the image of immortality. Every engineer still dreams of perpetual motion. In the information-biotechnical age, the vehicle of immortality is information. As we sit here there are human beings at Carnegie-Mellon and MIT who truly believe that they will be the last generation of mortals. They are attempting to download the human mind onto a computer that can live on forever, because they believe that information does not die. So we need to be conscious not only of the physical environment that's being replaced but of the fact that technology is literally all consuming. It takes up our metaphors, we redefine ourselves in its image, and we imbue it with immortality.

*⊘*STEPHANIE MILLS *obliquely suggests that absent megatechnology and transnational corporations, a land-based subsistence is our future:* If we're envisioning a future that goes beyond technological entrancement, what levels of business and private industry and what ownership of the means of production do we anticipate? There seems to be a moving into a progressive infantilization of individuals—no privacy, total dependency on large entities for our employment and livelihood.

When I told a friend I was coming to this Luddite party and that we were going to be criticizing the general technofantasy, she asked, "What would you do for an employment program?" The answer that occurred to me was land reform.

The U.S. Government's Promotion of High Technology

❷ *At the time of the 1993 conference, the Clinton administration's profile included a glamorous promotion of high technology, complete with proposals for government-corporate alliances to spur this development. Jeremy Rifkin and Langdon Winner therefore provided a briefing on the high-tech agenda, but quickly cut to the underlying ideas and popular notions that persist independent of the shifts in Beltway attention. The benefit of the populist mode of the Clinton administration's announcement of the program, Winner thought, was the implicit message that technology policy should involve public participation. It was downhill from there, though, with Rifkin anticipating even more massive unemployment as a result of advances in artificial intelligence, biotechnology, and robotics, all of which figured heavily in the administration's dreams. Rifkin concluded that then-Labor Secretary Reich's talk about workforce retraining was essentially cynical. Winner lamented that in what might be an opportunity for genuine national discussion of technology policy, instead of posing questions about ends and means, we fixate on means at the outset. During the discussion that followed, Helena Norberg-Hodge observed that such programs amount to vast subsidies for the infrastructure of increased globalization. The group's attention then shifted to the various implications of a decentralist future, and to the values, such as restoring the meaning and dignity of work, that would inform it.*

⊘JEREMY RIFKIN: Clinton and Gore are caught between world views. They're products of the sixties. They are enamored with high technology. They, too, grew up with Sputnik and the computer revolution. They love robotics and high tech. Their thinking has been tempered, though, by the deterioration of the biosphere, the loss of community, and the increasing alienation and disenfranchisement of the American people. Clinton and Gore want to heal the planet, restore community, and develop a sense of civic responsibility. They want a sustainable model of development. However, they have yet to see the inherent contradiction between a high-technology global marketplace in the twenty-first century and a sustainable development model for renewing the biosphere and reestablishing communities.

President Clinton has announced an economic recovery plan. It means committing $16 billion a year in research and development for high-technology industries, for robotics and biotechnology, fiber optics, computers, artificial intelligence, and the information superhighway. Over four years they hope to invest $60 billion and forge a new corporate-government alliance to promote high technology.

At the center of their program is the information superhighway. The goal is to develop an integrated, interactive information network that can connect the entire country and the world market in a single economic entity. To envision the tremendous impact that these kind of changes can have on demographics, values, employment, and ways of life, consider the effects of the transcontinental railway system, and, more important, the U.S. Highway Act.

During the 1992 presidential campaign Clinton attacked Bush rather effectively on his trickle-down economics. Ironically, he has trapped himself in the myth of trickle-down technology. The standing assumption of our economics has been that new technologies stimulate growth, productivity, and employment. Hitherto, when these new technologies were revolutionary and disruptive in scale, new sectors emerged to absorb displaced labor. At the turn of the century, when agriculture was mechanized, a tremendous rural labor force was disenfranchised but manufacturing grew to employ that labor. When manufacturing began to automate after World War II, that surplus labor was absorbed by the emerging service and white-collar sectors. The question now is, "What new sector might emerge to absorb the labor that's going to be displaced by the automation of those sectors?"

In agriculture, cloning techniques now being applied mean that food may be produced with no seed, no plant, no farmer, no soil, no cultivation, no harvest. They're now doing it with tomatoes, oranges, lemons, cotton, and tobacco. Forty years from now outdoor farming will be commercially eliminated. What becomes of the hundreds of millions of farmers in developing countries who have been pushed into the cash economy, who rely on exporting their foodstuffs, and who will not be able to compete? Tissue culture will reduce costs further, and its developers can synthesize and market biological commodities cheaper than farmers around the world can grow and export them.

Manufacturing, like agriculture, will in the next ten to twenty years with the new technologies be able virtually to eliminate labor from the economic equation. There's a 54,000-square-foot machine-part plant on Mount Fuji in which there are no human beings working. It is a jobless factory producing goods. Ten years ago, U.S. Steel required 120,000 people to produce the same quantity of steel that 20,000 people now produce.

The Postal Service just announced that it is going to eliminate 45,000 jobs in the next four years with computers that do signature recognition. AT&T has announced it's going to lay off 6,000 long-distance operators: A robot capable of voice pattern recognition is moving online this year.

Signature recognition and voice recognition are just two of the new technologies that will displace countless workers. Throughout the financial and service sector they're not just outsourcing, they're downsizing and replacing workers with computers. Employers do not want to pay for pension funds or health-care programs. Machines are cheaper substitutes in the global marketplace.

So what we have here is both the final triumph of technology and the debunking of the myth that technology creates jobs. It never did. The Clinton administration confronts the dilemma of the deficit. This time when technology displaces labor on the greatest scale in history, our politicians cannot bail out the system with social spending. This final triumph of technology not only means virtually the complete displacement of labor, it also means having to rethink the politics of the economy.

Robert Reich [then-Secretary of Labor] is in an unenviable position. He advocates retraining the workforce for new jobs in the "knowledge sector." This is a cynical move. This new sector may offer some employment. But those positions are very few. They're consultants, computer scientists, engineers, and teachers. How will it be possible to absorb tens of millions of Americans into an elite sector? Remember that 25 percent of the American workforce is marginally to functionally illiterate. These people cannot be retrained, in one generation, to be computer scientists. Enclaves are appearing all over the United States, from Palo Alto to Bethesda and Chevy Chase, to the North Shore of Chicago, and in the rest of the world as well. These enclaves are home to the new cosmopolitans of the global corporate workforce. Their loyalties are corporate, not national. Their affiliations have to do with the new institutional arrangements of the global market. The rest of us, not only the working poor, but the middle level in the managerial class in every country, are going to be increasingly disenfranchised. So we are in store for a tremendous political upheaval in the next ten years.

The opportunity is to provide an intellectual critique and, equally important, a political possibility for those millions and millions of people who are going to become increasingly resigned and increasingly cynical and skeptical about an economy that cannot provide them jobs. We need to be prepared to create a new political movement around jobs and a sustainable economy.

⊘ LANGDON WINNER *begins his remarks with a brief accent on the positive aspect of the Clinton administration's program, then finds it flawed, in a predictable way. Still, Winner sees an opening for more substantive national discussion of technology policy:* In the early days the Clinton administration recognized that technology policy is a matter for public choice, that it should not be left solely to the private sector as the Reagan/Bush people thought. Somehow the populace ought to be involved in talking about these issues, about which technologies are chosen and why. The implicit idea is that the renewal of society is wrapped up with choices about science and technology and that the nation needs to decide which avenues of development are truly wise investments in the future.

Beyond that, however, the picture coming out of Washington is fairly dreary. The model the Clinton administration is pursuing is an old and tired one. It projects all technological choices as components in a gigantic device: the national money pump. You turn the crank, out come more wealth and more jobs. What's appealing for many people about the Clinton and Gore proposals is that they reflect a high-technology wish list that recognizes the pet projects of university labs and Silicon Valley corporations, lame initiatives for smart highways, high-performance computing, magnetic-levitation trains, and the like. Certainly, there's need to debate questions about what kinds of communications and transportation infrastructure might be useful in the future. But instead of posing questions about social ends, Clinton and his col-

leagues begin with a set of prepackaged means. This is backward thinking about technology at its worst. The term "infrastructure" means
"deep structure." If we're going to ponder a transition from the kinds of
sociotechnical structures our society now depends upon—imagining a
future society that would be more graceful—issues about this deep structure are crucial. But questions about the relationship between basic
social, economic, and political ends and the choice of appropriate
means, however, are just not raised in today's policy discussions. A fascination with high technology renders the imagination mute.

In other parts of government, not to mention American society as a
whole, there are interesting signs that the premises of conventional science and technology policy are in serious doubt. Many people are beginning to ask, "If all this new science and technology is so good for us,
why has it failed so badly in the recent past?" If you look at areas where
massive infusions of scientific knowledge and high technology are supposed to bear fruit—industrial production, health care, education, environment, the quality of urban life—you find notorious symptoms of
stress and social decay. For the past year or so Congressman George
Brown, Chairman of the House Committee on Science, Technology, and
Space, has been giving talks in which he argues that Americans and their
political leaders have no idea, after the Cold War, what the basic purposes are for science and technology. Brown suggests that we need a
thorough national debate to reorient ourselves. We cannot continue
feeding ourselves on the old myths.

This is the man who controls a crucial set of purse strings in the U.S.
Congress, not a radical social critic. Yet he is asking many of the kinds
of questions that we would ask. Along with others, George Brown is saying that the post-World War II social contract about science and technology development—that the public supplies lots of funding and then
the scientific community gets to decide where the money will go—is no
longer good policy.

What I'm suggesting is that this deeper questioning is present even at
fairly high levels of government, a conversation waiting to be had. This
opportunity will be lost, however, if people persist thinking that technological innovation is important only as a way of revving up the great
national money pump. Unless there are other voices that speak up
about the pending technological choices and why they matter, then I
don't think we'll get much other than the collapse of the Clinton pres-
idency and a virulent reaction from the right.

   Ø JEREMY RIFKIN: Interestingly enough, the kinds of alternatives to the high-tech vision proposed for years by the New Age, feminist, New Left, and ecological communities could engender appropriate technologies and sustainable jobs. These alternatives could soon be politically possible.

⌾FRITJOF CAPRA takes the question of employment a step further: The long-term vision should include a separation of the concepts of jobs and of work. In the long run we are not going to have a full employment economy. Machines, supposedly, were invented to free humans from drudgery for more creative, more meaningful work. From that standpoint, it's not so bad if there's a computer reading envelopes instead of humans, but what do these workers do then? We need to create a society where people can work in a dignified way and associate their identity and their dignity with work rather than jobs. This would include a guaranteed minimum salary.

⌾SUSAN GRIFFIN responds with the thought that our attitude toward labor may be a cultural artifact, then turns to the subject of the suffering that joblessness is causing in the here and now: In *Genesis* and the creation myth, Adam is sent out of the garden, woman bears children in suffering and Adam labors, and it's all a punishment. This idea in our culture that work is punishment and drudgery is mixed in with everything we're discussing.

It's very urgent to address the immediate suffering of people in cities now, particularly people of color, people who started out on the bottom rungs, who were disenfranchised from the system. For our movement to be powerful, and also to be fully dimensional, we've got to be compassionate and concerned about this immediate suffering and come up with some immediate responses to it.

⌾HELENA NORBERG-HODGE urges that we get our systemic analysis of what is driving unemployment, and of what much public policy is subsidizing, to a broader public and that our policy recommendations stem from a long-term strategy: Yes, there will be a lot happening in biotechnology and information technology. Increasingly, the jobs are going to be moving to the South. Already computer engineers in India, who need only a fraction of the salary paid in Europe for such work, are being employed by aerospace companies. That means that our present analysis is quite incomplete. The analysis of how much energy we consume, for instance, suffers from the fact that the Gross Domestic Product is generated from global finance while energy statistics remain national. Because production is going on around the globe, we really have no idea. We have no global statistics. And yet many ecological economists

have fallen for the trap of believing that GDP and energy consumption have been de-linked because of modern information technology and production. In fact, what has happened is that less production is going on in the North, but on the other side of the world production is dirty and energy intensive, and energy consumption for transport has increased dramatically.

Investments in technology include research and development. Thus changes in universities are part of the shift toward larger-scale centralized production. These investments are thus used to fund "growth" or GDP. We should try to explain more clearly to the general public that this systemic interaction is leading to unemployment and to the suffering that Susan is talking about. If we only treat the symptoms of poverty in the cities, like unemployment, we're not going to get very far. We've got to be really strategic and clearminded about what the causes are and focus on those.

We need to spell out the future that continuing in the same direction will bring us. Economic policies on both the political left and right are subsidizing a process of growth that is a centralizing and urbanizing process. They are subsidizing trade and transport, which means that they are, in effect, subsidizing the TNCs. The end results are an erosion of the tax base that a fabric of smaller, national businesses and rooted capital provide, an erosion of democracy, unemployment, and ethnic and racial friction, all on a scale that we can barely imagine, in the South as well as in the North. Equally important and concurrently, we need to spell out the implications of diversification and decentralization. People want to hear not just the critique but the alternatives and the solutions as well.

⊘ SUSAN GRIFFIN *restates her plea for an immediate answer to the suffering:* I grew up in the sixties, began as a Marxist, and I remember the kind of thinking that put down reform. The idea was that we were going to transform society with radical ideas so we shouldn't bother about short-term solutions. I've shifted my thinking on that partly from having been in the position of suffering. Long-term solutions just don't do it.

What we're talking about is moving from the heart. We're talking about restoring that capacity for immediate response as a whole human being, which technology is robbing us of. We have a lot of imagination here, and we can include short-term solutions as well as long-term ones.

⊘ ANDREW KIMBRELL *seeks to mesh the long and short views, offering his insight and depth perception:* Craft is care. Too often in the sixties we thought that developing a craft was artificial or manipulative. But that is not true. If you truly care about something, whether it be poetry, pottery, or politics, you learn as much about it as you can and you develop a craft. This discussion's about how to use our intellectual and political craft to alleviate the suffering caused by the technological system.

Bear in mind that in critiquing technology and science, we're committing heresy to the surrogate religion of modernity. This new religion has its own trinity which has the force of dogma. We are told that science will allow us to know everything; technology will allow us to do everything; and that the free market will allow us to buy anything. Despite the supposed pluralism in modern religious beliefs, this trinity outlines the real religion of our time.

Now doubt about the modern religion is beginning to grow. That simple belief and trust in it has been broken. Science hasn't stopped disease; in fact, we are as concerned as ever about coming plagues. Technology has destroyed much of the environment and is now threatening the jobs of untold millions. The market hasn't decreased poverty; rather the gap between rich and poor is larger than ever. This growing doubt about the new trinity and especially technology allows us a unique opportunity to provide an alternate vision. However, we need to provide this new vision of society quickly. Otherwise destructive forces can take advantage of the situation. For example, the tens of millions who will now be permanently, structurally unemployed because of technology are going to blame it on the immigrants, on those taking the jobs. They are going to go toward the right, toward populism and fascism, unless a group such as this develops and provides a sustainable alternative future vision.

⊘ STEPHANIE MILLS *reiterates the contention that jobs are at best a short-term institution and that our long-term visions will of necessity be plural because local:* Jobs sound almost like a commodity. This perpetuates paternalistic relations. You're dependent on some larger entity than yourself for employment and livelihood. The ultimate future vision would be to have an independent livelihood that's located in a real place. A vision for the future that's generic is more of the same. Alternative visions are going to have to be place specific. There might be some principles that we could adduce, bearing in mind that bioregions are where this kind of political work can go on at a more palpable scale.

⊘ JEREMY RIFKIN *moves the focus to macroeconomics:* This broad topic does entail the sticky questions of ownership and redistribution of wealth. The whole question of the structure of the economy has to be

addressed. In addition to decentralization there is the question of who owns the machines. In the World's Fairs and all the Utopian spectacles of our society the publicity always said there would be no jobs, that we would all be free from toil. What was left out was that the benefits of this freedom from toil were going to go to the owners of the means of production and that we wouldn't have any way of surviving.

⊘ *Apropos the Clinton/Gore technology initiatives,* WENDELL BERRY *says:* The thing to do is to point out the amount of superstition that's involved in this enterprise.

⊘ SIGMUND KVALOY *segues from the subject of jobs and toil to the necessity of meaningful and genuinely productive [as of food] effort:* To be swallowed up by the European Union would virtually eliminate Norwegian agriculture, as all small-scale farming among our northern European neighbors is already disappearing. Connect this to the future, to the fact that we have a food crisis, actually a hunger catastrophe in large parts of the world, and to the fact that modern agricultural methods aggravate erosion, produce biological pollution at an exponential rate, and push people off the land and into the cities. Add the fact that countries like Norway, far north and with cool climates, still have the best soil quality and the most erosion-resistant landscapes in the world. Connect that with the concept of meaningful work. When you are rooted inside of a small-scale agricultural or fishing tradition you really get to care for your home place where meager resources are compensated by complex methods and you genuinely get to care for your home because that's where your body is constantly reaching a deeper and wider integration with nature's body, which is your own body, limitless in meaningful expansion.

I connect this with the world future where food will once more be the overriding global demand—barring catastrophes like an ozone layer breakdown, "free trade" infectious disease pandemics, et cetera. Here we have the possibility of meaningful work, work that brings us back to necessity, where nature is the great teacher; work demanding the unfurling of all the talents that we are born with and demanding that we get tied to a complex place while at the same time producing the needed food in an ecological way. Large areas in the world—particularly the North—can offer these kinds of meaningful employment, and to millions and millions of people.

⊘ GODFREY REGGIO *returns to the concept that technology has so pervaded and transformed human experience that it is beyond the power of governments to affect, possibly even beyond comprehension:* Ernst Jünger said that the metaphysics of the twentieth century was technology. We're using, with the best of intentions, old thoughts and old ideas in trying to analyze what is in fact a new world circumstance. We are not dealing with decisions that Gore and Clinton can make. We're dealing with something that is essentially autonomous in nature and has as its principal mode of operation the technological imperative. If we take that seriously, it describes a whole new response. If there is to be any possibility of balancing things, I think that our only hope is to be absolutely extreme, to be willing to rethink what we mean by political activism. People do learn in terms of what they already know. People do need jobs. Here is the basis for a political coalition. But not with old thinking.

What Susan said is extremely important. There is enormous suffering going on that we can't ignore because of the big picture. The big picture's causing it.

🖉 VANDANA SHIVA *is cognizant of the ultimate scope of the phenomenon we seek to address, and adamant that there be interpretations that allow for an active response by all persons, that there is a place to begin in the politics of the present:* We need to relate this to free trade. In engaging not so much the technology, but the victims of displacement, one does need to handle it at a different level, because to such victims technology is not autonomous. It is a Clinton-Gore decision. For them there's something they can do if mobilized in a different way. They'd be crippled in another discourse, unable to take their own destiny into their hands.

We owe it to the citizens of the world, and to American citizens, to point out that these billion-dollar investments are a subsidy given to one group of economic actors, which is totally against the declared logic of free trade. It is creating a bias. There's no self-provisioning possible in this industrial world. So even to create the conditions in which people could take care of themselves without the state requires that $60 billion not be spent in a way that cripples community self-provision.

In India the free-trade debate got distorted. People say, "Ah, freedom, the state is getting off our backs." But the state is getting more on their backs by helping the wrong people to take away even more of the resources and decision-making capacities that communities otherwise would have. We simply have to engage in that debate and worry about that strategy. How do we do it worldwide so as not to allow immigration and jobs lost to the Third World to lead to racist scapegoating and at the same time make enough sense locally for mobilization?

🖉 *Deep Ecologist* GEORGE SESSIONS *is at pains to remind us that the effects of technologies and development are not limited to our species, that the*

*survival of any undomesticated nature is now at stake and should be a pri-
mary concern:* It is crucial to emphasize the difference between the concept of "sustainable development" as promoted by the United Nations
Brundtland Report and at the 1992 United Nations Rio Earth Summit
and the concept of "ecological sustainability." The industrialized First
World is already overdeveloped. Its consumer patterns must be radically
reduced and further destruction of wild areas must cease. From both a
social and ecological perspective, the great challenge for First World
countries is to attain a "steady state" economics as rapidly as possible.
Third World countries need to develop, but along ecologically sustainable lines, not emulating the unsustainable consumerism of the First
World.

It is also easy to get caught in the trap of talking about "sustainability" in terms of "sustainability for humans." Arne Naess has proposed
the concept of "wide ecological sustainability," meaning sustainability
for all life on Earth.

It is also very important that we begin the process of ecological restoration throughout the world—restoring, for example, ancient biologically rich forests and not just planting monocultural "tree farms" as is
being done in many Third World countries. But there is a danger here in
that we may continue to destroy more wild areas, claiming that we can
restore an equivalent area elsewhere. Restoration should not be viewed
as just another technological fix which serves as a rationalization for
continuing to destroy what wild areas still remain on Earth. We are
going to have to try to restore what we can, which assumes that humans
have the competence to do this, but it's even more important that we
protect what's left of the wild now! The protection of wild areas and biodiversity has to be brought to the fore. We are on course to lose most of
the wild over the next ten or fifteen years, and there'll be no getting
most of it back.

 ℘DAVID SUZUKI *speaks from experience on the difficulty of conveying
such a message:* The problem we face is that 80 percent of us live in cities
and our disconnection from the natural world is profound. Kids don't
even know where their food or water comes from. The struggle we have
is trying to make wilderness something worth saving, because to them
nature is an enemy they are trying to tame.

 ℘SIGMUND KVALOY *essays another rationale for the preservation of wildness—that it is essential to the formation of the person within any autochthonous culture:* The Brundtland Commission's definition of sustainable
development is development that meets the basic needs of the present

generation without removing the possibility of fulfilling the basic needs of future generations. Of course the key word is "basic." One very clear basic need of human beings is the need to build an identity. To be able to do that you have to be raised inside of a local culture that is shaped by meeting the challenges of that singular place on this Earth. If you accept identity this way as a basic need, then you also must accept as a necessity protection of the wild, because that is an essential part of complex place integration on this Earth. That demands and creates meaningful work. And the enduring wildness of the place is basic to any viable culture.

⊘ GEORGE SESSIONS: And again, I have to insist that all of these sustainability documents must make an ecocentric claim. There has to be wide ecological sustainability for all species on Earth. An exclusively anthropocentric rationale is unacceptable.

Biotechnology, Biopiracy, and the Mentality of Science

๑ *At the heart of these gatherings throbs the conviction that the Earth and what it gives rise to are sacred and that technological interventions too often desecrate the land and its life. This conviction is variously expressed through plain animism, the science of ecology, respect for the creation, the Conservation Movement, ecophilosophy, aesthetics, and evolutionary biology. The quality of wildness, the integrity of landscape, the spontaneity of DNA are all sacred, aspects of the holy Earth. Arguments against further destruction of, or attempts to remodel, these bases of existence are among the most radical and essential positions of our technology criticism.*

Diverse and compelling arguments against biotechnology were made at both the 1993 and 1994 conferences by Vandana Shiva, Jeremy Rifkin, David Suzuki, Andrew Kimbrell, Martha Crouch, and Beth Burrows. Because Vandana and Andrew spoke on the subject at both meetings, I have consolidated each of their presentations slightly. All of the presentations on biotechnology are grouped in this chapter.

From the Third World perspective, what makes biotechnology so epochally threatening is the drastic extent to which it permits the privatization of lifeforms, and of the qualities of lifeforms. Vandana Shiva and Beth Burrows detail the politics and the economic implications of patenting genetic material and the way the doctrine of intellectual property rights is invoked to sanction this expropriation of organisms and traits.

In the developed world, biotechnology as a means is usually justified by its ends, particularly insofar as those ends promise a reprieve from morbidity and mortality. Lately even unfashionability is subject to "cure" by genetic engineering. Andrew Kimbrell, David Suzuki, and Jeremy Rifkin explore the eugenic future biotechnology portends: a future wherein human beings will be evaluated in terms of their genetic readouts, where correlation will be confused with causation, and where biotechnological cures will be sought for traits in social disfavor ("like Luddism," quipped one wag).

MARTHA CROUCH, a "deprofessionalized" biotechnologist, critiques the pursuit in toto: It's globalizing, the focus on DNA's linear sequence is effacing the diversity of organisms, it entails a cult of experts and an industrial infrastructure, and it "delays the creativity of living within limits." And in addition to its fundamental hubris, ANDREW KIMBRELL and DAVID SUZUKI note, biotechnology has appalling potential as weaponry—to be "the poor man's nuclear bomb"—one that could be tailored to afflict only certain ethnic groups or staple crops. This, truly, is a megatechnology that holds the potential to annihilate the integrity and commercialize the essence of life itself.

VANDANA SHIVA *begins:* When genetic engineering started, it used to be called that. Somewhere along the way, the public found this concept disturbing, so genetic engineering was renamed "biotechnology." Every biotech report begins by saying, "Biotechnology is a wide range of technologies from bread and brewing to the new technologies." Because no one has died of drinking beer or eating bread, "biotechnology" has become a deliberately confusing term that confounds the benign agricultural and food-processing technologies that worked with biological organisms with the new risk taking of genetic engineering.

Even prior to the emergence of specific applications, biotechnology is restructuring the way we think, the values we live by, and our imaginings. The new DNA language is becoming a basic mode of talking about the living world, which includes us. The DNA language has the power and the capacity to wipe out the history of the problems we suffer and to obscure what really needs to be done to deal with them. This is not an accident.

The real achievement of the new biotechnologies is that social control is so much a function of the fragmentation of living systems. What you are imagining is choice, but what is happening is control. You may have read about pharmaceutical companies investing in the human genome project. All the scientists have done is DNA screening of the human genome, but converting those bits of our life into DNA language becomes in effect the creation of life, and those fragments are made available by appropriation for the pharmaceutical industry, which is already starting to bid for patents and control. DNA language then creates property for one group of people.

When the Biodiversity Convention was being drafted, there was only one mention of genetically engineered organisms. Thanks to U.S. lobbying, it now reads "living modified organisms," meaning anything that has been modified. All selection for agriculture or forestry modifies organisms. With biotechnology amorphously redefined, the technologies of the South, of communities that have employed organisms in all kinds of ways, have just disappeared—at least from being *named* in discussions of technology transfers. These technologies get used all the time, though, because biotechnology as the new genetic engineering is working on terrain that it has no knowledge about. We've worked with chemicals so far. We've worked with machines. The engineering of life still needs some kind of guidepost. The guidepost comes from indigenous knowledge, from interviews with native farmers who know that this is a drought-resistant wheat or that a particular sorghum doesn't get this disease or that a particular herb has this property to cure illness.

Now that predation is being called "prospecting." But biological organisms are not like oil. They're not raw materials. They are things complete unto themselves with a life, identity, and intrinsic worth. Genetic engineering is turning life, biodiversity, into mere raw material through a misplaced agency. The properties come from nature and from centuries of village utilization of biodiversity. It's made to appear as if the desirable property is being created in the lab, whereas all that's been done is a relocation.

The biotechnology metaphor creates an imperative, makes trade the basic logic of existence. If genetic material can be moved around, then it has commodity value. If it remains in the organism, it has none.

Recently amaranth has been patented and genetically modified. Amaranth is a grain that needs next to no inputs. You can put it in drought areas and amaranth will still give you four tons of seed and of leaf per hectare. It's highly nutritious. A genetic engineer found that amaranth has high protein, so he's making transgenic rice and transgenic wheat with the protein characteristic of amaranth. As usual, the announcements are that we will solve the hunger problem. In reality, the introduction of transgenic rice will displace complex polycultures of as many as twelve crops together, which are already giving high yields. Transgenic rice requires about eight times as much water as traditional varieties and will require pesticide because it's an introduced species. It will produce far less nutrition overall than the original amaranth would have. Part of what the transgenic twist does is change the measure of the crop's merit: Protein in rice becomes the measure, whereas the measure should be protein in amaranth. Meanwhile, we've lost calcium, iron, and water. But because we've put protein in a place where it didn't belong, there's a sense of progress, and achievement, even though what's actually happening is a destruction.

In the new reports coming out of the United Nations Environment Programme or the United Nations Conference on Environment and Development or the General Agreement on Tariffs and Trade, what used to be a language of "rights to biodiversity" shifted quickly to "access to biodiversity" and is now "trade in genetic resources."

To talk of patents on life creates resistance, so the phrase is "patents to biotechnological invention." And what is merely a relocation of a fragment of life from one organism into another organism becomes a claim to the very reproduction of that organism and its future generations. In terms of formation of property, this is vastly greater than anything the enclosure of the commons could have achieved. It redefines living diversity with which cultures have always interacted, particularly domesticated crops, animals, and medicinal plants, into the realm of raw material.

Through the passing of knowledge from generation to generation, through building on all the surrounding diversity, the multiple technologies of the South have built very diverse agroecologies according to local conditions. Now such technologies are redefined into raw material. The technologies of sustainable agriculture, of knowing the uses of hundreds of medicinal plants, are devalued and erased. The capacity for communities to use their living knowledge is erased. That knowledge and that material disappears into a trade system.

I was invited to an area in India which is a center of diversity for rice, where they were launching a campaign against patenting and GATT and free trade. I was there on the day of a festival that begins the agricultural season. On that day, all the villagers, hundreds of families, bring their seed in beautiful cups made of leaves to the village god, which is just a rock under a tree. Each of those cups contains a different variety of rice. Through this amazing ritual they mix them up. Then the local priest, who is also the healer, distributes this mixed rice back to everyone. The ritual serves to erase the notion of private property, to honor diversity while doing agriculture, and to recognize that diversity makes its play only when it is given a chance to mix around.

Genetic engineering is really truncating time. By denying the history, denying where property came from, not recognizing it in nature, and not recognizing it as the contribution of Third World communities, by claiming it was created in the lab by white men in white lab coats, genetic engineering is reducing the past.

It's truncating future time, too, because the technologies are meant to end the production of life. If you take hybridization as a technology, for instance, its objective is to prevent seed from giving seed, to stop life from producing on its own terms. Patenting has the same objective except that it's through legal, rather than biological, instruments. Either way, you've killed the ability of nature to multiply its own seed ten thousandfold. That is a most crucial issue of sustainability.

Denial of the past is encapsulated in the notion of intellectual property rights. Native seeds have lovely names. They tell you which village they come from. The seeds carry memory and they carry gratitude. The new seeds deny both. The intellectual property-rights notion says we have originated these properties.

This assumption of creation is where the intellectual property-rights notion comes in. Genetic engineering has first to create a monopoly situation. Without intellectual property rights, genetic engineering fails to compete.

Piracy is a dominant metaphor of the biotechnology domain. In the last month, two Germans were arrested at Delhi Airport for attempting to take 30,000 insects out of the country. Every bit of life is now raw material. There will be patents on the soil bacteria from shovelsful taken from the tropical countries. Another example is the Indian neem tree. We've had knowledge of its medicinal properties and its use as an agricultural pesticide for centuries. Now there are patents on the biopesticide use of neem. So neem, which used to be available in every village, is being captured by the corporations that have the patents and are setting up factories everywhere. The cost of neem seed, from which the medicinal oil comes, has shot up more than one hundredfold. Now there's no neem oil available in local markets.

For us in India, the freedom of the seed—defined as the freedom of wilderness in the seed—has become the key issue. We don't see it as geographic. Wilderness is the ability of life to reproduce on its own terms. Wilderness means supporting communities that self-organize, that produce in their own terms what is necessary according to their own sense of values.

People know that our forest commons was stolen. They grasp the parallel: Our seeds as commons are being stolen through this notion of intellectual property rights and patenting. And the farmers are on the streets now protesting this issue. We've had demonstrations against Cargill—the world's biggest private corporation—which controls 70 percent of the seed trade of the world. The chief of Cargill has remarked that Indian farmers have had no genetic resources, that without Cargill (which came to India in 1988) we would have starved. He also touted brilliant new technologies that stop the bees from usurping the pollen. The farmers have taken that on in a big way—they say, "We are fighting for our freedom and the freedom of the bees—and the freedom of the seed—it's everyone's freedom we're fighting for—against the freedom of Cargill to create monopolies." This March [1993], 200,000 farmers came to Delhi, in spite of a ban on their rally, to protest against patenting. And that movement carries on. I don't think rural India can be stopped on this issue.

We're having tremendous conflicts within the scientific community in India right now. How do you retain for communities the rights, the capacity, and the continued use of their traditional agricultural knowledge, and its diversity as well? Our scientists have gotten sucked into the world of biotechnology and feel that they are denying value to their country if they don't run with a grant from a U.S. corporation to go and patent that indigenous knowledge. It's quite clearly a transfer of knowledge and power to the corporation. Yet many scientists are thinking they're somehow empowering the community by usurping this birthright of diversity.

The poor sleep on the floor; they have one sari, nothing more. Yet every year they put aside something for the birds in the rainy season when the birds can't find grain. It's that largeness of heart that seems to be lost every time we go for the wrong notion of growth and the notion of abundance as being something that's created by technology.

Intellectual property rights and genetic engineering are both denials of rights of species and rights of other cultures. Life cannot be owned.

⊘ ANDREW KIMBRELL *brings to our attention the reality that the large capital investment required to genetically engineer a novel organism requires that scientists develop methods of cloning organisms. Natural reproduction is inadequate in that it allows for unplanned genetic material to enter the germline of the offspring of genetically engineered organisms. Cloning technique is well advanced, and the cloning of larger animals, even human beings, has begun.*

He also talks about the slippery patenting slope. In 1980 courts allowed the patenting of a genetically engineered bacterium. Now plants, animals, human cells, genes, and tissues have been patented. Most patented lifeforms have been genetically engineered, but recently the Patent and Trademark Office allowed the patenting of animals merely infected with a disease. He says this raises the question, "What are the limits of patentability?" He proceeds: Biotech-nology is based in genetic engineering. What is happening here is the application of traditional engineering standards, quantifiable measure-ment, predictability of outcome, standardization, and utility to natural living substance, including genes. Just as our industrial-age predecessors soldered and molded and heated inanimate matter to create the machines and products of the industrial age, we're editing, program-ming, recombining, and deleting genetic material to create the new liv-ing products of the age of biotechnology. Scientists have mixed and matched the genes of microorganisms, plants, and animals and created hundreds of thousands of novel lifeforms in the hopes of finding more profitable organisms for agriculture or research. Since natural reproduc-tion is not efficient, they are also now cloning their newly created crea-tures. Cloning allows for producing lifeforms in industrial amounts. Biotechnology is based in a reductionist, mechanistic view of life. In a recent keynote speech, Dr. Robert Haynes, president of the 16th Inter-national Congress of Genetics, firmly reminded his audience that the doctrine of mechanism is the central organizing principle of the age of biotechnology. He said, "For 3,000 years at least, the majority of people have considered that human beings were special, were magic. It's the Judeo-Christian view of man. What the ability to manipulate genes should indicate to people is the very deep extent to which we are bio-logical machines. The traditional view is built on the foundation that life is sacred. Well, not anymore. It's no longer possible to live by the idea that there is something special, unique, or even sacred about living organisms."

Haynes's proclamation was not some isolated view. Genetic engi-neering has really propagated the concept that all living things are bio-logical machines. A few years ago we organized a religious coalition to fight the patenting of life and had a press conference. The religious lead-ers objected to the Patent Office's legally defining life as a machine or manufacture, and therefore patentable. In response the *New York Times* ran a lead editorial against the religious coalition, titled "Industrialized

Life." The editorial said, "Life is special, humans even more so. But biological machines are still machines that now can be cloned, altered and patented. The consequences will be profound but, taken a step at a time, they can be managed."* Biotechnology's revolution in the way we think about life is simply the ideological underpinning of the current massive engineering of virtually every segment of the biotic community. We can observe biotechnology's invasion into life in three general areas: its use in warfare, agriculture, and human health and reproduction.

Most are unaware of biotechnology's military role. Perhaps the key moment in modern history was when the military got nuclear technology. Many in the world got their first horrific glimpse of the nuclear technology revolution when the bombs were dropped on Hiroshima and Nagasaki. It took a long time for the nuclear industry to shake off this image, which they originally tried to do in the 1950s with the "Atoms for Peace" propaganda campaign.

We've had the opposite problem with biotechnology: It's been used for warfare since its inception, but almost nobody notices.

This newfound ability to recombine or delete genes from organisms did not escape the notice of the Department of Defense. Since the early 1970s when Nixon signed the International Convention against Biological Warfare, the U.S. drastically reduced its funding and research in this area. But in the early 1980s Reagan's Secretary of Defense, Caspar Weinberger, realized that there was potential in biotechnology to begin a whole new era in biological warfare research. He began a significant and well-hidden expansion of the U.S. biological warfare program. During the Reagan-Bush years, over $120 million a year was being spent on biological warfare research in over 100 labs across the country. They were taking the most dangerous pathogens known to humankind—the plague, anthrax, botulism, snake venom—enhancing their virulence often through genetic engineering, and then cloning large amounts of these new biological weapons.

The Department of Defense insists that all this genetic engineering of biological warfare agents is really defensive. We have to do it in order to find cures if some other country decides it will genetically engineer pathogens. They do admit that in the early stages there is no distinction between offensive and defensive use, since you have to come up with a new biological agent in order to find the antibiotic or antiviral agent that will stop it. In reality, with genetic engineering you can make end-

*"Life Industrialized," *New York Times*, February 22, 1988, editorial page.

less changes to disease, causing microorganisms to avoid any interventive attempt. The idea that even spending billions would provide for cures is ridiculous. What we are seeing then is a new arms race—the genetics arms race—where nations are using biotechnology to create thousands of new pathogens targeted to people, animals, or plants. It is a very scary scenario, and international action to halt it is urgently required.

We have been able to stop some of this research. We successfully litigated against certain of these laboratories because they had failed to prepare environmental assessments, and these labs were working on incredibly dangerous organisms in some of the most populated areas in the United States. That program has also been trimmed somewhat by the Clinton administration under the force of our litigation and by some very careful scrutiny by the Congress. The Persian Gulf War showed that while we were spending billions on exotic genetically engineered biological warfare agents we did not have vaccines against simple basic biological warfare agents. But the U.S. is still leading the world into the new genetic arms race, and this must be stopped.

Another major area of public and private investment in biotechnology is in the agricultural sector. Agricultural use of biotechnology is very wide ranging. In general terms the idea is to genetically engineer microbes, plants, and animals to make them more efficient for agriculture. Years ago scientists debated the ethics of genetically engineering plants and animals with foreign genes. Did we have the right to alter permanently the genetic inheritance of plants and animals at will? I argued against it as did many of my colleagues. We lost. Soon the government was spending billions of our taxpayers' money on permanently altering the germlines of animals and plants. And this investment was being matched by biotechnology companies. In one well-reported example Dr. Vernon Pursel inserted the human growth gene in a pig. Pursel hoped to create giant pigs that would be major meat producers. The problem was that though the human growth gene was in every cell of the pig's body it did not act in the manner the scientists expected. Instead of making the pig larger it made it squat, cross-eyed, bow-legged, smaller than an average pig, with huge bone mass, a truly wretched product of science without ethics. Pursel tried to find a silver lining in his experiment gone wrong by claiming that the pig was leaner. Pursel's argument was that people are worried about cholesterol, so maybe we can sell this as lean pig. Did he really think the public was ready for pork chops with human genes?

Clearly biotechnology brings up unprecedented and grave environmental, economic, and ethical concerns. Here you are creating millions of novel organisms, organisms that the Earth has never seen, and then releasing them into the environment. They are exactly analogous to exotic organisms like kudzu vine or those responsible for chestnut blight or Dutch elm disease. Any time you introduce an exotic organism into a new environment you are throwing the ecological dice. With the deliberate release of thousands of genetically engineered microbes, plants, or animals, you're putting something into the environment that could be very deleterious. Many of us have spent much of our working lives addressing the terrible ecological problems created by chemical pollution. Now we confront a whole new concept in pollution: biological pollution. Biological pollution is very different than chemical pollution. Chemical pollution, however horrible, does dilute over time, and it can often be contained. However, once you release an organism into the environment it cannot be recalled or contained. It will not dilute but rather will reproduce, disseminate, and mutate. It is unstoppable. My colleagues and I have sued many times to prevent the release of genetically engineered organisms and have often been very successful. However, with thousands of new releases planned every year we need a moratorium on any new releases and new national and international laws which protect us from the very real threat of biological pollution.

Biotechnology research could also have disastrous impacts on human health. In one example Dr. Malcolm Martin of the National Institutes of Health genetically engineered mice so that they contained the entire genome of the AIDS virus in every one of their cells. The experiment was hailed in front-page stories across the country as a major breakthrough in AIDS research. Once again, however, nature was far too complex for the scientists to predict. As it turned out, the AIDS had melded with native retroviruses inside the mouse to create a new virus, a kind of super-AIDS that could even be transmissible through air. This was reported with great alarm by Dr. Robert Gallo and others in *Science* magazine. One can only imagine the devastation if this new AIDS were spread by a researcher or by the escape of one of the mice. Once again our organization sued to stop this experiment, and a few others have been suing and petitioning. We've even organized locally to get counties to declare themselves genetic-engineered free zones, so as not to be subject to these kinds of dangerous experiments and hazardous environmental releases.

Another highly publicized biotechnology controversy surrounds the use of genetically engineered bovine growth hormone (rbGH). RbGH is injected into cows to make them produce 15 to 40 percent more milk at the height of their lactation cycle. The economic consequences of this technology are disturbing; we already have a glut in the milk market. The use of this hormone is destroying the small dairy farmer in America in one fell swoop. It also has hideous impacts on the cows and may cause some human health problems as well.

As we mix and match the genetic makeup of virtually the entire living kingdom, an ethical question arises: Shouldn't creatures be allowed some biological dignity or integrity? Adding insult to injury, the industry since 1980 has been allowed to patent genetically engineered organisms. That year, a five-to-four Supreme Court decision allowed for the patenting of a genetically engineered microbe that was supposed to eat oil. At the time Jeremy Rifkin asked, "What does the microbe eat for dessert?" And it turned out that the microbes did have a nasty appetite. The microbe was never commercially released, but the ability to patent all lifeforms has been decreed. By fiat the Reagan-Bush administration extended it from microbes to plants, and animals to human cells, genes, and cell lines. Now there are more than 200 genetically engineered animals standing, figuratively speaking, in line at the patent office. Over a dozen animals have already been patented.

Recently a scientist at the National Institutes of Health applied for patents on 2,000 brain genes he had isolated. His idea was that one of these might be the key to IQ or to cure brain cancer. He didn't know what he had, but he was hoping that some of the genes would be massive profitmakers. The race to patent lifeforms has reached extraordinary proportions. One European corporation is trying to patent women who have been genetically engineered to produce valuable biochemicals in their mammary glands. This technique has been mastered in animals, and they want to make sure that in case it's ever mastered in human beings they've got the patent. It is important to remember in the midst of the patenting frenzy that patenting is the trigger for the biotechnology revolution. If you halt the patenting of life you take the profit out of the technology. Therefore this must be a key in any campaign to halt the onslaught of biotechnology on life.

Human health and reproduction is another important biotechnology area. It is here where we are seeing the full force of this technological revolution affect the most basic definitions of life and death. Recently a California Supreme Court decision separated for the first time the birth process from legal rights of motherhood. A surrogate mother, an

African-American woman who had been implanted with the embryo of a white couple, decided after the nine-month pregnancy that she wanted to share the parenting. This went to court and the court decided that she was not the mother, that she was a new class of woman, a paid "human incubator." It is an extraordinary decision because it allows the commodification of childbearing. Combined with the new techniques in gene screening of embryos, that will create a whole new industry in the selection of embryos to be implanted into surrogate mothers. Nine months later the yuppie couple can have their perfect children delivered. This is no longer science fiction but fact, and now the law in the State of California.

We are also seeing the human equivalent of the bovine growth hormone controversy. Last year Genentech sold $200 million worth of human growth hormone. Genentech genetically engineered industrial amounts of the growth hormone that is naturally produced in our pituitary gland. Since only a few people suffer from dwarfism, Genentech immediately began an aggressive marketing strategy, claiming that children totally normal in every respect, but in the bottom 3 to 5 percent of their height range, need therapy: genetically engineered growth hormones. Tens of thousands of parents—primarily in the U.S.—with the approval of their pediatricians are now injecting genetically engineered human growth hormones into their children three to five times a week. As you might expect, it's a costly therapy. Nine out of ten of these kids are boys, since we like our boys tall. Needless to say, shortness is a cultural stereotype, not a disease. We are seeing a new situation emerging where the solution to prejudice whether based in height, weight, skin color, eye shape, or the like will be not to educate the purveyors of discrimination or to outlaw it but rather to change the bodies of those being discriminated against. Human growth hormone is a sign of things to come. The most profitable drug in the biotechnology industry is being used to modify the bodies of the victims of prejudice.

Genetic privacy is another major issue and may become the central civil rights issue of the coming century. The Human Genome Project, a $3 billion government program, is trying to decipher over 100,000 genes, purportedly to cure disease. They're also looking at the functions of all of our genes. They claim they've got the genes for alcoholism, for shyness, schizophrenia, and depression. Is Luddism next? Is the explanation for this meeting genetic inferiority?

It is easy to see how privacy becomes a central question. Once we have a catalogue of genes which may predispose an individual to phys-

ical or mental diseases, can an insurance company use genetic screening
to change your insurance rate? Can an employer insist on seeing your
genetic readout? The Office of Technology Assessment just revealed that
many of the Fortune 500 companies already do genetic screening to
avoid liability for workers who may be predisposed to a cancer or disease
that might be a hazard of a given workplace. Rather than making the
workplaces safe, we screen our workers to make sure they are not predisposed to the risk of occupational illness. Prenatal screening creates its
own dilemmas. Prenatal screening has already caused a worldwide rise
in sex-selection abortions. That may only be the beginning of a new
type of eugenics. Recent polls said that 11 percent of Americans would
abort a child that was genetically predisposed to obesity.

 *David Suzuki elaborates a bit on the potential applications of genetic
engineering in war:* When the Reagan administration supported a lot of
this research they bought a front-row seat at the action. They were funding the *best* labs in the United States. The military was deeply attentive
to what the state of the art was. When the U.S. was in this grubby little
war in Vietnam, an article titled "Ethnic Weapons" was published by a
Swedish geneticist in 1970 in the U.S. journal *Military Review.* At that
time, he proposed a cocktail of chemicals that would be ethnically specific. But today, with fancy molecular techniques, it should be possible
to design a retrovirus that would be absolutely ethnically specific. The
military would never admit to doing that, but I don't believe there is
any way that you could ever out-imagine the horrific possibilities of the
military mind.

 *Andrew Kimbrell points out that genetically engineered pathogens
could be employed in salt-the-earth strategies:* The destruction of a particular plant or animal that formed the basis of a particular Third World
country's economy could be accomplished through biological warfare
involving genetic engineering.

 *David Suzuki expects that the reductionism of modern genetics will
engender a pseudoscience of social engineering:* Modern claims by molecular geneticists are fostering a terrible biological determinism, the notion
that virtually every aspect of human behavior has a biological basis. As
soon as the genome is pretty well specified, scientists will no doubt
determine that a high proportion of people with certain kinds of diseases will also carry particular sets of genetic markers. Don't think for a
minute such discoveries will lead to immediate cures. But geneticists will
very quickly run out of disease groups to compare DNA sequences. So no
doubt they will turn to the socially difficult categories and look, for

example, at people who are on welfare, homosexuals, criminals. No doubt they will find that people in these troublesome categories share subsets of DNA sequences. The problem is, *correlation* does not mean *causation*, but even scientists often confuse them.

If you examine a group of people who died from lung cancer, and found that out of 100, 90 of them have yellow-stained teeth and yellow fingers, that's a correlation. But it would be wrong to conclude that yellow-stained teeth and yellow fingers cause lung cancer, yet that is what scientists are already doing in some of these projects.

⊘JEREMY RIFKIN *thinks it likely that genetic engineering will usher back in some venerable forms of discrimination and abuse and set back the philosophical clock:* With genetic engineering we are on the verge of a new Eugenics Movement. When we think of eugenics we think of what happened in America at the turn of the century—the sterilization laws and the new immigration laws—that set the basis for what happened in Nazi Germany in the thirties. That was a social Eugenics Movement. Many of our ethicists are hoping that a new Hitler doesn't come along and abuse this new technology.

Unfortunately, what they miss is that the new Eugenics Movement is already here; it is endemic to the new technology. This time it's not social eugenics, it's commercial eugenics. People want healthy babies, we want more efficient means of production, we want plants and animals that are predictable, quantifiable, and useful. So in the attempt to imprint engineering standards into the life code, we are automatically involved in a Eugenics Movement. The motivation of the scientists in the lab makes no difference. They are making eugenics decisions and doing so on criteria that we have not yet debated or understood. We have to understand the tremendous social import of this revolution in terms of the body politic.

The entire philosophical paradigm is shifting radically to the old prerevolutionary concept that one's role in life is predetermined by biological destiny, by nature. And that while the environment—nurture—is a mitigating factor, one's genetic predispositions are the key to the kind of social performance that an individual can expect in life. This is going to set up a form of discrimination more virulent than anything in the past, because now there is a technology whereby to implement it. By the end of this decade we are going to see people judged by their genetic readout. We will see a new form of prejudice based on genotype, not just skin color, race, or ethnicity. The new global civil-liberty campaign superseding human rights will have to do with genetic rights. We have moved from anticolonial struggles to civil rights to human rights. By the end of this decade we are going to see the struggle for the right of every person in the world to genetic privacy as protection against genetic discrimination.

⊘ SUSAN GRIFFIN *finds it appalling that the response to the problems in human reproduction caused by various forms of pollution is to redesign the process of generation rather than to cease polluting and destroying. She also makes quite an interesting point about deconstructionism:* Cancer is part of the portrait of immune-system failure in this country. But another major system that is under attack now from environmental degradation is the reproductive system. And so we have something called reproductive failure, which is hidden by the fact that miscarriages, stillbirths, and congenital problems are all studied separately. Not being able to conceive at all is also studied separately. But in fact they are all one phenomenon.

One might say that they are moving from nurture to nature in genetic engineering, but in postmodernism they are moving the other way. Rather it may look like it's different, but in fact the extreme end of deconstructionism holds that any time you make a statement about any group of people or any person or any category, that that is essentialism, which is arguing that something has an essence. I think that goes back to eighteenth- or nineteenth-century thought of *tabula rasa*, that somehow there is no human nature, you can just write whatever you want there. And I think both genetic engineering and postmodernism are moving toward the belief that nothing has any essence, and therefore we can just manipulate things and make them whatever we want because nothing has essence to be violated.

⊘ CHELLIS GLENDINNING *seems to say that postmodernism is an effect, not a cause, and that we might find some realities that are nonrelative in the indigenous experience of cultural interchange:* I would like to propose that the postmodern thought patterns that tout the absence of values, that define all of reality as socially constructed and then revel in meaninglessness, that these states of mind actually *spring* from the latest stages of technological development.

One of the first times I met Kirkpatrick Sale was in 1991 at the Institute for Policy Studies roundtable on technology. He made a comment about postmodernism that has stayed with me. He said, "There's nothing new about postmodernism; it's just the same old rationalization from the dominant world."

And so it is! The postmodern dictate that virtually everything under the sun is relative and therefore meaningless is intertwined with the processes of expansion, conquering, colonization, and appropriation that have propelled Western technological development for centuries. It is the perfect expression of the mind-body, human-Earth split. Today these processes have reached the point where the entire world is encapsulated within the technological web. No culture in the world is exempt from the meddlesome hand of the techno-marketplace that picks up fragments of a culture in one place and carts them halfway around the world to sell in the Great Mall. You can watch Yanomami tribespeople protesting mining in Brazil on your Japanese television screen while doing yoga in your Guatemalan peasant pants. You can jump on United Airlines and be in Tahiti in a few hours. I know a Dine' man who lives with his extended family on his nation's land, speaks his native tongue, practices traditional ceremonies *and* listens to the Bob Dylan bootleg tapes, flies Tibetan prayer flags, and drives a hot black car with tinted windows. The Associated Press photo that impressed me the most during the Rio Summit was an Amazon Kayapo Indian dressed in his jungle garb standing by a food booth drinking a Coca-Cola.

The disorientation, uncertainty, ideological conflict, and sense of homelessness that result from such experiences lie at the base of postmodernism's grandiosity. But the driving force behind these experiences remains the imperial endeavor with its reliance on technological development to pull off its global vision of superiority.

So many aspects of life within the corporate techno-world get confused and removed from their origins that we forget what is truly human and truly healthy. Cultural exchange is, of course, a natural human activity. Yes, social construction has validity—to a point. What we need to be asking ourselves, to make reasonable sense out of the insistences of the postmodern ideologues, is, "How do indigenous people do cultural exchange?" "How do they view the origin of culture?" "How do they trade and give of themselves to other native people?" In other words, "What is communication when the playing field is leveled?" "What is truly human?"

⊘ MARTHA CROUCH *elucidates the fundamental politics of biotechnology, its logic, and its ineluctable outcomes:* Built into the way of thinking that developed biotechnology, and built into the technology itself, are monoculture, imperialism, and industrialization. You can't tease these attributes out, and you can't abstract the technology from its context to use in a way that doesn't have these kinds of consequences. If peasants in Mexico or sustainable agriculture researchers in Kansas developed a tool for agriculture or for reproductive technologies, it wouldn't be biotechnology. Biotechnology is not something that we want to support. In fact, it's something we want to oppose as a whole. Analyzing each little application isn't necessary, and biotechnology as a whole is going to have these inevitable consequences.

To convince you of that I'm going to talk about my own experiences. For about twelve years I ran a research lab that genetically engineered rape seed, an oil crop. We worked on seeds and pollen particularly. I had the opportunity to see some of our work applied and was horrified at the results. In consequence I had a chance really to think about how basic science, applied science, and the economic system are all integrated.

Biotechnology is born out of a scientific vision of control over nature, control over reproduction, and from the desire for man to be able to reproduce without nature and women. As a scientist I was trained to think in a very specific way. The training started young and it was very normalizing; the types of questions that were allowed were linear, reductionist, objectifying. They teased things apart into components that could then be controlled and commodified. Other kinds of inquiry were not allowed.

From the very outset of the enterprise, the type of thinking required to develop scientific tools, of which biotechnology is one example, predicts that the only kind of technologies that can use this thinking will be those that reduce the world. The idea of genetic engineering is to reduce an organism to little bits of information in a linear sequence. All organisms have the same elements in their genetic code, so it's a globalizing logic that makes all organisms part of the same soup. I can take a gene from an elephant or a bacterium and combine it with my genes and prove that we're basically the same stuff. It maximizes similarities and minimizes differences.

If with that kind of logic we develop a tool, it will suit the type of agriculture and the type of industry that we do. We take land that might have a different slope or be north or west facing, or have different amounts of rainfall or a different soil type, and reduce it. We do this using irrigation, mechanization, and fossil fuels so that the whole world can be treated in a uniform way. Where things used to be different, we make them the same. So the tool is developed out of a thought process aimed at monoculture rather than specific local applications. In order for something to be adapted to a local environment the people developing it must be able to modify it quickly. If we plant out our tomatoes and notice that they're doing better in one part of the field than in another, we save the seeds from that part, and we keep planting those tomatoes in the same place. To do that requires constant interaction and direct control.

In training to be a scientist and develop generic tools, we become more specialized—and more placeless. We're in an educational system where people from India, China, and Africa all rise above their home places, often traveling to centers in Europe or the United States to become part of a global educational system. They may become unable even to talk to the people in the places that they came from. I could never talk to my mother about my work: My mother is an intelligent woman, yet I couldn't explain to her what I was doing. Even though I had the knowledge, I wouldn't have been able to do my work in my own backyard, because of the infrastructure required. So biotechnology becomes something that is developed in a way inaccessible to local communities and beyond their control. If it breaks or if it doesn't work in this little part of the field, it can't easily be modified. There's an elitism, a cult of experts that's integral.

The infrastructure required to support it is not only global in terms of the computer networks that store and link all the research data and the necessity for library systems; materially it requires an industrial infrastructure. Biotechnology requires purified enzymes that come on ice via two-day air; it requires ultra-centrifuges; it requires good air conditioning to keep all the equipment going; it requires lots of electricity. The result is that it maintains the status quo so that only the people who are already doing high-tech agriculture, or are already in medicine, can manipulate this infrastructure and extract resources with it.

The technology appears to extend limits: If we have a drought area, runs the thinking, we'll insert a gene for drought resistance so we can still grow plants there. Then we don't have to worry about why the rain isn't coming. We have a disease problem: We'll put in virus resistance, so we can keep doing monoculture, keep distancing the food system, and keep doing industrial medicine and so forth. It makes it appear that you're able to overcome the limits, but really you're just extending the time before you have to deal with them. That's dangerous: It delays the creativity of living within limits.

I can't think of a single human problem that can't be approached alternatively with local solutions that are more effective than biotechnology. One example in the United States is bovine growth hormone versus rotational grazing in the dairy industry. The dairy industry has economic problems from having surpluses and because of the high cost to farmers of intensification. The genetic-engineering solution is to invent a hormone that yields more milk per cow, thus further intensifying production. Rotational grazing is where farmers themselves have decided to get rid of the whole structure of expensive inputs and intensive farming. They just move the cows around on pastures managed optimally. They don't have to buy supplemental feed, or antibiotics, or go to the vet so often, or be around as much. They compete by lowering costs. This is a farmer-initiated solution, a method spread by farmer-to-farmer networks. They control it; they decide when to move the animals around the pastures. It requires very few industrial inputs.

There's always an alternative. The debate over the specific applications of biotechnology obscures the larger issue of what is inherent in the technology. We could as a group confidently oppose the entire proposition.

⊘ BETH BURROWS *talks about the particulars that she, as an activist, had to understand in order to work on international trade agreements, biotechnology, and property rights. Shortly after she began, she became especially curious about a provision in GATT and NAFTA called TRIPS—Trade Related International Property. The biotechnology industry was advocating for these measures because, they said, "at least one sector of the U.S. industry relies heavily on effective patenting protection for its competitiveness and ultimate survival." There was a lot of evidence, Burrows says, that "patent protection was the knee-cap of capitalism."*

The material was multifarious and complicated. The responsibility Burrows assumed in studying it and grasping its implications was fearful. What would be the effect of these sections on consumers, biodiversity, and ecology? "What would be the effect of intellectual property sections on how we understand who we are as human beings?" was for Beth Burrows the most troubling question of them all.

She had to look at U.S. legislative and judicial actions relating to biodiversity patents, such as a case before the Supreme Court where a seed company sued a farmer for selling seeds to neighbors. "The effect of that case is to get the Supreme Court to punish people for exercising what used to be considered rights and now are being considered privileges and soon will be memories that computers will not be able to encode," *she says.*

⊘ *Burrows learned of the Human Genome Diversity Project, where scientists will fan out all over the world taking genetic samples from indigenous peoples —labeled "isolates of historic interest"—ostensibly to understand the migrations of peoples and languages around the world over time. At about the same time that she became aware of the Human Genome Diversity Project, appli-*

cations to patent cell lines from indigenous people came to light. There also surfaced patents on species-wide characteristics of plants and animals, which would make any organism with such a characteristic private property. Burrows also learned that with such patented resources laboratories could create synthetic replacements for commodities that might be the entire basis of a nation's export earnings.

At one time, Burrows says, patents were awarded to human creations that had to be new, nonobvious, and useful. But the trend has been away from these criteria—"Patents are not rewards for inventions; patents are protection for investment." *And therefore the ratification of these patenting requirements in these trade treaties is a very serious business.*

Burrows concludes with a story from an international conference on the future of intellectual property protection and biotechnology in the U.S., Europe, and Japan. She was struck by a remark of one of the eminent speakers who bewailed the difficulty, in Europe, of obtaining patents on lifeforms. He hoped, according to Burrows, that his colleagues elsewhere would not have to face "environmentalists and those who would bring *ethics and other irrational considerations"—*Burrows's emphasis*—"to the table!" Which pairing, says Burrows, went entirely unchallenged.*

MARIA MIES *talks about the successes and strategies of a number of small interconnected groups in Germany in creating resistance to the patenting of life:* It is very important that we do this kind of mobilization. We are not scientists, but we are citizens—we take our citizens' rights to oppose what we don't want. Public mobilization may not hinder the industries from proceeding with their technology, but it may mean that they won't find the people to purchase their products.

Really mobilize your public; don't address yourself only to the scientific community; it is possible to undermine the acceptance for these technologies. As a method it is important to link up our concerns: We are not only talking about women, but also about animals and plants, and not only about white people but about the Third World. Though ours is a small group, we publish, we talk, we make a big fuss whenever we can.

⊘VANDANA SHIVA *highlights the widening gulf between common sense and orthodox "evidence" in public debate on biotechnology and other such issues:* With regard to "the ethics and other irrational considerations" bearing on biotechnology and trade agreements, all kinds of ontological shifts are taking place, some extremely crude. It may work among negotiators—but you bring it out in the public domain and thinking people will laugh at contentions such as that an animal gene is not animal-like, which would mean that you can put a pig gene into a carrot. Ask the Muslims of the world. Imagine what consternation it could create if we could get this in the hands of some good Islamic theologians!

Every time a problem occurs with biotechnology and opposition is mounted, the response is characterized as irrational, emotional. International scientific bodies are run by corporations, so only their scientific evidence will be counted as evidence to resolve any kind of public debate. None of the work that we've done in the Environmental Movement has been reflected in the formation of any of these governing agencies. Under these global conventions and agreements, environmental issues will be resolved by a body called the International Standards Organization. It used to work only for industry. In five or six years it's become the big standards-setting institution for international environmental issues.

Chapter 5

The Prospects for Sustainable Agriculture

⊘ *Clearly, one of the most dramatic discontinuities precipitated by the expansion of commerce and technology into every sphere is in the realm of human sustenance. In the briefest instant of history, agriculture has been mechanized and commoditized, and has ceased to be organic. Corporate intermediaries have taken over the provision of food, the most basic of needs, and have helped most householders forget or lose their ability to grow their own.*

Wendell Berry and Martha Crouch each make a presentation to begin with raising plentiful opportunities and possibilities for individuals and communities to regain some control over the food systems of their bioregions. A diversified, localized agriculture can be the foundation for the economic life of a place, and also for remembering the practice of mutual aid.

Berry speaks of the ethics of the social relationship to land, and of the soul of community, which flourishes best when engaged in some real work. Crouch, a bioregionalist, talks about the tremendous empowerment that household food gardening can effect, in the overdeveloped countries especially, and of the educative value of growing what you consume. Martha Crouch's stories of starting a community-supported agriculture program in her home town, and of farmer-to-farmer information networks, reveal a wealth of common sense on the farm, and that once alternatives are demonstrated there's a willingness to abandon chemical agriculture and corporate food distribution.

After both speak, other participants comment, and the conversation broadens to consider the role science has played in the devaluing of homegrown

intelligence and the economic ideas that have sanctioned and promoted the
commodification of just about everything that lives or can be invented.

WENDELL BERRY: As has been testified by implication over and over
again at this meeting, economic life is life. If you have no economic life,
you have no life. So who controls your economic life is as critical a question as any that has been raised. Your economic life is your bodily life,
and so when we talk about these economic issues we are really talking
about the issue of tyranny. And it's tyranny with a vengeance that we
are up against.

The principal illusion that I started out with as a young man was that
if you spoke convincingly to reasonable people they would change. To
find that it didn't make any difference whether you were right or not
was a bitter pill for me to swallow. I can testify that it doesn't matter a
bit whether you've got the best argument or not. The people in universities and the people in the governments and the people in the corporations don't care about your argument. They don't have to argue;
they've got power. If you've got power you don't have to argue.

The next turn in my understanding of these things was that it didn't
make any difference whether they understood your argument or not,
because they couldn't make the solution. There is no big solution, for
example, to the problem of agriculture.

I realized that the problem that I am trying to address is one that is
not going to be answered by a university or a government or a corporation—and is not going to be answered by a movement. The categorical
thought of movements is hopeless.

There is no big solution and, furthermore, there is no expensive solution. My first criterion is cheapness. The first thing I ask about anything
new is, "How cheap is it?" And my advice to my kids and any of the
young farmers that I can get to listen is, "Don't spend any money that
you don't have to. If you've got too much money, throw it away rather
than put it into the hands of the global corporations."

While we may use these words—"anthropocentric" and "biocentric"
and other geometrical metaphors—what we are talking about is that we
want to preserve a many-centered world. What we are trying to preserve
is not just nature but ourselves as human beings in the fullest sense—not
as people just living for ourselves along the line of least resistance as
defined by popular and fashionable public expedience and graver necessities, but as people able to live from the heart and to be motivated by
affection. The real question is, "If I love this person, this child, this
woman, this man, this place, what then must I do?" This is specific. The
abstractions and statistics evaporate away from that question.

The great enterprise of the industrial economy has been to capture the functions of our real humanity. What we do for each other in a neighborhood doesn't cost anything. The people of the old communities didn't have insurance; they had each other. The industrial economy takes us away from each other and then sells us insurance. What concerns me about the agricultural economy is that if the wrong people control it, it's the worst tyranny you can imagine. Agrarian people have always understood this. I grew up surrounded by people—farmers— who'd say, "They may get me somehow but they'll never starve me out." They were going to do for themselves. Most of them are dead now, but they didn't starve.

The food economy is probably the most recapturable part of that captured economy. People can do things for themselves. They can either grow food themselves or they can deal directly with other people who grow it. People can beat the industrial food system by getting out of it, leaving it hanging.

The industrial food economy has so filled its various layers with parasites, people raking off profit for transportation, advertising, pesticides, and herbicides, and all the rest of the things they make us pay for, that it becomes thinkable that direct dealing between consumer and producer might provide cheaper food for the consumer at a greater income for the farmer. This can be done by two individuals; it can be done by church groups or conservation groups in the city making connection with groups of small farmers.

Here is a way it might go: If a city, say in the Midwest, began to live from its own landscape as much as possible, the agriculture in that landscape would begin to diversify. Because of diversification, work would increase, employment would increase. If you begin that kind of commerce between a city and its tributary landscape, other things also would follow. The people in the city would be getting out into the landscape, not for what we now call recreation, but to see friends, to picnic on a friend's farm. This idea of direct dealing—and it's already going on —is the right kind of a solution because it leads to other right solutions.

☞MARTHA CROUCH: Once you give people the idea that they can reclaim a little bit of power over the basic needs in their lives, it becomes something they can't live without. The food system is perhaps the easiest to reclaim. Even a child can participate in it. You can participate at some level no matter where you live.

Expansion of the economic system requires distancing food producers from food consumers. Thus the average food item now travels a couple of thousand miles before it's eaten. A quick way to collapse an economy would be to reunite the producer and consumer. So the idea of providing things within a community and reestablishing the local connections is a nice direct way to not participate in the globalization of the economy.

If you're talking about changing your story to a story of relationship instead of divorce, consider that the most intimate relationship that we have with "the other" is to eat them. It's more intimate than sex. You take another organism, you kill it, and you put it inside your own body and gradually disassemble it into molecules and absorb them into your flesh. To obscure that relationship to the point where children and adults alike have no concept that they even have a relationship with cows and soybeans and corn is the ultimate denial of the interrelatedness of life. If you can start getting people involved in those fundamental relationships, then the whole idea of a relationship story as central to our lives becomes easier to imagine.

Taking food out of the category of the global commodity and thinking of it not as a commodity but as a relationship is possible in many situations. Community-supported agriculture—CSA—is a simple linkage between urban eaters and outlying growers. We've just started that in our own community. It's elegant and requires no intervention from government.

All we had to do in our town was announce that we were going to have a meeting at the public library. We invited a lot of local farmers. We said, "What would you think if we could get ten to twenty families who would subscribe to your farm and give you some money ahead of time, say in January when you're planning your planting, and then at harvest time you would divide the produce that you grew according to their shares?" We found an interested group of farmers who saw that it would allow them to diversify and not have to worry about what to do with the excess production or the things that they didn't sell at the market. We had an education campaign to tell the consumers in town about it, and the CSA just took off. Through it people learn what can be grown locally. They learn about seasonality. A lot of them are surprised to discover that strawberries are only available for three weeks. They have no idea that there are seasons in their area or that the harvest varies from year to year. So community-supported agriculture reestablishes human relationships to the cycles of the weather and the cycles of the seasons.

All around the country farmer-to-farmer networks have been forming. These are organizations where farmers share their ideas about how to get off of the chemical and industrial treadmills. Since it's been a long time since they've farmed that way, they have to teach each other how. They don't need experts, universities, or research programs. There's nothing they can't do for themselves and adapt to their own local conditions. For example, as a result some dairy farmers are getting away from any need for the agrichemical industry. Taking those steps doesn't require anything except a little communication.

In the Plains states several different groups of Native Americans are reintroducing buffalo. In a lot of the buffalo reintroduction programs the idea is not just to have a new market commodity but to reestablish a cultural identity based on the relationship with food.

Amateur associations to preserve traditional seeds and fruits and nuts are springing up everywhere. We have such a group. These are mostly rural people from all over the state. They locate old homesteads and collect the old fruit and nut varieties they find there and graft them to their own rootstocks to keep these old varieties going. They develop their own techniques for growing different kinds of fruit and nut crops and mainly choose for themselves and their local communities. This collecting and propagating is done out of love, not to be part of some big marketing scheme.

In my community one of my own efforts is articulating the relationship between domesticated and wild lands. The idea of wilderness as being somewhere people don't go, or something separate from humans, can be a problem. Without some connection people can't know enough about the forests to really care about them. In our community, the only thing that people forage for in the forests other than ginseng and yellow root is wild mushrooms. You bring these undomesticated organisms into the local markets and introduce the city people to them. The city folk begin to realize that these mushrooms are seasonal, they are limited in supply, that they come directly from the forest, and that if the forest is not healthy there won't be wild mushrooms to eat.

That's a tangible relationship with the wild, between forest and town. Finding medicinal or ceremonial or other uses of forest products—uses that don't involve destruction of the forest, that allow these harvests to be appreciated and savored locally—is important for the protection of the forests. That's been shown over and over again around the world.

⊘ANDREW KIMBRELL *responds to Wendell Berry's implicit criticism of political movements. Without denying that work in localities is crucial, Kimbrell sees an urgent need for a mass political movement to act from a clearer understanding of the world than liberal capitalism provides. He raises the idea of bioregionalism and reinhabitation and mentions Gary Snyder's essay on the*

subject in The Practice of the Wild. "The defense of the vernacular culture is key along with the defense of the wild," *says Kimbrell. He continues:* Ideas do have consequences. The most important thing that happened in 1776 was not American Independence but rather the
publication of Adam Smith's *The Wealth of Nations.* Prior to that particular system of ideas, none of the things that we are referring to as commodities, including labor, land, or money, had ever been thought of as
commodities. In traditional vernacular societies, medieval Europe for
example, you did not sell these things. That concept of making self-
interest and contract law the substitute for every other kind of relation
—kinship, tribal, religious, and spiritual—was an idea with enormous
consequences. It immediately commodified labor. A profession used to
be a profession of faith. Land was considered a gift, and usury was for-
bidden because time belonged to God. The ability to sell money created
the capital accumulation that was required for the entire technological
age. As this system breaks down, we're going to have to come up with
ideas that have other consequences, that restore some of those vernacular relationships.

This is not to say that all solutions and movements have to be local.
I think that there's a real need for mass movement and political strategies. The Environmental Movement and Feminist Movement show that
there is an enormous role and need for mass movements. Local solutions are terribly important, but it would be a tragic mistake to ignore
the larger political realities and fail to take advantage of our current situation.

⊘VANDANA SHIVA *talks about the way in which the economism of
Cargill-style agribusiness works against traditional farmers:* The farmers
don't treat this as economics; for them it's life. They never do this budget. The credit is at one time of the year. The return is at another time.
They have never been businessmen; farmers have been farmers. *Shiva
goes on to observe that in her area while the return on globally traded crops
dropped 50 percent in a year, the locally traded staple crop provided a consistent return. So, for farmers, she concludes:* Insurance is not in hooking up
to the multinational global trading system; insurance is in local community.

⊘LANGDON WINNER *adds that the provision of a number of other basic
needs and services could well be devolved to towns and municipalities but that
public investment has long been headed in the opposite direction:* There are
several areas of our lives where we might actively seek to reclaim power.
Historically speaking, the infrastructures that are now huge systems in

water supply, electrical power, sewage disposal, and the like started as small, local operations and were later aggregated and reaggregated. Throughout the nineteenth and twentieth centuries people have, in the name of efficiency, reliability, and safety, allowed decisions that were at one time close at hand to be organized within megasystems that remove them from the home and from local communities. It is worrisome that in the current debate about infrastructure there are proposals to do this yet again in all kinds of ways: to build an information superhighway, a system of magnetic-levitation trains, and "smart highways" which would remove control of the automobile from the driver to a computer. At the very moment when signs of social breakdown are so obvious, we are preparing to engage again in the same strategies for disempowerment that we have followed for the past 150 years.

There are alternatives one can find, however, in each of the areas now occupied by our society's megasystems. One can explore ways of managing water, waste disposal, energy, transit, and introducing technologies in the workplace and find ways to bring decisions and useful tools closer to the control of individuals and local communities.

HELENA NORBERG-HODGE suggests that the notion that humanity is now subsumed in technology is parochial—it may be true for the rich world, but not for surviving folk cultures and economies. Referring to Godfrey Reggio's argument that we live technology, Helena begins: Enormous differences still exist between North and South. Asserting that *we live* technology makes it sound as if this were true for all humankind. Really what this speaks to is the urbanized or suburbanized minority of the world's population. When we imagine that everyone on the planet is "living technology" and that it's all pervasive, we lose hope. It is heartening to realize that the majority of the people in the world today are not "living technology." So the first order of action is to protect the vernacular, the noncommoditized, the decentralized, diversified peoples where family and community still have power, where the economy's based on relationship and the land, and where so much of the alternative vision that many Westerners are trying to aspire to is still lived.

The strategies for North and South are different. In the North, we're losing a basis of comparison for a healthy ecosystem. We've forgotten what community really looks like. The strategies must include protecting the wild wherever it still exists and countering this acceleration of the technologization and commodification of life, which is being done with enormous investments. We should be insisting of our governments, "Don't spend our tax money to distance producers and consumers even farther and to support the big middlemen. Let's have a new definition of progress."

⊘WENDELL BERRY *responds to Andrew Kimbrell's earlier point about the usefulness of movements:* Some ideas have direct consequences, but those often are bad ideas. Good ideas don't work in exactly that way. I have willingly taken part in movements. Critically enough, I hope, but I have done it. And one does it simply because one understands that there are certain needed things that a movement can do. The thing it's best at is forbidding. But when the movement begins to prescribe positively, then you're in trouble. You're not going to have a movement for local adaptation because that's a contradiction in terms. A *good* idea spreads this way: "Well, that worked there. Now, let me see. My situation here is a little bit different. Is there a way that that can be varied so as to work here?" The idea becomes good when it's kindly adapted to local conditions.

It's easy to go along tugging at the coattails of power and saying, "Wait! Wait! Wait! Stop! Stop!" But when power turns around and says, "All right, what would you do?"—that's your crisis. Then you've got to begin to think specifically, and the movement rhetoric won't work anymore.

⊘ANDREW KIMBRELL: Sometimes we fall into the jargon that those using and benefiting from megatechnologies and technocracies are the minority, and that the nontechnologized majority can somehow gain power and destroy the current system. Technology-living Northern suburbanites may still be fewer in number than those still living in traditional or simple technology environments, but technology equals power both in productivity and military might. Further, the world's governments are conforming their societies to the techno-market paradigm through power structures like the World Trade Organization proposed under the General Agreement on Tariffs and Trade. It is difficult to see how the powerless can effectively usurp the current technological and political juggernaut of globalization.

⊘SUSAN GRIFFIN *connects with Vandana's remark and articulates the vast cost of abstractions like world markets. She also encourages us to seek further for more comprehensive responses to seemingly unrelated problems:* One of the things that gets destroyed in this abstracted system is that people no longer have an understanding of something in an intuitive, sensual way, which is the way most people on the Earth have known things for centuries. Yet with this abstractive economy they no longer understand what the real price is of what they're selling.

Preserving the wild, wanting to have communities, and addressing the urgent questions of social justice and urban suffering don't have to be opposing concerns. In fact, they are allied. The alliance has to be made fresh. How about some of us working to set up a program to employ a certain number of urban kids who would not otherwise be employable and employ them in helping to preserve the wilderness? We can take concern and care for their lives so that they have this work that they also learn from, and we learn from them at the same time.

⊘ASHIS NANDY *makes the necessary point that in the relationship between "haves" and "have nots" there are disadvantages to the powerful, also, and that it is vital to keep these in mind:* Most of the people in the world still see and understand intuitively, but those who do have been disempowered and marginalized. At conferences like this, there are two main modalities of speaking. Either you speak like an archaeologist or an ancient historian trying to recover something from the past, or you talk as a futurist of transcending modern systems to bring something new, better, and more human. Whereas, when I go back to India, it seems to me that the political and moral choices are right there in front of me. It is no longer something which you have to excavate from the past or create in the future.

We have been talking of those who exercise power. At one level this image is true. But I have some discomfort with it.

There is a direct relationship between what we are calling victimhood and that other implicit victimhood that befalls the beneficiaries or the powerful. Unless we recognize that victimhood somehow, our exercise is doomed, because if we do not recognize it, we are granting the superiority of the other system.

⊘VANDANA SHIVA *mentions an encounter with a young man who was organizing drug addicts, dropouts, and welfare recipients in Germany. Meeting him brought her into contact with the dispossessed of the North:* "We'll meet at the battery door," *said the young man, meaning that subsistence peoples, who know how to graze around and find a little food, are being pushed into industrialized systems like factory farms, or chicken batteries, while people in the developed world are increasingly being displaced from their industrial niches and needing to learn how to feed themselves.* "We have to create our alternative at that door," *says Shiva.* "Even though everyone's surrounded by technology, so many people are being pushed out of that system, with no place at all, having forgotten that you can feed yourself."

⊘FRÉDÉRIQUE APPFEL-MARGLIN *details some of the range of knowledge involved in the everyday life of village women and describes the seamlessness of life in vernacular cultures—then reflects on the demeaning of these by industrial-era categories and concepts:* In vernacular ways of life women are the preventive doctors of the family, of the household. The cooking, in the villages of India where I've been going for eighteen years, entails an incredible amount of knowledge. It involves knowing the constitution of each member of the family, their state of health, their energy requirement, which foods will give them that energy requirement, which food, at what time of the season, what time of the day, which medicinal herbs to use when, and at what time. This of course has all been taken away with industrialization. The response for women should be to reclaim this meaningful, necessary, and useful work.

In India, peasant women's activities of cooking, healing, feeding the cattle, having intercourse with their husbands, as well as ritual activity, are all spoken of as *káma,* work. These activities, along with the agricultural and ritual activities of the men, generate and regenerate their world. They are thus at the heart of things and cannot be separated into a private and a public domain. These activities are very different from what we today call "reproduction," be it biological or social. The word "reproduction" emerged in nineteenth-century Europe and signals the effects of the Industrial Revolution and the commodification of life. There is here no separation between a purely natural—that is biological—realm and a properly cultural realm. These separations do violence to the noncommodified world of the peasants.

We should not see generation as mere reproduction, as a biological phenomenon, and give it away to biomedicine. The act of generation is deeply rooted in community and in the nonhuman world and should not be seen as only the work of women. In vernacular society, of course, the cooking is ritualized, the generation is ritualized, and we have to reclaim that.

⊘ Never one to mince words about the severity of the situation and the seriousness of response required, JOHN MOHAWK *lays it out:* We're talking about nothing short of a cultural revolution. And some of the concepts we're discussing are untranslatable. Yet these ideas have long been predicted. The Indians had cultural expectations that the technological society would self-destruct and leave people in disastrous situations. Their antidote was to revitalize the culture. Of course they're talking about the culture of the village. We're talking about that, too, but in a new way.

On the one hand, it's depressing to hear that the power elites are finally getting their way and are going to run the world. On the other, it means that people are going to be free from the illusion that they're participating. So we can get on with the job of rebuilding societies. That means everything—music and dance, art, stories, food, plants—it means all of it. Everything's been commodified. And everything has been despiritualized to the extent that it can be and rendered effectively dead. Now what we're going to do is to respiritualize and revitalize the world, render it alive, and meaningful and interactive.

⊘ELISABET HERMODSSON *affectingly brings the discussion to a close with her reminiscence of the violation of her own sense of nature's vitalism precipitated by her schoolgirl encounter with Galileo, hero of science and rationality, and how such reductionist thinking about nature accounts for the brutal quality of so much of life today:* Susan Griffin mentioned that we as women identify ourselves with nature more than men do. I think this is what I was doing when I felt hurt by the statements of Galileo Galilei. Namely, he took the spirit from nature through his division of the primary and secondary characteristics of nature. When I learned this, I must have felt as if he took my soul from me.

Looking at early society where science "grew up," we see that no women took part in creating the scientific theories with which nature began to be researched. It was men in a patriarchal society who invented the concept of knowledge. It is not difficult to see how sexist many of the scientific ideas about nature are.

Already when I was a schoolchild I had an aversion to Galileo Galilei. It's a little curious, and painful. The teacher said Galileo was the hero of the modern world. He had been threatened by the Catholic Church and I was no friend of the Catholic Church and its Inquisition. Nevertheless, Galileo had said something that was bothering me. He had said that the constitution of nature is of two kinds, the primary and the secondary. And the primary characteristics are measurable quantities, such as weight, extent, volume, and they belong to nature itself. But the secondary, the unmeasurables, what would be called the qualities—color, taste, smell, beauty—they do not belong to nature itself. In this philosophy, or in what's called science, the flower's color is not the flower's own, and nature's beauty is not nature's own.

I felt hurt when I learned this, but I was fifteen years old and I had no argument against what the teacher said and what Galileo said, because this was science. And I could have objections against religion, poetry, literature, or politics, but not against science. I was more or less conscious then, but I hid my protest. When I became a student in philosophy my protest reawakened. At that time analytical philosophy, which regarded itself as science, was dominant. By studying this philosophy I found the argument against it. Through working with art and through my personal experience, especially of the growing technocracy, and through my mourning for destroyed landscapes, I found my arguments against Galileo Galilei.

It is not that man's biology makes him more aggressive; it is that the patriarchal system forces him to oppress woman. Then he becomes enemy to his own female nature, and to woman and to Earth. Why has modern high technology become so brutal? It has its root in a patriarchal society that once made all the symbols and all the myths about nature. And all methods with which you research nature were created from the idea which says that nature has only quantities and no qualities.

Concluding Dialogue

᠙ *The final session of the conference began with a recap by Fritjof Capra of the preceding discussions. The purpose of the session, as announced by Jerry Mander, was for the group to begin to articulate a set of criteria for assessing technologies, unearthing their covert politics, and anticipating the unadvertised side effects of new technologies—which effects have the unfortunate tendency not to remain on the side.*

The resulting criteria were considered and augmented at the 1994 conference. A distilled version appears at the end of this book, titled "78 Reasonable Questions to Ask About Any Technology." It was our hope to provide activists and citizens of every stripe with a list of queries as well developed and pointed as a gathering of the world's leading technology critics could make it.

What follows, then, is an assortment of comments: the reasoning behind certain criteria, strategic considerations, further philosophical premises—from and for activists in the field, responses to ideas voiced earlier in the discussion that only found their way into the conversation late in the day—and a moral coda.

Apropos the maxim that "technology is power," which has been proposed for the list, HELENA NORBERG-HODGE *comments that it's more complicated than that:* For the majority of us who have been encouraged to use modern technologies, we are actually being robbed of power and choice.

᠙ PER GAHRTON *provides some insight into the form and character of the scientific establishment we would confront:* From my older brother, who is a member of the Swedish Nobel Prize Committee for Medicine, a very powerful, very nice guy, I get the impression that science is enormously well organized. It's completely global. He goes to every country—China, Japan, India, the United States, everywhere—and everywhere he goes he is inside a global organization. Science is also a community. Whatever is known, anywhere on Earth in that science, is always a basis for the research of new scientists, which gives them a certain ever-growing strength.

⊘ Gahrton goes on to contrast the Ecology Movement with science, business, and the state, observing that Greens are not nearly so well organized but that Green-minded movements exist all over the world. "It's important to know that this kind of thinking is not the luxury of the rich world," *he says. And that the necessity for organizing and global networking is clear.*

JERRY MANDER *succinctly states his sense of our mission:* Langdon Winner has used the phrase "technological somnambulism" to describe the condition of sleepwalking through the world oblivious to the problems of technology. Society, scientists, the intelligentsia, the media, and policymakers need to be awakened to these problems. We have to recognize and name the creature—megatechnology—as well as speak about its specific elements. We have to refute the misconception that technology is neutral. Technology must become a subject that is considered in its own terms.

⊘ JOHN DAVIS and ANDREW KIMBRELL offer some brief comments about points of focus and tactics. Says JOHN DAVIS: We should give at least as much attention to natural communities as to human communities. A couple of the fundamental criteria in evaluating a technology would be its effects on land and wildlife, which in many cases can be measured fairly easily. On that basis it would be easy to condemn some technologies like cars, computers, and chainsaws that almost all of us unfortunately are using right now. We should be willing to go to that extreme, to condemn some specific technologies.

⊘ PER GAHRTON: I am quite prepared to specify certain technologies which are main evils and have really brought enormous adverse structural change and to condemn cars and even water closets on condition that people would understand that it's different to fancy a society without these technologies at all than it is for an individual in a society where this technology is dominating to withdraw from it.

⊘ JOHN DAVIS: Time is a consideration. If we call for the elimination of TV, computers, cars, and such, to suggest it be done over the course of many years or even many decades might sound more tenable than calling for immediate elimination. Seeing it as a long-term project might be one way to make our ideas radical yet politically feasible.

⊘ANDREW KIMBRELL: Most of us have come to the conclusion that technology is the primary engine of social change. So you can't promote social change without changing technology. You cannot have democracy on an assembly line, something Marx didn't understand. Changing the politics of the means of production is the only way to begin to address our basic social concerns.

⊘SIGMUND KVALOY, *in this discussion and elsewhere, envisions a synergy of environmental monitoring technology and global computer control/sensing —an ominous cybernetic world brain—as one possible outcome of present trends, many of which are insidious in their appeal to the environmentally concerned.*

KVALOY *agrees with* JEREMY RIFKIN *that we are moving into an age of biotechnology, but that computers and the resulting mindset are the foundations of this epochal change and make that kind of thinking and those kinds of solutions a self-propelling process. Other participants contribute brief comments.*

HELENA NORBERG-HODGE: The majority of environmental organizations are now ready to question the economic paradigm, but most of them don't see megatechnology as a root cause and root issue.

⊘DOUG TOMPKINS, *out of his own experience, expands on Helena's observation:* The larger environmental community is, more often than not, obstructing the very change in world view that we advocate. These big groups are acting as a total voice of the Environmental Movement. The Environmental Movement has been slow to pick up on trade issues, and many in the movement are middle-of-the-road when they do. Governments and politicians try to take a compromise middle ground and thus marginalize the vanguard which may have very different positions, even opposite in substance and strategy from the big groups.

⊘VANDANA SHIVA *remarks that this latest generation of monopolizing technologies comes advertised as lending themselves to decentralization, which makes information and action campaigns trickier, especially systemic assessment of technological impacts.*

MARTHA CROUCH: That people actually can control technology at the community level is a radical concept. Most people I know don't think they have a choice. They think that technology just falls out of the sky like rain and they have to respond to it. Jerry Mander's writing on television and computers was instrumental in giving me permission to assess and ultimately condemn technologies I was involved in creating, like biotechnology. Because I live in a culture that pretends that we don't have that control, I wouldn't have thought of it myself without having such a role model.

☙The question of whether or not it is possible to assess technology rigorously is raised.

DAVID SUZUKI: Our knowledge base is so minuscule that we can't assess the consequences of technology. Consider nuclear power. If in 1945, before or after the bomb was dropped on Hiroshima, there had been an environmental impact assessment, nothing would have been said about radioactive fallout, because it wasn't discovered until after the Bikini Atoll bomb test. Biomagnification of contaminants through the food chain was discovered years later, as well as electromagnetic pulses of gamma rays, and the notion of a nuclear fall or winter. The idea that we can manage technology by proper assessment is a trap. We have to recognize how complex the world around us all is, and how little we know.

The problem is that the benefits of technology are always immediate and obvious; that is why we create technologies. Those who want to promulgate an area such as biotechnology say, "So what are your objections to biotechnology?" And you end up by speculating, "Gee, maybe a monster is going to crawl out of the test tube," and sounding like a whining party pooper. We don't have the knowledge base to be able to predict precise consequences, and so we are stuck sounding vague.

There is no such thing as a problem-free technology. So can or should we continue buying the obvious immediate benefits, knowing full well that there are going to be consequences that we can't even predict?

☙JERRY MANDER: David Brower says, "Guilty until proven innocent."

☙DOUG TOMPKINS: Wes Jackson once put this question to a group of technophiles—If chemists took 150 years or 100 years to come up with ozone-depleting substances, how long will the biotech industry take to come up with their equivalent? It's just a matter of time before something as disastrous as the ozone side effect will appear in biotech. You don't have to confront any specific technologies on their own merits, but simply on their informing values. In my opinion we need to define the bioregional vision. The assessment starts there. Whatever technologies develop out of those visions and values will tend to be beneficial. Trying to make blueprints, or to guess precisely what a technology will do, is unimportant. We have to adopt a whole different value base.

In short, when you truly put ecologically and biologically sustainable objectives first, then the social, economic, *technological*, scientific decisions, programs, and systems will conform to keeping our planet healthy, rich, and diverse. We will focus on abundance and diversity of *all* species, health in water, forests, air, and soils and discover the wonderful *byproducts* that accrue to human communities. It is, oddly enough, marvelously simple. Its elegance, as many know, was embodied by the original bioregionalists, indigenous societies—many of those societies had it right.

⊘VANDANA SHIVA: Incapacity is growing. More people know what they prefer to do than are able to do it because of the context that technology is creating. We have to stop that incapacitation somehow. We need to think what is the kind of *meaning* that creates restraint on the system.

⊘WENDELL BERRY *identifies the Achilles heel of technology's promoters and how to take aim at it:* What David Suzuki says about us—that we have inadequate knowledge to assess the impacts of these innovations—is equally true of the proponents. They don't have an adequate knowledge to assess these impacts either. So our debate strategy is not to prove that they are wrong but to force them to reveal that they don't know. We don't have to know anything except how to phrase the questions. And it seems to me that the right questions would be appropriately phrased versions of "What will this thing do to our community?" By "community" I mean simply all that we have in common: the world, the natural world, the wilderness, our humanity, each other, the rest of it.

⊘HELENA NORBERG-HODGE *advocates the use of an epistemological criterion for judging technologies:* The alternatives are plural—sustainable ways of living are based on diversity. One criterion for assessing technologies would be to distrust anything that is born of such reductionist knowledge as our late twentieth-century science. The Second World War was an enormous watershed. Just about everything produced after that is questionable; the side effects are only now beginning to be recognized. So another criterion for a healthy type of technology would be that it be born of bioregional, rather than reductionist, laboratory knowledge and research.

⊘JOHN MOHAWK *enjoins us to expose the partiality of the megatechnological agenda:* Law is political. People have to understand that it's not neutral, not something that arises out of nature. It's something that's designed for a specific end. Of course the politics of law, and the politics of technology, are intertwined. You can't really imagine these technologies without a superstructure of law to protect and advance their agendas. Yet technology is regarded almost as though it were organic, as if it weren't invented by some people for some purpose to serve some interests at the expense of other interests. We have to unmask everybody's claims that they don't have a position. We have to define and deconstruct those things that people think are irresistible and irremediable.

🖉 SIGMUND KVALOY *suggests that awareness of the distinction between the complicated and the complex provides a basis for criticizing or assessing technologies. And he observes:* The attack on all the localities in the world comes from a force global in character.

🖉 FRÉDÉRIQUE APFFEL-MARGLIN: The third industrial revolution is based on the colonization of life itself. All our concerns have to do with reclaiming or decolonizing life. Ritualized technology is noncolonizing. It is dialogical, in dialogue with the Earth and people. So that's the politics and that's the kind of technology.

🖉 JERRY MANDER *returns to the question of whether technological assessment is possible, answers in the affirmative, and explains how:* It most certainly is possible to assess technology. The corporations that invent these things have to know what you can do with them in order to sell them. As the MIT Studies on Retrospective Technology Assessment showed, at the time of the invention of most technologies, a great deal is known as to ultimate effects. At the time of the invention of the telephone, for example, scores and scores of its potential effects—from the death of farms to the migration to cities to the growth of highrises—had been described.

So the question is not so much whether we *can* assess technologies, it's what kind of assessment standards we employ, who controls them, and to what end. When I hear about food irradiation I know categorically that it's a quintessentially industrial approach to food, that it is part and parcel of a hazardous centralized system of packaging, marketing, and distributing food. From the standpoint of democracy and local self-reliance—from a holistic viewpoint—I can know that the technology's bad even before hearing from scientists.

🖉 WENDELL BERRY: We haven't said anything at all about the vulnerability of a completely technologized world—nothing at all, when in fact it is the most vulnerable that you can imagine. Our country here is already just sitting and waiting for a few terrorists or saboteurs to figure out where the wires cross.

🖉 JEREMY RIFKIN *contributes a telling phrase and some strategic—and moral—intelligence:* Trickle-down technology is the notion that technologies that benefit those who own and control them will somehow wind up benefiting everyone else. . . . Justice is the entry point for masses of people to understand the technology issue.

⊘ At the end of the day SUSAN GRIFFIN *reminds us of Gandhi's conviction that intent is crucially important, that the way we proceed and the feeling we hold toward the people we would reach should be a feeling of love rather than of making enemies, that corporations may be evil but they are different from human beings.*

Griffin continues, proposing that our objection to technology is comprehensive and rooted in fundamental beliefs: This confusion of technology with something natural reminds me of Hannah Arendt's observation that every totalitarian system argues for itself that it is historically inevitable. And that's what technology is arguing for itself now. It is the new form of totalitarianism. So it's not simply that we have a technological objection to technology or that we have an economic objection to technology, but that we have a deep philosophical objection to technology which involves issues of the spirit and of the soul and social justice.

Megatechnology and Economic Globalization

⊘ Devon, 1994

The 1994 meeting was held in early October in a storybook place—Dartington Hall, a medieval manor in Devon, England. Home of a charitable trust, Dartington Hall was lovingly, lavishly restored in the twenties by an Englishman, Leonard Elmhirst, with inspiration supplied by Rabindranath Tagore and support supplied by Elmhirst's American wife, Dorothy. In addition to hosting conferences such as ours, Dartington Hall is also home to Schumacher College, an arts college, a concert series, and efforts to restore the vast farmlands of the estate to organic agriculture.

Great stone buildings, simple elegant salons for some of our meetings, plainer, cozier quarters for others, a medieval churchyard with a 1,000-year-old yew, and a rhapsodically beautiful formal garden of perhaps 100 acres, one of which had been, it was speculated, a jousting tilt—these provided the setting for our meeting.

One jet-lagged morning I woke before dawn and walked out on the grounds in the crepuscular mist, pressing out toward the margin between gardens and fields where I encountered looming ancient oaks and beeches, dwarfing any I'd ever seen in America. They were here, I thought, because for generation after generation, some person had decided to let them continue to stand. That sense of the landscape's charm and depth in time as human effect was strange. These oaks and beeches were like pet Druids in a court of converts and one could only speculate as to their sense of the matter. All this was in certain contrast to the San Francisco venue of the meeting a year before.

Chapter 7

Opening Remarks

⊙*The majority of the participants gather after dinner Thursday night for brief introductions and some presentations by the conference organizers.* SATISH KUMAR, *once a Jain monk, now editor of* Resurgence *magazine and a founder of Schumacher College, gives a welcome to Dartington Hall and supplies a bit of the history of the place:* Dartington was established to regenerate and renew all facets of local economy—farming, craft, arts, culture, and education—out of Elmhirst's vision that rural life should be rich and that we should maintain it so. So Dartington can fitly be used for creating a new consciousness which is sustainable, local, ecological, spiritual, and artistic. All those elements come together here. On behalf of Dartington, I would like to welcome you.

⊙ *Next, the other conveners of the conference speak, beginning with* JERRY MANDER: I was in the advertising business originally. Working daily with the power of images I began to understand that it's possible to put an image into hundreds of millions of human beings' minds at the same time, and to persuade huge populations to behave in a certain way that I wished them to. This kind of power—now expressed to the scale of some $200 billion per year—explains much about our culture, its amorality, its values, its homogenized quality, its commodity orientation, and the drives to massification of consciousness and behavior.

Out of that understanding, I decided to write *Four Arguments for the Elimination of Television*, a book which has proved to be surprisingly popular; more than a quarter of a million copies have been sold. It was only after working on that book for some time, and finding the hundreds of dangerous effects that are clearly present, that I began to think society would be better off without television. I started to research who else had drawn that conclusion and found that though 6,000 books had been written about TV at that point [1977], none had thought to recommend that, on balance, it might be doing more harm than good, and that we'd be better off without it. Given the immense number of harms attributable to TV, the idea of saying "no" to the technology seemed to remain in the realm of the unthinkable thought. Unfortunately, that is characteristic of our society; once a technology is upon us, we do not permit ourselves to believe that its negative aspects are more profound than its positive, or that there is really anything we can do to stop it. People lose the ability to imagine doing without the technology, as has already become apparent with computers. Technologies like cars, computers, and TV make profound changes in the world in the end, they have far greater impact than the politicians we elect—yet we remain utterly passive to the process of their introduction, leaving it to corporations to define the technologies for us. We don't think to address the metaquestions about technology, and we have no training or practice in even knowing what questions to ask. And if we do ask questions, we find we have little process or means or power to reject technologies on the grounds of their social, psychological, political, or ecological consequences.

Marshall McLuhan's 1965 saying, "The medium is the message," may be the most important statement of this century, and yet it remains profoundly misunderstood even to this day. He meant that the technological form itself has far more consequence than its content or apparent function. The TV programs may be important, but more important is the fact of the existence of TV in society—how it changes power arrangements, how it changes what we know and don't know, how we think, and even what we are capable of learning. How it alters community life, family life, and human health. We need to develop questions about all these and more—to think about the machine systemically in all its dimensions. Who gains? Who loses? What characteristics of humanity and society are amplified? What characteristics are diminished? Most of all, are we better off with it or without it?

The few people who do attempt to create systemic critiques of technology now tend to be dismissed out of hand as Luddites. At one time I was reluctant to be called such a term as "Luddite." But then I heard Langdon Winner embrace that epithet on a radio program because, he said, the Luddites had accurately anticipated what technological change

—the mechanization, mass production, and concentration of their cottage industry—was going to mean. It did in fact destroy their families, their livelihood, their communities, their prosperity.

Lately it's become apparent that there are also technical forms that are not machines but institutional expressions of technological culture. Trade agreements, global communications, and political and economic arrangements catering to transnational corporations are made possible by machines, aggrandize the machine, and vice versa. The result is a radical transformation of politics, economies at every scale, and cultures everywhere. We're about to be sucked into a homogenized global economy that makes every place on Earth look like Phoenix, Arizona, and share nearly identical values and behaviors. This is a formidable new colonialism that isn't usually perceived as such.

My colleagues, Teddy and Helena, and I began to realize that the integral role of technology in this onslaught of globalization and destruction of the natural world had not been directly addressed. People didn't recognize that computers, television, transport, biotechnology, automation, robotics, and satellite communications all are working parts of this juggernaut and that transnational corporations and trade agreements are themselves technological forms. Our work together here is to articulate a multidimensional technological assessment that will be as encompassing as possible.

⊘EDWARD ("TEDDY") GOLDSMITH *crisply articulates how, in his view, technology is irrelevant to the solution of our most serious problems, and that the conventional idea of progress is in error:* In a recent book—*The Way: An Ecological World View*—I have tried to describe an ecological world view, and to contrast it with the world view of modernism. In terms of an ecological world view, all real benefits and hence real wealth are the product of the normal functioning of the natural world, that is, of the biosphere and the ecosystems that compose it, and the traditional communities and families that were once part of these ecosystems. Natural or real wealth must include a stable and favorable climate, fertile soil, free-flowing rivers, cohesive and self-governing communities, and the cultural patterns with which they are imbued and which alone make it possible for them to be self-governing.

A society imbued with an ecological world view must seek above all to preserve the natural world—on which human welfare depends. Significantly, this was the case with the tribal and archaic societies of the past that saw human welfare as dependent on maintaining the order of the cosmos—that included their society itself, the natural world, and the world of the gods—to which task their behavior patterns were specifically geared, in particular their rituals and ceremonies.

The first tenet of the world view of modernism, on the other hand, is that all benefits and hence all wealth are humanmade, being largely the product of science, technology, and industry. Accordingly, we interpret all our problems in such a way as to make them appear amenable to a scientific, technological, and industrial solution, that is, one dependent on economic development or "progress."

In this way we rationalize and hence legitimize the sort of "solutions" we have decided in advance to apply to these problems: the only ones that our society is organized to provide and the only ones that are compatible with that world view.

The second tenet of the world view of modernism follows directly from the first: If all benefits are humanmade—are the products of science, technology, and industry—it follows that the only way of maximizing these benefits is by economic development, since it involves systematically substituting for the real world that provides us with natural benefits an artificial or surrogate world that provides us with humanmade benefits. Thus you have to increase the capacity to provide humanmade benefits.

In terms of this world view, whatever problems a society is faced with are thereby interpreted as evidence of underdevelopment, that is, of our failure to fund sufficient scientific research, technological innovation, and industrial development. Progress is thereby seen as not having proceeded fast enough, for if it had the problems would quite clearly not have occurred. Thus, increasing floods are seen as occurring because we have not built enough dams and embankments. If the crime rate goes up, this is because we have not built enough prisons, hired enough police, or installed enough burglar alarms. If people are sick, this is because they have not consumed enough pills or have not built enough hospitals.

In general it is assumed that there is a technological solution to every one of our problems. However, in reality, technology can only solve technological problems, like repairing an automobile or flying to the moon. The latter is obviously a very impressive achievement, but it is not clear that it solves any of the increasingly serious problems that confront us on this planet. Humans have never really suffered from not going to the moon! In any case, if we were to draw up a list of the problems that confront us today, "not going to the moon" must be fairly low down on that list.

Our real problems are not technological problems and are not amenable to technological solutions. There is no gadgetry, however ingenious and however elaborate, for instance, that can reconstitute a family that has broken apart, or can re-create a disrupted cultural pattern that once held together a society, or can, for that matter, restore a tropical rainforest that has been felled by a logging company.

These problems are caused by the breakdown of natural systems— biological organisms, communities, and ecosystems—under the impact of that highly destructive process called economic development or progress, of which technology is one of the most important ingredients. Only nature can reconstitute these natural systems. More precisely, they must reconstitute themselves, and our role can only be to re-create the conditions in which this is possible—which above all means putting progress into reverse.

⊘ *Next,* HELENA NORBERG-HODGE *takes the floor:* After *Silent Spring,* when the Western world was alerted to the environmental crisis, there was an awareness of the need to rethink science and technology. It became apparent that decontextualized, reductionist knowledge is dangerous, because it allows humans to intervene in the complex web of relationship that is the natural world without understanding the overall impact of such intervention. In almost every industrial country there was a push for a more holistic and interdisciplinary approach, and many universities started interdisciplinary departments.

However, these responses to the environmental crises were relatively short-lived. Probably on account of a whole range of "systemic" pressures—partly because many narrowly trained specialists felt threatened, and partly because funding steered research in a direction that suited big business—these interdisciplinary departments have either closed down or become narrowly reductionist.

There was also an attempt to develop "decentralized," "appropriate" technologies with the aid of small independent research institutes like Farallones and the New Alchemy Institute in America and their counterparts in Europe. Then, perhaps because of the seduction of computers and electronic technology—which masqueraded as decentralizing, benign, and clean—that whole attempt was undermined. Now almost all those little institutes are also gone.

Over the last decades, I've been trying to alert people to the impact of economic centralization—more recently joining campaigns against Maastricht, GATT, and NAFTA. In the last couple of years there's been an encouragingly rapid turnaround as far as the trade issue is concerned, but before that there was little awareness throughout Europe and the U.S.A. that economic centralization is undermining virtually all the efforts of the environmental and social movements. However, Western science and technology, which you can't really separate, is the missing piece. Science remains the religion of modern society, dangerous because unspoken. From left to right, from political to grassroots movements, the faith in science and technology has been absolute.

It is generally thought that the knowledge is universal, that technology is neutral, and that, if people using them have the right intentions, then the technologies will be beneficial.

As people become more aware of the implications of GATT, and the globalization of the economy, there inevitably will be a growing awareness of the role technology has played in making this globalization possible, and therefore we will see more questioning. Nevertheless, there's a real urgency to promote this critical awareness. We're rapidly obliterating evidence of other ways of living, and other ways of knowing. Those other ways were characterized by a closer relationship to reality, a closer relationship to the living world. The great danger today is that through our separation from the living world, we become easily manipulated by the Orwellian doublespeak of the media. We become increasingly enveloped by a humanmade world in which scientific knowledge and modern teaching become more and more essential for survival. But that very "technosphere" is eroding life itself.

ᘒ ᘑ ᘒ

ᘑ *The next morning the conference begins in earnest with each participant present making a full statement of their concerns arising from our subject or an update on their current work.*

MARTHA CROUCH *picks up a thread from the year before:* I was looking out of the window as we flew above the huge heartland of North America and was struck by how much of the landscape had been stamped with the geometric patterns of agriculture and suburbia, straight lines, perfect circles—the mind of Descartes writ large on the land. It was a visual reminder of how powerful ideas can be. The ideas of a particular kind of economy, or land use, or land ownership can be a technology that can have vast influence and effect.

In my former work, in biotechnology, we used organisms and tools and described them as systems. We would talk about the "corn system," the "tomato system," or the "cow system," regarding the organism as an indistinguishable part of a whole set of interactions, including the reagents and the tools that we used in our experiments. Now I would like to think about going in the other direction—re-animating rather than mechanizing. Science and technology have placed ideas, tools, and organisms in machine-oriented systems. I'm not only a Neo-Luddite but a neo-animist; I like the idea of the tables and the chairs and the airplanes being re-animated to reflect their individual characteristics and the human intentions that went into their being.

One of the questions related to neo-animism is, "When you consider a technology like biotechnology or a computer or a plow, can you ever separate out the particular characteristics that are built in with the ideas and intentions of the creators of those technologies?" I used to think of turning swords into plowshares as a very peaceful idea. Now I think of it as turning the war against the land. The intent of making a sharp object out of ore that has been wrenched from the guts of the Earth is still in the plow. It is still a tool for disembowelment, but now it disembowels the soil. Can that original intent ever be escaped? Can you take a computer with systems theory and binary logic, put on a façade of software that makes it converse with you, and then use it to solve problems in a holistic way? Can we absolve these tools of their origins, or do we have to somehow begin anew and create new artifacts that incorporate the intentions we would like to see in a world we would like to build?

*⊘*Andrew Kimbrell *begins by questioning some of the linguistic, philosophical, and political misdirection that confounds us now:* During the anti-Vietnam War days, you had to preface anything you said as a political activist with, "I'm no Communist but what we're doing in Vietnam is wrong." Or, "I'm no Communist, but we really must have workplace democracy." Now that has changed and people say, "I'm no Luddite, but I have a real problem with biotechnology."

I was brought up in a very Progressive environment with the central political chore being to create more justice in the ownership of the means of production. It was a great struggle, in which many courageous people died. But the ownership of the means of production wasn't the real issue. We were being a little naïve in thinking that you could have democracy on an assembly line or inside a corporation or inside a whole system of totalitarian technologies.

Totalitarian technologies have two aspects: They are unresponsive to individuals and communities, and we are incapable of taking responsibility for them. When you turn on the electricity, you cannot take responsibility for your action. You can't demand that energy come from solar power rather than nuclear power. You can't take responsibility for the food you eat, for how your taxes are spent, for what's being taught to your kids, or for the air they breathe. Nor can the centralized technologies and technocracies of our time be responsive to us and our individual desires for environmental or human health protection. These intrinsically totalitarian technologies have made us servile.

The paradigm shift from concern with the ownership of the means of production to dealing with the politics of the means of production—not just the machines, but the whole complex of technologies and technocracies required for production to take place, including corporations and trade organizations—has not happened, at least not in the United States, and certainly not among Progressives in Washington, D.C.

There seem to be very few taboos left. The most graphic sex and violence has become routine. But there is one great taboo, and that's against assuming that nature has an inside—a soul or mind. Whenever we see intelligence or emotion in other lifeforms we call it "instinct" in a desperate attempt to hide the fact that other lifeforms have intelligence and interiority. It's an enduring consequence of the Cartesian de-souling of nature.

Another great de-souler is the doctrine of efficiency: No one seems to be against efficiency. Our whole society is based on its tenets: minimum input, for maximum output, in minimum time. However, if I were to apply the efficiency doctrine to my family and provide my children with minimum input of food and affection for maximum good grades and obedience, you would say this guy needs therapy in a major way! Do we hang up on our friends because a conversation at a certain time may be inefficient? Do we turn our pets out into the street because we realize they are totally inefficient? No. Of course not. In fact, we never apply this ethic of efficiency to those we really care about. Rather we use empathy or, dare we say it, love. Yet policymakers insist that efficiency be the sole manner in which we treat nature—always referred to as "natural resources." Just try bringing up love and empathy for a river or tree when attempting to pass legislation or win an environmental lawsuit. We must realize that when we allow our struggle to be characterized as an attempt to be more efficient in the use of natural resources or human resources—which is you and me—we've already lost the argument because we're using that de-souling paradigm and language which allowed for the destruction in the first place.

Another unfortunate reductionist term is the use of "consumer" and indeed the idea of a "Consumer Movement": As a consumer, you consume the world. Tuberculosis used to be called consumption because it appeared to consume the body. In struggling against the "consumption ethic" technologies, what we want is not a "Consumer" but rather a "Creator" Movement. In every decision you make, everything you buy, everything you do, the technologies you utilize, you're not a consumer, you're a creator, creating a future for the entire biotic community.

⊘JOHN MOHAWK *sketches the disastrous chain of events that follows from the policy of enclosure, begun hundreds of years ago and continuing today. He thinks the "technology" of which we speak here is a late-stage manifestation of that definitive power relationship:* In looking at these issues, we're talking about nothing less ambitious than challenging the very foundations of Western civilization. The process of moving people off the land that started in England six centuries ago is the major reason why we have the growth of populations, cities, and the rise of hunger in the world. Hunger is about the lack of distribution of wealth and not an inevitability of technological process. It is the single most important result of the issues that we are dealing with. Driving people off the land, impoverishing them, and forcing them into cities is exactly what renders them subject to all of the next round of strategic implementation of technology and implementation of experimental social forms. In our discussions, we really have to start asking ourselves, "What is happening to the people most disempowered by these technologies and social projects?"

What was talked about centuries ago in Thomas More's *Utopia* is still happening today. The sheep are still eating people, except now it's cattle doing the eating. The difference in Latin America and other parts of the world is that this situation is the result of something that's on automatic pilot. The technologies create chemical changes in the environment, which in turn cause social disruptions. The chemical changes cause a slight warming of the planet; those small variations in climate cause deserts to expand; desertification drives people in the Third World who lived on marginal lands into the cities. The huge rise in the population of Third World cities is a result of the current stage of the Industrial Revolution.

The people who are planning the rape of the planet can adjust and take advantage of that. They're still colonizing forest areas, promising land to people, when what they want to do in fact is clear the land for more cattle. We see the rise of social violence in order to make that happen; fascism rises fast when all you have to do is hire a bunch of *pistoleros* to go out and beat up the poor people who are not yet crowded into wherever it is they will be crowded.

When we talk about technology, what we're really talking about is the maturity, in our century, of a process that has been going on for a long time.

₢CHARLENE SPRETNAK: I've been working on a book called *The Resurgence of the Real: Body, Nature, and Place in a Hypermodern World.* It considers the ways in which the ideologies of modernity—the mechanistic world view that will supposedly deliver us to technotopia— are being challenged in the 1990s by the very elements of life on Earth that were most devalued and marginalized. The knowing body, the creative cosmos, and the complex sense of place are asserting their real nature and thus poking through the overlaying ideologies of denial.

₢SIGMUND KVALOY *provides us with a little good news about successful resistance to globalization and an awful lot of bad news that could result if that resistance flags:* Let me just say in passing that I'm very pleased that the connection between technology and globalization is being articulated. These two are so deeply entwined and presuppose each other so much that, in my view, our work would be fruitfully served by the joining together of the anti-globalists and the Neo-Luddites. Let me say, too, as a quick report, that we are winning the struggle to keep Norway outside of the European Union. A few days ago [September 1994], the whole collective of Norwegian trade unions voted "no." For the last six months I've been working on and finally finished the booklet "Nature's 'No' to the European Union," which says a "no" to its enormous increase in volume and speed in the mobility of things, animals, foodstuffs, people, et cetera, across old borders, and its corresponding removal of border controls. The specific point of the booklet is that nature doesn't like this because it means mixing ecosystems and replacing order by chaos.

A lot of elements interact all at once, propelled by the competitive industrial system as it is globalized—with consequences like the emergence and dissemination of displaced or ecologically dislocated organisms—everything, from viruses and bacteria to algae and fungi to insects —simultaneous with the sudden, almost explosive increase in resistance to drugs and vaccines in a lot of these organisms. We have a new global situation! Most people are unaware of the threat produced by the synergy of all these elements, since the knowledge of it is fragmented, possessed by specialists who don't communicate with one another.

Simultaneously, the gap between food production and human population will keep widening. We have the explosion of urbanization and the growth of slums, also exacerbating the spread of infection. We have rising temperatures which, according to some of the research, will mean that tropical and subtropical diseases will invade Europe, America, and Japan; and, mind you, *we*—the rich Northerners—have lost much of the natural immunity to these diseases, still possessed by the Third World. *We* are the vulnerable now.

So some people are now saying that nature is hitting back at us, after all our years of brutal abuse. Aggravating the situation, we have at the same time a fantastic rise in global unemployment. We are back to the Great Depression, and it will be permanent this time and will deepen due to two factors: the replacement of humans by machines and the free-trade system allowing the big companies to move production to areas where labor is cheap. Finally, we have global and local computerization, which means that—at the very moment when we need to be down on the ground in order to understand with our senses and concrete, bodily interactions what is happening—we have created an abstract sphere and are removing ourselves from a concerned, locally rooted understanding of what is going on: We manipulate model worlds on screens instead of involving ourselves in the challenges posed by Earth-reality. The total situation says that this is the worst possible moment in human history to introduce global free trade and further increase travel and create those inner markets, like NAFTA and the Union. It is like opening up a global draft for fanning the fires of unemployment, hunger, and disease.

⊘ Viennese septuagenarian PAUL BLAU, *still recuperating from a serious fall, nevertheless is able to contribute his wisdom, with courtly gravity. He speaks of his lifetime involvement in resistance to authoritarian regimes and of the horrific realization, after Hiroshima, that nature itself could become a casualty of war:* During the last weeks of the Second World War, when there were heavy air raids on Vienna, I used to bicycle out to the woods in order to escape. Naïve as I was in those days, when the houses were destroyed by bombing I would say to myself, "Look at this forest; they can destroy the city, but they will never destroy this." In August 1945,

we learned about Hiroshima and Nagasaki and from that moment knew that even this nature can be destroyed. That reality was a strong motivation for my work.

During my life I found that whatever your arguments may be, whatever the wealth of figures you present, you can't reach people in the bottom of their hearts without there being a door open; and the door is to be opened only by emotions—not by figures.

Coming to the subject of this conference, one of the greatest difficulties which we meet today is that the thinking of those in power is entirely different from ours. Before having any hope to change the course of events, we have to change the way of thinking in the broad public. I remember that once at a disarmament seminar in Japan, a Japanese physicist who was a witness to the bombing of Hiroshima and Nagasaki said, "We did the wrong thing. We thought we could convince those in power of the madness of the nuclear war. Instead of this, we should have tried to create an enlightened public. Then those in power would be forced to bring their politics into agreement with the feeling of the broad population."

⊘ Oregonian CHET BOWERS, *with scholarly precision, tells us that he has been trying to point out to his colleagues in education that there are other ways to understand the world than those we're accustomed to, and that these kinds of understanding may inform far less destructive ways of living than our own:* I'm interested in how the cultural assumptions underlying modernity are coded and reproduced and become taken-for-granted attitudes of the next generation. I'm in the field of education, where I've been trying to look at how it is that culture gets reproduced in consciousness. Part of that task has been to sort out cultural assumptions that are encoded in metaphorical language, encoded assumptions that "think" people as people think within the language, assumptions that shape their natural attitudes. Some of these cultural assumptions, root metaphors that underlie modernity, assume an anthropocentric universe, view the individual as the basic social unit, regard change as progressive, and encode a mechanistic way of looking at the world. Within the field of education, particularly in universities, these root metaphors are the basis of high-status knowledge. They shape how we understand relationships. I've also been trying to deal with the question of what are the alternative patterns that contribute to ecologically sustainable forms of culture. So I've been writing on the possibility of re-metaphorizing our understanding of the nature of human intelligence. Right now in the field of

cognitive psychology and cognitive science and in the field of education itself, where constructivist thinking reigns, the notion is that intelligence is an individual attribute, that individual intelligence is empowered through data. This view of intelligence leads to the argument that computers are needed because they make data available on a massive scale. I've tried to articulate how it is that the individual is nested in culture, that cultures are nested in ecosystems. Therefore, to understand intelligence we have to understand it in terms of whether it contributes to sustainability rather than thinking of intelligence as an individual attribute, which shifts the focus away from different forms of cultural intelligence.

I've also tried to write on the ecological view of creativity. In the field of education, one of the god-words is that the purpose of education is to foster creativity in all areas of life. The search for the new, the experimental, the innovative is based on the assumption that it's all progressive. Whereas I've tried to articulate how it is that in traditional cultures creativity is the aesthetic part of cultural coding in stories and communication about relationships. In traditional cultures creativity is used in ways that transform the ordinary into the extraordinary and connect the people to a larger symbolic spiritual world.

Another of my interests has to do with articulating why we need to recover an ecologically responsible form of transgenerational communication within modern cultures. Old people in mainstream cultures, at least in the United States, do not really have a clear understanding of their responsibilities to the next generation and have no sense of what knowledge and wisdom they should pass on. And we keep telling our young children not to listen to the old people, which means that if we did have old people who were in fact elders there wouldn't be a dialogue, because you can't have a dialogue without knowing how to participate in the process of cultural renewal.

In terms of public education, when you talk about the ecological crisis and the problem of modernity, there is always the question, "Well, what are the alternatives?" I've been trying to make the case that the marginalized, despised, and essentially subverted cultural groups may have ecologically sustainable cultural patterns that the mainstream can learn from.

As computers become a more dominant aspect of our coding and communicating process we are losing the possibility of recovering these other forms of cultural knowledge. We're in a double bind. We need to understand how to live in terms of relationships. However, computer technology reproduces a form of language, an epistemology that represents our relationship to life as essentially instrumental.

⊘ BETH BURROWS, *a high-spirited, stunningly lucid activist and biotechnology critic from Washington State, begins her truth-speaking thus:* The more busily I advocate for the splendor of the Earth, the more my own garden becomes wild or dried out. I'm an organizer.

When the failure of what I try to do gets to me and I can't take it anymore, I organize direct actions, usually at midnight. *(She adds:* A friend of mine in Vermont tells me that these are not technically "direct actions" but "stunts." If he is right, so be it. I organize stunts.) My favorite was our last one in which we put 1,800 stickers on fire hydrants in downtown Seattle at dogs' eye level. The stickers read, "Lift your leg on GATT." I'm concerned with trade, I'm concerned with biotechnology. I've made myself into a kind of expert on intellectual property. My hobby is toxic-waste cleanup, and I'm really not very good at what I do because all of those things I oppose—free trade, technology out of control, toxic waste—continue.

⊘ RICHARD DOUTHWAITE, *who comes from County Mayo, soberly explains his sense of the historic pass we're in, what actions ordinary people may find necessary to undertake for community survival, and the opposing forces they—and we—may contend with:* I'm currently writing a book about the ways in which communities can achieve a higher degree of economic self-reliance for themselves. Such an approach is necessary because, for the first time in history, as a result of the technological developments, the rich are today able to manage without the poor. The poor are no longer needed to produce their food, to clean their houses, to manufacture or provide their goods and services. Moreover, they are no longer needed to fight their wars. And because they are no longer needed, the poor are increasingly being consigned to ghettos where, in the industrialized countries, they are being maintained economically on the lowest social-welfare allowances which keep crime and social disorder at levels acceptable to the rich.

The task I have set myself is therefore to find a way by which the poor can manage without the rich. This is necessary because the change in the power balance between those with money and those without will not be reversed by the democratic process within the foreseeable future —which is, for these purposes, the next ten years. This is because multinational corporations and international investors are now more powerful than national governments and have the political policies firmly under their control. And even if they did not, politicians who have spent much of their time over the last quarter century building a world economic system based on international free trade and the free movement of capital are not going to scrap that system now unless a trade war breaks out. In any case, the majority of politicians genuinely believe that the world economic system is highly efficient, and that if they can finally remove the few remaining barriers to the free movement of goods and capital their creation will begin to work perfectly and a general prosperity will be restored. Very few politicians admit, even to themselves, that this will not be the case and, unfortunately, we haven't provided this group with suitable alternative policies to adopt. No politician likes being a pioneer and introducing an untried policy for the first time, so before we can urge any change, we have to find a way of demonstrating that the change will work and is completely practical.

I've been visiting communities around the industrialized world which have adopted one, or perhaps two, of the sort of changes that are going to be necessary. I've been able to find enough working examples of the necessary social techniques in use to make a total strategy, but no community anywhere has yet used enough of these techniques simultaneously to build an independent parallel economy strong enough to resist the pressures of the world system. And these pressures are going to be considerable, because if we demonstrate that there is a realistic alternative to the world system we will be challenging existing power structures and are likely to provoke an extreme, oppressive reaction.

So this is another reason we can't rely on the politicians to help us: The best we can hope for is that they remain neutral. Only when communities have adopted a number of these techniques and made them into a workable alternative that exploits the synergies between them can we expect the politicians to move in our way.

⊘ *Oaxacan* GUSTAVO ESTEVA *relates parables of "the ruins of development" and what may rise from them—the rediscovery of hospitality:* I no longer dispute development for the same reason I avoid religious fights —development is a question of faith. When you find a believer in development it's useless to discuss the point. They're believing that they're *seeing* something. They're *seeing* that we are underdeveloped, assuming that we are in the undignified condition of those who can no longer trust their own noses, or dream their own dreams, that we are in the undignified situation of those who have not, of those who-are-not-yet-but-will-be.

The world view of development is constructed around some key words which operate as a web of meanings. Beyond development you are first mute: if you refuse to use those words that were distorting the perception. You will discover that they were covering most of the territory of meaning of your thinking and your conversation. You will also discover that you've become blind because you were using the lenses of development to see "the reality"; when you take off those lenses at first you see nothing. It's very difficult to start seeing the real world around you again.

The opposite of development is hospitality. With hospitality you *do not* need to follow your guest, to admire, to understand your guest; you open your arms and you accept the other. Perhaps the other is a complete mystery for you, but he or she is your guest, and you open your arms and have a place for him.

In Mexico we are trying to reclaim, or recover, or regenerate our commons. It's not to go back to the old commons; the old commons were completely dismantled by 500 years of colonization and development. We are reclaiming the commons to create something completely new, which has hospitality, rather than development, at the center.

For the experts, Indian peoples represent only 10 to 15 percent of the population. True, no more than a fifth of the Mexicans consider themselves as Indians. But half of them, or even more, share their world view, the same horizon of intelligibility which gives meaning to their thinking and behavior. They constitute the social fabric for the social majority in Mexico. That's why we can talk about reclaiming the commons and thinking in a different way, beyond development.

In Tepito, a neighborhood in downtown Mexico City, the center has been under permanent threat because all developers want that space for their own projects. The people who live there, though, have created a marvelous culture. You can see a lot of destitution around, but no social worker will ever find malnutrition because they are eating very well and enjoying life and they have a magnificent life there in spite of the physical and social restrictions. I was there once with Wolfgang Sachs and other friends. At the end of our visit, Wolfgang Sachs said to one of my friends in Tepito, "You have a marvelous culture and many beautiful things here, but still you are very poor," and immediately my friend reacted, "No, we are not poor, we are Tepitians." This man was telling Wolfgang, "You call me poor because I don't have some things that you have. You think you are rich and you say I am poor. I can do exactly the same. I can say, 'You don't have my leisure time, my music, my conditions. There are many things you don't have.' But I am not doing that.

I am saying, 'You are American or German. I am Tepitian. Let's express this dignity in our relations, instead of accepting this qualification of the other.'"

In reclaiming the commons, we are about something that I cannot but call techno-fasting. It is making a very careful selection of the techniques that we want to use and very clearly limiting both the economic sphere and the technological sphere. In such an endeavor, we are trying to exclude the whole idea of power as something "up there" that some people have and others don't. We have a completely different idea of what the power is; the power with the people has a completely different meaning.

⊘ SANDY IRVINE, *a good Socrates from Newcastle-Upon-Tyne, provides these mental calisthenics:* Conferences like this can do a lot to enrich our thinking and to help us develop a much better case to take out to the wider world if they avoid six pitfalls. One is the treatment of technology in isolation. It can only be understood as part of an interacting trinity, the other two corners of which are population growth and per capita consumption. People mentioned the Amish folk in America. The Amish have one of the fastest-growing populations in the United States—they must at some point become deeply unsustainable. Consider one of the most hated of modern technologies, the motor car. The ecological impact of the transportation system in the U.S. is well known, but the biggest source of that impact was not the switch from public to private transport nor the fact of increasing affluence, accounting for more journeys, but simply the fact that there were more Americans operating more motor cars.

Consider this: If England were to switch from the technology of caging and factory farming of chickens to free-range egg production, we would no longer be self-sufficient in eggs. Therefore the key factors become per capita consumption and overpopulation. Even though technology is a critical determinant in this context, I think one is wasting one's time looking at technology in isolation.

The next thing we must avoid is populism. There's a tendency to treat the ordinary man and woman as though they are passive victims, rather than as active and knowing participants in what is going on. For example, last time I was in a bookshop I saw two books on permaculture which use the argument that if you care for people you automatically care for the Earth. There are countless examples one can cite to prove that in any concrete policy sense this is simply not true, though in a general sense it may contain a deep truth.

Nostalgia is the third pitfall. Many traditional and vernacular societies were failures, were bad places in which to live, and did massive ecological damage. Humankind, with stone-age technologies, exterminated entire faunas, vast numbers of wildlife.

The fourth pitfall is defining "anti-technology" far too loosely. The Luddites were not opponents of technology. In many ways they welcomed the new technologies of the time. It was the way technology was being introduced that they opposed. We have to be very careful in our use of language. Last night we heard a long list of adjectives used to describe technology: I'll use another one, which is "comfortable." I slept in a technology, a bed, last night and it was very nice. We have to be realistic and not indulge in sweeping generalizations.

Fifth, I would caution against conceiving of technology as an unstoppable juggernaut. You can look at nuclear power and see the example of a technology which contains contradictions that are there to be exploited and can bring the technology to a halt.

Last, I think we have to avoid the either/or logic which we've inherited from the other side. People are wont to say the solution is local. Yet the solution could be local, regional, national, or international, depending on the circumstances and what works at a particular point in time. Phrase mongering about top-down versus bottom-up is equally meaningless: It poses false dichotomies and doesn't actually tease out what needs to be done.

☙ JOHN LANE, *an artist and a trustee of Dartington, makes a contribution to our discourse that is part lyric, part historical, and part Blakean reminder of the necessity to attend to particulars:* I'd like to talk about poetry and commitment to place. The antidote to technology is poetry, by which I mean myth, imagination, beauty, and creativity. These are the elements that move mountains. Paul Blau talked about people being touched by emotion: It's at that level, I think, that the changes will come. It's vision that moves people, the vision of a better world. It's the vision of progress which has ensnared the Western world. We have to have another vision, and that vision won't come out of force—it will come out of poetry.

Commitment to place is another way of saying, "Don't let the weeds grow in your garden." Rather than trying to save the world, I think we have to save where we are.

You mightn't have known, but it was at Dartington that scientific agriculture was introduced into England. The first tractors were introduced here, hedgerows were ripped up, and artificial insemination of livestock was brought from Russia. Scientific agriculture developed here because it was believed that in order to stop the hemorrhage of people from the country to the towns, the life of rural areas had to be based on a sound economic foundation. That economic foundation was seen to be scientific agriculture. It was an honorable vision even if it's taken us in directions which we now regret and would reverse. Accordingly, beginning next September, a commitment has been made to farm here organically, and following that commitment will, of course, come the development of cheeses, yogurts, flours, and breads which will be sold in the local economy.

In the last two years, Dartington has started a six-acre organic market garden, which within five or six years should be feeding the hundreds of thousands of people who come through here. That's an enormously important step forward: Instead of buying our food, we'll actually be producing our food.

Another instance of change: In the thirties, Dartington's work in the field of forestry management undoubtedly contributed to the formation of the Forestry Commission and was committed to the development of coniferous forests. We've reversed that policy and are now replanting broadleaved trees.

It's important to begin where we are and to do what we can with our actual responsibilities, however small and modest this may seem. This is not to suggest that we shouldn't work, as activists, on a broad scale, but I do think that we shouldn't let the weeds grow under our feet.

⊘ ANDREW McLAUGHLIN, *who lives in upstate New York, draws our attention to the dire consequences of industrialism for more-than-human nature, and having acknowledged that, to steer toward creative engagement rather than hopeless inertia:* I'm excited to be here, though I'm not sure I should be, since being here means I'm not in my community. I take quite seriously the point that one has to take care of the place where one is.

I'm a philosopher by profession and a social activist by desire. I've shared some of the struggles in the war against Vietnam and in the Civil Rights Movement. I am currently active in local issues surrounding the preservation of forests and farms. I've always considered activism as being somewhat incompatible with philosophy. As a philosopher, you've got to go sit in the woods and contemplate and allow the space for new ideas to come in. With activism there are always demands and issues pressing for immediate attention.

In my philosophical mode, I wrote *Regarding Nature* to say clearly that our problems in respect to our mismatch with nature are urgent, long-term, and profound. Conservation biologists are talking about the loss of one-third of all species on Earth in the next forty years. There are lots of other sufferings besides the human species' suffering that we need to address. There's a whole lot of life that hinges on what we do collectively as humans.

As I was writing *Regarding Nature*, the plot kept getting worse and worse. I examined capitalism and then socialism and asked what was wrong. I realized, not originally, that it was the industrial system underlying all modern societies that was the problem. I have problems invoking the term "technology" in such a way as to include almost everything, yet I guess I use the term "industrialism" to include the economy and culture of modern society, which is pretty inclusive usage also.

I think analyses of our situation should lead to suggestions about what should be done to change it, to what I call the requirement of agency. Yet another dire portrayal of our ecological problems leads, for me at least, to numbing despair. Both kinds of analyses, those that look to the agency of transformation and those that lead you to the path of no action—either could become true. It's not a matter of truth or falsity here; it's a matter of trying to see what might be done. In these issues we create the truth through our actions.

In my life and work I deal with two sorts of people: urban citizens—I teach in a working-class university—and Republicans—I live in a community which is, in American political terms, largely Republican. Neither of these constituencies has the foggiest notion of the cascade that we're about to go over.

☙ Ralph Metzner *speaks of his scholarly interest in fathoming the collective psychopathologies alienating us from nature and of experiential practices for reconnection with nature:* This area which some call ecopsychology might better be called green psychology. Rather than a new subfield of psychology, it's a fundamental revisioning of psychology to take the ecological context into account.

My original field was consciousness studies. In the sixties I was involved at Harvard University in some of the early research on consciousness-expanding drugs. The expansion of consciousness and its role in personal growth and transformation has been a central interest. In the last ten years or so I've begun asking, "Changing of consciousness for what?" and raising the question of the relationship of human consciousness to nature, especially the nonhuman parts of nature. From psychedelics my interests have changed to sacred plants and their uses in shamanism: the techniques, or the technology, of ecstasy.

I see the revival of shamanism taking place as an example of a grass-roots attempt to reestablish an experiential connection with the natural world. I'm very interested in the nature of the collective psychopathology that alienates us from the natural world. I use the interesting but poorly understood psychological concept of dissociation in analyzing the situation. Also, the concept of amnesia is interesting: the amnesia which we as human beings have about our original place in the natural world.

In my book, *The Well of Remembrance*, which is about pre-Christian Nordic-Germanic mythology, I discuss the story of this well at the roots of the Tree of the World. It is the well from which you drink in order to recover the lost knowledge of your origins, what the Buddhists call "primordial mind." Ecological consciousness—what Gary Snyder calls "the practice of the wild," being in wilderness alone and, for me, working with sacred plants—has become my main spiritual practice, the means to recover a sense of our origin in nature.

I hope we can discuss the history of culture. How did this human alienation from the natural world come about? We may look at the beginnings of industrialism and the scientific world view, then back to the Judeo-Christian tradition and the kind of transcendentalism, a split between spirituality and nature, which is endemic in European, Western culture. This transcendental spirituality is in marked contrast to that of indigenous society, which sees spirituality and the natural as identical. One could go back even further to locate the origins of transcendentalism in Greek philosophy and the invention of writing and back to the origins of the patriarchy and finally back to the beginnings of domestication. This was the first step away from hunter-gatherer consciousness of being embedded in nature toward the beginnings of managing and controlling nature.

ⓈMaria Mies voices her conviction that patriarchy and its belligerence animate the problem of technology as well as the violence of capitalism, colonialism, and imperialism. She shares insights derived from her experience in feminism and from growing up in, then studying, subsistence economy: I come from a peasant background, a small farm of twelve acres in a poor area south of Köln, Germany. There were twelve children in my family. Our farm existed for about 300 years, but my brother has had to give farming up because of GATT and the European agrarian policy. He gets the same amount of money for 100 kilos of grain as my father got in 1937. I was born in 1931, which means I know what work on a subsistence farm is. It was, of course, work, but it was not misery. My mother

died at the age of 87. When she looked back at her life she used to say, "Wasn't that a happy life! Of course, it was a lot of work. But I liked to work."

I lived in India for five years. When I came back I did my Ph.D. on Indian patriarchy. That was at the end of the sixties. While I was study-ing the Indian patriarchy, I discovered the German patriarchy, and thus patriarchy as a system. I became actively involved with the new Women's Movement. In trying to understand the cause of patriarchy, I came to an observation relevant to us today: Patriarchy is based not only on a certain relationship between men and women, but that relation-ship is based on a certain technology, namely that of war.

The patriarchal man-woman relationship is central to this whole question of technology, which is basically war technology. The tribes and societies that were the most successful economically and politically were the ones who had the most successful means of destruction rather than of production. Militarism was and is the secret behind these tech-nologies and these societies. Even now we have to discuss how the man-woman relationship became what it is today and how that is linked to a certain war technology. Violence is the secret of this society, of this economy, which I continue to call capitalist. I refuse to talk only of cul-ture. This whole drive toward growth and expansion has much to do with a mode of production based on patriarchal conquest, colonialism, and warfare. It has shaped male identity even today.

Reproductive and gene technologies are the latest weapons in this war against women, nature, and foreign peoples of the South. In 1984 feminists started FINRRAGE (Feminist International Network of Resis-tance to Reproductive and Genetic Engineering). From the beginning we've made it very clear that we are not just talking about this technol-ogy, we are *against* it. It's a small group—twenty to thirty women—but we have organized big conferences and have made our voices heard. We have had, in Germany particularly, some success. We were able to stop surrogate motherhood agencies some years ago. There is a lot of resis-tance against biotechnology, particularly against gene technology, among the German people. The politicians complain that the German public is against it; that is part of our doing. Although we are a small group, we just continue to mobilize people. I'm quite optimistic that a small group can do something to change the world.

It was but natural that this struggle led to the questioning of the whole concept and paradigm of modern science. On the other hand, however, one can not only criticize something. What my friends and I have done for years is to try to develop a kind of alternative as well. We call it the subsistence perspective. Many people in the Third World have no other alternative but to defend their subsistence base; they have no welfare state to support them, so they have to fall back on something which we call the self-reliant, subsistence economy. You may call it a communal, or local, economy. People in the South are already doing it; it's not something we have to dream of, it's not just a vision; it's a necessity which people are already putting into practice. One can't change the world just by talking about change, we have to practice it, and then we will understand more. In order to understand the world you also have to change it.

⊘RICHARD SCLOVE, *self-styled "samurai policy wonk" from Amherst, Massachusetts, finds it more useful to deal with technologies, rather than technology as monolith, and is hopeful that the public and community groups may find this an opportune moment to intervene in national and global policies concerning research, science, and technology:* In my conceptual work I deal with many technologies at once. But I don't aggregate technology into a single homogeneous megatechnology juggernaut, which is disempowering. I'd rather look at specific technologies because that allows for specific interventions. The end of the Cold War, and the Clinton administration's interest in technology policy—although I don't like a good bit of what they want to do—create an important strategic opportunity to understand and act on technology in the U.S. at the national level. There's an opportunity, in principle, to get some public interest and grassroots voices into that domain. There's a rare, and likely brief, opportunity to try to mobilize interventions at the national level, and critiques and manifestos are extremely important and useful.

Beyond critique, I think we have to engender more creative opportunities for grassroots involvement in decisions around science and technology. Unless they're in a totally oppressive regime, everybody can work toward a more locally self-reliant, sustainable, democratic economy. There are hundreds of initiatives around the world that empower communities to address larger issues and larger power structures and to be somewhat buffered from larger power structures and from corporate might or corporate penetration. I also think we want to consider ways to create greater opportunities for grassroots participation in translocal activism. For relatively modest money one could give grassroots groups around the world access to the Internet and have an ongoing global dialogue as a counterforce to the state-dominated dialogues of the IMF and U.N. As far as we know, about one-quarter of world research funds are still going into the military. So in a post–Cold War world we have to contend with that ongoing stream of military research and development. Perhaps there's an opportunity there to enlist the help of elite scientists of conscience.

🔊 SULAK SIVARAKSA'S *pacific simplicity of means models Buddha nature and barely hints at his extraordinary career as editor, social critic, political exile, international organizer, and pioneer of moral, small-scale development strategies:* I come from Bangkok, which is one of the worst cities in the world because we are caught up in these megatechnologies and globalization. The country wants to imitate Taiwan, Hong Kong, South Korea, and Singapore. This is the wrong trend. My activities in opposition are first of all to synchronize my head and my heart, and to live peacefully with my family, my people, and to cultivate the gardens. My house is in the middle of Bangkok. Despite the pollution, I still live there, but create peace there. Over the last ten years I have established an ashram where activists can come and retreat, to meditate and to be aware of the environment and the perils of development. This ashram was started for the Siamese, but now people throughout our region come for small workshops. Thus the grassroots activists are being empowered nonviolently. I should like to sow these seeds of peace wider and deeper. These sorts of activities need to be linked as a movement, and as a Buddhist I should like to work more closely with Christians and Muslims to create communities against consumerism. Consumerism is linked directly to greed, and it's a new demonic religion. Whereas in the Buddhist context, friendship is the most important thing.

🔊 *Psychologist* CHELLIS GLENDINNING *brings a lot to the party, having accomplished much creative intellectual work to make Neo-Luddism sensible and significant to a wider audience, including her bold "Notes Toward a Neo-Luddite Manifesto," which appeared in* Utne Reader *in the spring of 1990. At this meeting, she outlines the theory expounded in her third book and relates, with feeling and immediacy, what she is learning about technology, racism, and imperialism:* I spent a great deal of time in the last decade developing critiques of technology. I laid out some of the going principles for thinking about technology in my Neo-Luddite manifesto. In my second book, *When Technology Wounds*, I interviewed people who had been injured or made sick by different kinds of technologies—from nuclear weapons and electronics to the Dalkon Shield intrauterine device—and I examined the psychological effect of that experience. I found that it doesn't really matter what the technology is, what the disease is, or what

the injury is. The psychological effects are similar because they are generated by something that doesn't have to happen, something that is
humanmade and human-disseminated.

This work led me to the view I put forward in my third book, *My
Name Is Chellis and I'm in Recovery from Western Civilization*. In this book,
I examine the psychological consequences of the systemic separation
from the natural world that lays the base for technological society.

Before domestication, for 99 percent of our existence as a species,
human beings lived in unmediated participation with the natural world.
Domestication is a fairly recent invention: about 10,000 years old, about
300 generations. Through agriculture and animal domestication, people
in the West forged an unprecedented relationship to the natural world
by attempting to manage and control what previously had been "wild"
and free. The changes were at first slow, hardly noticeable, and yet as
time went on all major social catastrophes we are now addressing were
born: technological development as the answer to address technological
problems created by previous technological fixes; the population explosion; the rat race; the expansion of domesticated livelihood and therefore war, colonization, and imperialism; sexism, racism, slavery; environmental overuse and degradation—all of them!

The thing that struck me about this transformation in the human
relationship to Creation was that the changes taking place on the outside—basically the fencing off of human activity from natural processes
and the control of everything within that new human sphere—were
mirrored by changes going on *on the inside*, in the psychological world.
This insight led me to speak of the external symptoms of technological
society using psychological language.

I see mass technological civilization as the product of trauma: the
human dissociation from the natural world. This is what I call "original
trauma." You can see all the resultant symptoms of post-traumatic stress
disorder—PTSD—rampant, and even institutionalized, through contemporary society, among them addiction—addiction to so many things:
alcohol, drugs, sex, shopping, travel, "experience," money, power, *technology*. It is so strange to me that, even though repression and denial
stand among these basic PTSD symptoms, so many people who live
within the technological world assume this world to be the way life *is*,
the way it is *supposed to be*—when in fact, in the grand scheme of things,
the techno-world represents just a fleeting moment.

Having been born into this moment, I am outraged when I realize that the technology is *inside* me. So I have embarked upon an attempt, as serious as anything else I have ever done, to rehumanize myself, to reindigenize myself, to adopt a more organic and natural being.

I live in an indigenous village in northern New Mexico that, up to a generation and a half ago, was isolated from the modern world and self-sustaining. I am one of the only European-Americans in the community. The people in the village have a marvelous heritage. They came from Spain in the 1600s and lived in Mexico before moving north. They have Mayan and Aztec blood. When they got here, they mixed with Tewa and Apache Indians. And some were Moorish Jews who escaped Spain when the anti-Semitic proclamation came down in 1492. In the village, the old ways are going on alongside the recent inculcation of cash-economy demands; telephones—half the villagers have them now —cars, "Baywatch," and the tourism that is pouring into the West from the global economy. We dig a thousand-year-old *acequia* system for irrigation. We use horses for transportation. Some of my neighbors eat only the meat they hunt themselves. We grow vegetables, pick our medicines from the forest. And at the same time, what was once sustainable living now becomes poverty. People see fancy cars on TV driven by fancy Caucasian people, and self-esteem plummets. Heroin addiction is big in my village, along with self-violence, murder, robbery, loss of traditional values.

One of my daily concerns is to relate well with the people around me. I've become keenly aware of both the blatant and the subtle domination inflicted by Europeans and European-Americans in this world. I think that our work addressing technology and the global economy naturally must grow to include work on the effects of imperialism and racism. I have become terribly aware of what I call the "imperial mind" and how so many of us who have been educated within the dominant society reiterate aspects of this mind. Let us be especially careful about our use of the word "we." I have heard, right here in this room, echoes of the "we" that thinks it sees everything and will create all the solutions! The vision of a nontechnological, nonimperialist world is the vision of a world returned to locality, the mass is broken down to human-scale communities. In such a world, the word "we" takes on a totally different significance. It becomes more respectful, humbler. The connectedness it suggests becomes spiritual, no longer political.

And speaking of breaking down the mass, one aspect of this task, I think, is the deconstruction of "whiteness." This is a new horizon being pioneered by some insightful European-Americans who see that the concept of "white" merges with the "mass" of technological society to create a hegemony of power. As long as we "whites" identify ourselves in a big pure mass of cohesion, we will continue to be alienated from others and used in the dominator role. If we can unearth our original land-based heritages, or at least know that they exist, and nurture relationship with the place where we live, then we can further the possibility of a genuine human connection—to our "nonwhite" comrades and to the Earth.

⊘ STEPHANIE MILLS *does her part to remind those present that Thoreau's dictum, "In wildness is the preservation of the world," is being borne out by conservation biologists, and that this has big implications for our visioning process:* I recently finished writing a book, *In Service of the Wild*, on ecological restoration and that wholesome potential for restoring some of the damage that civilization has done to the land. Restoration has to address the question, "What do we restore to?" Part of the investigation is deciding what quality of landscape you're trying to reinstate, insofar as it's possible, given the number of extinctions that have taken place, trying to decide what quality of social life we restore to. How far do we dispel our technological entrancement, or can we?

Predicated on the best intelligence of conservation biology, the bottom line is that if you're serious about dealing with the problem of extinction, a tremendous amount of land—half of North America—has to be consecrated to wildness—enough land to support representative ecosystems with their big, wide-ranging predators. I went with a sixteen-year-old friend to a conference explaining this. She said, "Where are all the people going to go?" After you draw the maps of these ecosystem preserves, it's clear that a lot of places, ideally, would be depopulated. So there's information that needs to be reconciled with our work here.

One thing that keeps me going is knowing that our species is capable of making huge transitions. We've gone from being hunter-gatherers to being farmers; more recently we've had the experience, as Langdon Winner pointed out at the meeting last year, of deconstructing the dependencies that monarchy created, moving into democracy. So there is hope that we can move from our present megatechnological condition into communities beyond civilization.

⊘ *A brief discussion follows on the round of introductions, with an interesting tussle over the questions of which civilization might be held culpable for the problems we're considering and whether or not the C-word—capitalism— is useful to describe a certain complex of destructive tendencies.*

MARIA MIES: Most of you refer to Western civilization as being the problem, but looking at the world as it is, I think we also have to include in that critique Eastern civilizations and civilization as such. For instance, why is it possible that globalization of capital takes place in these Chinese or Japanese or Indian civilizations or cultures? There is something which I call patriarchy which has already been there for a long time. In India there is the caste system; in Japan there is the Samurai system. It's not that Western culture alone created these dichotomies, these dualisms, these hierarchical groups. At the base of it all is militarism, expansionism, conquest.

⌀HELENA NORBERG-HODGE *responds:* The global market is the single most destructive force behind the social and environmental breakdown we are witnessing. Western civilization is based on an expansionist economy which has risen at the expense of thousands of other cultures and peoples. The Chinese, the Mongolians—all expansionist civilizations—have destroyed other "smaller" cultures and their local, more diversified economic systems. However, we shouldn't cloud the fact that Western civilization has expanded across the globe in an unprecedented way to destroy other ways of being and seeing—more sustainable ways of living that were healthier and richer than what has supplanted them. Today this process has reached another level of destruction—now threatening the right to life of future generations around the planet.

⌀MARIA MIES: Why not call it patriarchal capitalism?

⌀HELENA NORBERG-HODGE: That seems to imply that communism was not guilty of many of the same problems. It seems more appropriate to speak of an "industrialism"—rooted in an attitude toward knowledge and the natural world—which is based on the notion of specialized knowledge and centralized control. Today this system has developed structures and institutions that are exploiting all of us. The transnational corporations' stranglehold on the global economy is now impoverishing the Western middle classes as well. This means that it is no longer appropriate to speak of the West exploiting the less developed countries. The economic system that blindly promotes transnational trade is exploiting all of us.

⌀GUSTAVO ESTEVA: I would like to discuss one specific technology that is of fundamental dread for Mexican Indians and peasants. We have many ideas and much action in Mexico now about how to deal with NAFTA, GATT, biotechnology, and the electronic revolution. But we don't know how to deal very well with the technology that is really destroying and dismantling communities all over Mexico: democracy.

Most Mexicans are clearly interested in improving our use of an imported technology: universal suffrage. But not at the price of sacrificing our own vernacular tools for governing ourselves, in our own political spaces, in both urban and rural settlements. In the name of political modernization, however, both the government and the political parties now want to root in Mexico a kind of representative democracy which will reduce or eliminate the political autonomy of our communities.

We gladly accept the challenge of articulating our own "democratic" experience, our own ways of government at the local level, with the modern technology of "democratic" elections, while trying to limit the latter. We are thus trying to avoid the parties' monopoly of political activity and reduce the scope and functions of the so-called "democratic governments," to protect our cultural self-determination at the grassroots.

This, any way, is but an example of the prudence we are applying in the selection and use of modern technology.

⌖ SANDY IRVINE: The paradigm of anti-capitalism has got some truth to it, but it's inadequate. To blame things on patriarchy, also, has got its limits. One could have gender equality and still have a human-centered culture that treats the rest of nature as lifeless and devoid of intrinsic value.

⌖ JERRY MANDER: The reason for addressing globalization in this context is that the GATT, which is a horrendous transnational corporate conspiracy against the planet and its peoples, may not be the end of the story. So we are trying to encourage a new paradigm among activists, to try to get them to realize that the machine disastrously keeps aggrandizing itself. So we must directly confront massification, globalization, and homogenization as causes of human and ecological destruction.

⌖ ANDREW MCLAUGHLIN: There's a way to talk about capitalism from an ecological perspective, if not necessarily from a political perspective. From an ecological perspective, the capitalist system is any system that makes decisions about the relationships of society to the rest of nature through the mechanism of markets. [With GATT] we're talking about reducing the restraints that individual localities can put on the market as it goes about making decisions as to how nature is to be consumed and disposed. So GATT destroys the capacity of a community to make ecologically sensible choices.

But don't think then that you are going to be able to find a culprit. If you go into the boardroom you're not going to find the devils who are doing all this devilish stuff. Those devils are easily replaceable and probably experience themselves as being under the constraints of the markets. It's the market that is an ecological disaster.

Chapter 8

Technology, Employment, and Livelihood

◎*Throughout the conferences, the wisdom of traditional and subsistence cultures was generally regarded as, if not superior to, certainly far more suited to life on Earth than that of modern urbanized societies. While all cultures must meet material needs, traditional societies avoid the modern error of rampant individualist materialism which is so terribly corrosive of generous, reciprocal relationships, whether they be among different clans or between a people and its bioregion. Community itself is sacred, forms the person, determines the group's relation to the land. It helps order life in decent ways and considers the generations to come.*

In sharp contrast to the commoditized, alienated labor performed in the global factory, there is the whole sustenance provided through meaningful work and right livelihood. When technology undermines these, it desecrates the body, the person, and the community.

We resort to technology to facilitate, or eliminate, work. Toolmaking is a pronounced (though not exclusive) characteristic of our species. The essential question facing critics of technology is to determine the point at which this human trait of invention goes astray and does harm. The uses of energy, the wielding of technological power, the value—and vanishing—of craft, the extirpation of meaning from work, the politics of mass production as shaping experience within the factory and without, the spread of automation and robotization, and the tidal wave of unemployment they unleash long have been prime subjects of Luddite attention.

Effective blue-collar labor organizing has been heavily confounded. Electronic technology now is displacing pink- and white-collar workers as well. Thus "rising productivity" translates directly into permanent joblessness for all but a few technocrats and a body of menials.

The unraveling of the developed world's socioeconomy as a result of the combined effects of megatechnology and economic globalization, and the massive unemployment these cause, are not nightmare fantasies but uncomfortably realistic extrapolations of the consequences of the continuing acceleration of technological application and the centralization and globalization of the human economy.

In this discussion, panelists TEDDY GOLDSMITH, *editor, activist, and author;* ANDREW KIMBRELL, *author and litigator; and* RICHARD DOUTHWAITE, *journalist, economist, and manufacturer, proceed from the assumption that claims that technology development leads to employment are false. On the contrary, they show it is resulting in massive joblessness, deracination, and misery around the world.*

TEDDY GOLDSMITH *begins with a round of all-too-plausible prognostication, broadly sketching the causes and consequences of the destruction of small-scale human communities and arguing for revival of such communities, his arguments leaning heavily on common sense:* Economic development, dependent as it is on science, technology, and industry, is totally out of control and is transforming the world at a truly terrifying rate. The corporations that control this suicidal process, in their frenzied rush to maximize their share of the spoils, seem to show no interest whatsoever in the innumerable implications of all the things they are doing. In particular, they refuse today to consider the implications of creating a global free-trade economy dominated by a small number of vast stateless, transnational corporations, whose increasingly destructive activities have been freed by the recent GATT agreement from all social, ecological, and moral constraints.

Nor have they asked themselves whether it will in fact be possible to cater to the needs of the hundreds of millions of peasants in the Third World—in particular in India and China—who will be forced off their small marginal farms. We must not forget that something like 600 million Indian peasants fall into this category, and possibly a billion Chinese peasants. What is going to happen to all these people? The highly automated global economy that is coming into existence has no need for them. It will probably be able to function with no more than 20 percent of the world's labor force. The poor are surplus to the requirements of the economy. They are merely an embarrassment, and the fate that awaits them in the slums, in which most of them will seek refuge, is too awful to contemplate.

An associated problem is going to be growing impoverishment even among those who do find jobs. If the West is to compete with the Chinese and the Indians, it clearly cannot afford to pay people the wages they get today. These will have to be drastically reduced just as long-term contracts will have to be replaced by short-term contracts and full-time jobs by part-time jobs. Nor will we be able to afford the welfare state, which is being systematically dismantled throughout the industrial world.

In England, we have already gone a long way toward dismantling our lunatic asylums. The pretext is that people with mental problems are better looked after by the community than by the state. This is probably true. Unfortunately, however, we no longer have any real communities capable of doing this. As a result, people with mental problems have been largely abandoned to their own devices, and many now sleep on the pavements or on park benches. Indeed, about 40 percent of the homeless in London today are people with mental diseases. But this is probably only the beginning. As the welfare state is systematically dismantled, the old, the sick, children abandoned by their parents, and all sorts of other needy people are likely to suffer the same fate.

If neither the market, the formal economy, nor the state can now provide for the needs of the vast bulk of society, who can do so? The answer is no one, unless we restore the family and community, which until very recently have always assumed this important task—and usually very much better than either the formal economy or the state could conceivably do. Unfortunately, the restoration of the family and the community today is very difficult, above all because economic development or progress, to which just about all governments are totally committed, involves the systematic usurpation, commodification, and monetization by the corporations and the state of these functions. Once families and communities have been divested of the functions they were designed to fulfill they necessarily atrophy, just like a muscle that is no longer used. What is more, to return to them even a few of these functions would have economic consequences which our governments would never accept.

Nevertheless, one can predict that families and communities will eventually reconstitute themselves. Indeed, if economic globalization marginalizes 80 percent of humanity, what are all the marginalized people going to do? Many of them are bound to revolt. We can look forward to massive protests, strikes, revolutions, and civil wars all over the place. But one thing that the bulk of the marginalized people will simply have to do is reorganize themselves and create their own informal economies, for if they do not they will simply starve. What is more, these local economies must eventually provide the economic infrastructure for renewed families and communities, which, if we are lucky, could slowly increase their political clout. This is the silver lining on an otherwise black horizon.

If local community-based economics are alone capable of providing people with a livelihood, it is also only such economies that can conceivably be sustainable. The reason is clear: If we have an environmental crisis today it is because the impact on our environment of our economic activities is far greater than the environment can sustain. This means that we have no alternative but to reduce this impact, and this can only be done by phasing out the global economy in favor of a network of local economies. The idea that a global economy run by vast transnational corporations can be made even remotely sustainable—as is currently assumed—is simply farcical.

It is also only by setting up these local community-based economies that we can reverse the present very rapid erosion of democratic government. If democracy is government for the people by the people, then it is clearly not possible at a national, let alone at a supranational level, where the common person can have no conceivable influence, but only at a communal level, where everybody can really take part in government.

⊘ANDREW KIMBRELL *first examines the Enlightenment origins of the abstraction and commoditization of the elements of the community commonwealth—labor, land, and society—and the successive waves of alienation resulting. Like Goldsmith, Kimbrell sees no hope of any mass reemployment of displaced workers by transnational corporations or nation states. At best this unremediable and widespread joblessness, thinks Kimbrell, could represent an unprecedented organizing opportunity:* Teddy has ably outlined the remarkable break in the capitalist social contract, a contract which had its origins only two centuries ago. Francis Hutcheson, a seventeenth-century philosopher, was so impressed with Newton's discovery of gravity that he was convinced there had to be some scientific principle of human behavior which could be seen as the universal basis for human action. Christian dogma suggested that benevolence might be such a principle. This was not going to suffice for Hutcheson, an enlightened thinker. Rather he called self-interest the gravity of human society. Adam Smith, the great prophet of self-interest, vastly expanded his teacher Hutcheson's ideas in *The Wealth of Nations*.

The new rule of law was the contract, supposedly between free individuals. Forget kinship, community, religion, customs; now all binding relations were governed by contracts and based on the laws of supply and demand and each side's self-interest. This dictatorship of self-interest, according to Smith, would work as a divinely inspired "invisible hand" which would, without humans intending it to, lead to the public good. If everything is going to be run by contract, then everything has to be a commodity. There was a problem, however. Even to the early capitalist thinkers, it was clear that everything is not a commodity—everything is not an item produced for consumption.

Smith, for example, knew that labor was not a true commodity, but he felt it could be treated as one. He realized that few societies had ever sold labor as a commodity. He understood that human energy and emotions were inseparable from work. You don't just buy labor as a package of energy, you buy human beings, their emotions, their families. Further, there is no way to distinguish the work we do for pay from that which we do without pay. Yet the new factory system demanded that farmers working for subsistence be enclosed off their lands and be turned into wage slaves.

Of course after the enclosures, when the common lands in England were closed off from the peasants by wealthy landowners, countryfolk were shoved into the new workplaces, and they did sell themselves like commodities just as Smith envisioned: Children, women, and men all became commodities. One of the ironies of the enclosures is that land is also a fictitious commodity—land is not produced for sale, and yet it was treated as a commodity. When you have a whole system based on this central idea of contract and self-interest, then these fictitious commodities, as Marx called them, have to be treated as commodities. Soon there was a crisis as children were used so brutally in the new factories that the first laws on child labor were instituted, and unions began to spring up. By 1913, in the U.S. you had the Department of Labor, a whole new bureaucracy that tried somehow to defend society from the complete disruption that resulted from treating labor as commodity. Later you had minimum-wage laws, workplace safety regulations, and so on. Workers could not be treated as so much saleable energy without revolution taking place. The same, of course, happened with land as commodity. By the turn of the century land and resources were being used up at such an alarming pace that even the capitalists understood that regulations had to be put in place. Zoning plans came about. National parks were created, environmental regulations were put in place lest the commodification of nature destroy it so quickly that nothing would remain. It is ironic that the free marketeers constantly complain of bureaucracies and regulations. It is the very nature of the free market and its fictitious commodities to require such government interventions if society and nature are to be preserved. Massive bureaucracies are needed to defend society, land, and labor from the free-market system itself.

Smith and his followers turned work into commodified "labor." Now, however, the short history of "labor" is coming to an end. Worldwide, the population explosion has provided far too much supply, and technology has significantly reduced demand. It is becoming far cheaper to invest in capital—machines and technology—than in human labor, particularly with the attendant costs of health care and other expenditures on human welfare. This represents an extraordinary crisis for the capitalist system. What will happen to society when work can no longer be treated as a commodity?

Modern societies have avoided this inevitable crisis in the past because some new sector always emerged to soak up the dispossessed labor pool. When mechanization hit agriculture, the manufacturing sector opened up; people flooded into the cities and got factory jobs. Then automation took over the manufacturing base. Over the last twenty years, the service industries soaked up workers displaced by technology. Now they're automating the service industries. For example, 145,000 Postal Service employees are being made redundant because there's now a machine that can read envelopes. The services once performed by telephone operators have been turned over to machines that synthesize human voices. The key question is, "What new sector is going to emerge to provide jobs for the next wave of unemployed?"

People say, "What about the new industries such as biotechnology? Surely they'll employ these people." Well, the idea of an unemployed steelworker or middle manager becoming a molecular biologist is a little farfetched. More to the point, however, biotechnology and other new industries are being created as technology- and not labor-intensive. It seems clear that we are looking at the very real possibility of mass unemployment in the coming decades caused by the increasing use of technology. At the same time populations continue growing and the social safety nets are being destroyed.

Given this employment crisis there are some government "solutions." One of them is the possibility of a new wartime economy like the wartime economy that got the U.S. out of the Great Depression. Who the war would be against or what it would be like are matters for grim speculation.

Another possible solution is all the rage in Europe. For years, every time there was a productivity gain, the work week was decreased—ultimately from sixty to forty hours. With the new technologies people were saying cut it down to a thirty- or twenty-hour week. Some European corporations have done that. So far, corporate America has not. Outside of those solutions, there's little the government can do at this point. As environmentalists, we are in serious trouble. Now there's going to be such a scarcity of jobs that virtually any environmental or social initiative that seems to threaten jobs will be rejected.

Environmentalists are only too familiar with "jobs blackmail" on our issues, and it's going to get worse. Also, people are going to be looking for scapegoats. A demagogue who can exploit our xenophobia can blame the U.S. jobs problem on people coming over from Mexico, rather than on the technology.

Massive unemployment presents enormous problems but also some opportunities as far as localization is concerned. As Teddy mentioned, when people do stop racing around after vanishing jobs, they will find themselves in their communities and could organize a whole new community movement.

⊘ RICHARD DOUTHWAITE, *who's been extensively chronicling existing practices of community-based economics, concludes the briefings by exposing some fallacies of current economic thinking and provides concise directions for building the parallel economies so necessary to sustain people in the postindustrial world:* On a national or international level it is going to be extremely difficult to do anything about these problems within the short term. So what should we be recommending that people do for themselves? People are increasingly being excluded from the mainstream economy. How can we enable the poor to live without the rich who have discarded them? How can the poor regain power over their lives? We can't hope that the politicians, at least in the short term, will help the poor with their problems. We have to build, in effect, a parallel economy, not least because the mainstream economy itself is becoming increasingly unstable and is no longer a reliable source for the things that we need to survive. Certainly, if you look at the changes in commodity prices, at the values of currencies relative to each other, and at interest rates, the present degree of instability in world markets is unprecedented. This creates a climate in which only big business, which is well diversified, can survive. It is craziness for a small firm to depend on exporting because circumstances can change so rapidly.

The hardest part of what we need to do is to take the first step. That is, to convince ourselves that it is necessary to build an alternative. Too many of us still think that if we tinker around with the mainstream economy it will return to the relatively stable days that we knew in our childhood. Those days have gone.

The next thing we need to do is to adopt a new approach to what we think of as economic development. If there's poverty in a community, or unemployment, our thinking generally consists of trying to assess what resources that community has—its comparative advantages—and then to package its natural resources or the skills of its people in some way, turning those resources into goods and services which can be sold to a wealthy market elsewhere. But because of the fluctuations I just mentioned, this is a very high-risk strategy. With the money that these external sales earn, we hope to be able to buy the goods and services which the members of our communities really need from wherever in the world they're cheapest.

This indirect approach to development and the satisfaction of needs has created our present difficulties. We need a much more direct route; we need to look at the resources of our own areas and see how they can be applied locally to making those goods and services without which we cannot survive. Then we can trade with the outside world on our own terms: out of a desire to get a wider variety of goods, but not because we will starve otherwise. We need to produce within our communities a much wider range of goods and services than it's possible to make under the existing system. We need to do a lot of things which it would be uneconomical to do at present because, within most of our communities, the weight of competition is so great that very few economic activities are possible. So we need to widen our repertoire considerably. How can we do this? As politicians aren't going to give us the protection that they could have twenty or thirty years ago by imposing tariff barriers or import quotas, there's no way we can avoid world prices ruling in our communities. How then can we produce this wider range of goods and services at prices which enable local producers to compete with goods and services from outside? We have four very powerful answers.

One is to recognize that the claims for efficiency in the mainstream system are grossly exaggerated. Even in highly competitive areas, like the sale of electronic goods, the distribution chain absorbs at least 50 percent of the price that the consumer pays. Just getting the goods through the maze from the factory to the consumer takes as much as it actually costs to make the product in the first place. If, therefore, we are to make a wider range of goods in our communities, we've got to short-circuit this process. We're obviously going to be producing on a much smaller scale, and if our producers try to put their goods through the distribution system that is used by the transnationals, then they will get the same cost penalties imposed on them. However, if you're making furniture and selling it directly to your neighbor, you're getting the whole amount that the customer pays. In agriculture, there are already modes of doing this: Community Supported Agriculture is all about the farmer getting the whole price that the consumer pays.

Method number two is similar: We need to make capital available in our communities at rates of interest which are comparable, or even better, than those available to the transnationals. At present, if you deposit money into a British bank, you may get a ¼- or ½-percent interest, whereas if you're a small business borrowing money you're probably paying 11 or 12 percent. There's at least a 10-percent gap. So we need to set up locally owned banks so that the savings can be recycled to businesses in the area at an interest rate based on the potential for profit in that area and not on the potential for profit in a faraway part of the world, a rate which is very unstable because of fluctuations in international markets.

Third, we need to consider giving local producers a subsidy by working for them for less. Throughout the world many firms are already forcing their workers to take pay cuts, but these pay cuts have a domino effect, and if one company gets its workers to take less money, its competitors have to get theirs to do the same. We need to be in a position to resist that in our communities. However, if we agree to work for a local enterprise for less money than we would accept from a transnational, our sacrifice stays within our communities and goes as a subsidy to our neighbor, who may, in turn, subsidize us. On the other hand, the wage subsidy workers give to the transnational gets distributed all over the globe. That money has no way of coming back to them.

The fourth way is that local enterprise can be protected from outside competition by setting up a local currency. If your community has something equivalent to a Local Employment and Training System (LETS) and the company can accept at least part of its sale price in the local currency, then it has an advantage over an outside competitor that has to demand complete payment in the national currency. Similarly, if you are paid part of your wage packet in the local currency, then this enables a local firm to succeed, where one which is completely governed by the national currency couldn't.

 The discussion that follows begins with JOHN MOHAWK *raising two themes that twine through the rest of the conversation—first, there must be some cultural base undergirding the values necessary to postindustrial life; and second, that focusing efforts on the parallel economy might unfetter the mainstream robber barons completely:* In the future, large numbers of people are going to be required by circumstances that they cannot control or reverse to subsist on less wealth than they have previously been expected to subsist on. One of the overall strategies must be to address the cultural consequences of reduced income and how people can learn to live well and happily on less. How are we going to enable people to think about life in the postindustrial wage-earner condition?

It has to be done. When I heard that we would build local banks, right away I could see the local bankers sneaking off into the night into the faraway market and fooling around with our deposits. People need to have something that enables them to behave in ways that are coherent; culture means something greater than the stick and carrot of economic motivation. Attention needs to be paid to what would help motivate people to do what is right and proper and supportive of community.

 The trenchant GUSTAVO ESTEVA *raises the idea of community-level liberation from the very semantics of economics:* A few years ago somebody used the expression "re-embedding the economy into culture." In our communities, we are trying to do something different. We are not constructing an economy at a local level; we are trying to limit the economic sphere. We know by experience how the economy, as an autonomous sphere disembedded from society and culture, now permeates everything, even in the most isolated of our villages. However, economics is but a set of assumptions adopted as principles to organize and regulate social life, putting the economy at the center. By adopting other assumptions, we are trying to decentralize the economy, to marginalize both its assumptions and the activities and institutions associated with them. What we are trying to construct at the local level is a completely different view. No formal category of the economic language can be used to describe that local culture and livelihood.

 As a Malthusian feminist, STEPHANIE MILLS *raises a question that provokes a bevy of responses whereby she discovers that many of her colleagues (although not the sociologist Maria Mies) regard traditional women's roles as optimum for women and their communities:* While I do think that some kind of intimate human grouping would be a good basis for regenerating community economies, I'm highly suspicious of the family as it has existed under patriarchy for goodness knows how long. Also, with human overpopulation, from the planetary ecosystem's view very few women are going to need to be mothers. That whole predicate of women's identity needs to change.

⊘ MARIA MIES: I appreciate what's been said about the communal economy. But I have a few questions. Who does this voluntary labor? Would the new extended family be just a replica of the old one? Would the women do this unpaid labor and the men do whatever paid labor there is? That wouldn't be good enough. In the context of building up new communities we have to talk about a new sexual division of labor. Otherwise, I think women would not accept these new communities.

⊘ HELENA NORBERG-HODGE *vigilantly reminds us that global communications technology represents a vast infrastructure that, like highways, is of no, or negative, utility to localized economies:* The expansion of the transport and communications infrastructure is moving the economy in exactly the opposite direction from where it needs to go. Computers particularly have expanded and extended the communications infrastructure that is serving the needs of transnational production, trade, and capital mobility. Consider Wal-Mart. It sells everything from shrimp to plastic buckets. They use satellite technology and computers to keep track of every Mickey Mouse T-shirt in every shop. They have fleets of lorries using the highways to replenish their stock. That infrastructure doesn't serve a local producer. What's the small shop going to do with this expanded computer technology? In effect this infrastructure is yet another subsidy for the large producers over the small.

I cannot go along with the notion that "family" is detrimental to women. The "nuclear family"—cut off from community and the local economy—has become a prison for many women. However, from what I've experienced in Ladakh and other traditional cultures, I think the extended family unit corresponds with deeply encoded needs for continuous emotional support and nurturing. I think this bonding is particularly important for more female needs and instincts.

⊘ SIGMUND KVALOY *affirms Richard Douthwaite with experience from contemporary Norway, then reaches back into the Middle Ages for evidence of the sturdiness of rural economies based on small farms:* We had a bank crisis a few years back in Norway. Because the big banks tried to get into the world market a whole series of small local banks arose. They offer higher interest rates and people have been flocking to put their money into them.

A Norwegian expert on the Middle Ages, Professor Kåre Lunden, went through the journals of the courts of that era and up to the time of the Renaissance and compared them with modern Norway, *à propos* the idea that to survive in the modern economy we have to "rationalize the structure" of Norwegian agriculture, that each farm, to be viable, must be monocultural. He found that, on the contrary, in the "flat Earth economy" of medieval *continental* Europe, where the people were so poor many of them had to go to the big monasteries and estates to sell themselves and their families to them, the farmers of western Norway worked on tiny farms on the steep mountainsides between five and eight hours a day to earn a decent living. Those who had fewer than six cows weren't obliged to contribute to the common brewing of festival beer (!) and all kinds of little farms survived; it shows the strength of the local economy when based in democracy and self-rule. But all that deteriorated during the 400 years when we were occupied by Denmark and the Danish kings colonized the Norwegian economy to fight their wars in Europe. Self-reliant freedom was gradually removed and *that* resulted in hunger and misery, illustrating how self-rule is more important than size of property!

⊘ *Sharp* SANDY IRVINE *probes the soft spots in the arguments for a devolution to small communities—the indifference, or positive antipathy, to community on the part of many today; the tendency of small-scale enterprise to pollute; and the ongoing utility of some very large-scale manufacturing facilities:* I can see a few transitional problems—one is the collapse of community itself. Recent research in Britain demonstrates that large numbers of people don't want community. People don't want that sense of obligation which is central to any notion of community. So reaching out to individualistic, hedonistic people—and we're not all free from those vices ourselves!—is incredibly difficult. For example, there is now a layer of young men who go around creating lots of children with lots of women and then abandon them; they also engage in a great deal of mindless violence. They go around terrorizing old people, making life miserable for people on housing estates. In the near term it's difficult to know how we're going to keep those young men in check.

Another problem lies in rebuilding the economy. In the European Union, small- and medium-size enterprises are the biggest source of pollution, for the obvious reason that often they don't have filters and other gadgetry that multinational corporations can afford. In the short term, during the transition to smaller-scale activities, we might actually be boosting pollution levels, which are drastic already.

Finally, there is this problem of large-scale job redundancies. On Tyneside all the shipyards are shutting down—it's a hell of a lot of people to absorb at any one go. There is scope for old-fashioned job creation. Shipyards could be used to build wind turbine machines and offshore platforms with wind systems. There could be energy-efficiency programs for people living in cold and damp housing. We could do a hell of a lot of good for a lot of people.

⊘JERRY MANDER *first interjects some plain speech, then reads Wendell Berry's precepts for coherent, enduring community:* As a Neo-Luddite it's my job to state simply that this current elimination of employment is effected by machines. Robotics, computers, and biotechnology are three major reasons that workers are becoming redundant. The substitution of those machines for human beings is conventionally called "gains in productivity." And it does increase productivity in one sense, but it throws a lot of people out on the street.

Wendell Berry has contributed an essay with a list of considerations for local communities that seems relevant here:

1. Always ask of any proposed change or innovation, What will this do to our community? How will this affect our common wealth?
2. Always include local nature—the land, the water, the air, the native creatures—within the membership of the community.
3. Always ask how local needs might be supplied from local sources, including the mutual help of neighbors.
4. Always supply local needs *first*. (And only then think of exporting products, first to nearby cities, and then to others.)
5. Understand the ultimate unsoundness of the industrial doctrine of "labor saving" if that implies poor work, unemployment, or any kind of pollution or contamination.
6. Develop properly scaled, value-adding industries for local products to ensure that the community does not become merely a colony of the national or global economy.
7. Develop small-scale industries and businesses to support the local farm and/or forest economy.
8. Strive to produce as much of the community's own energy as possible.
9. Strive to increase earnings (in whatever form) within the community, and decrease expenditures outside the community.

10. Make sure that money paid into the local economy circulates within the community for as long as possible before it is paid out.

11. Make the community able to invest in itself by maintaining its properties, keeping itself clean (without dirtying some other place), caring for its old people, teaching its children.

12. See that the old and young take care of one another. The young must learn from the old, not necessarily and not always in school. There must be no institutionalized "child care" and "homes for the aged." The community knows and remembers itself by the association of old and young.

13. Account for costs now conventionally hidden or "externalized." Whenever possible, these costs must be debited against monetary income.

14. Look into the possible uses of local currency, community-funded loan programs, systems of barter and the like.

15. Always be aware of the economic value of neighborly acts. In our time the costs of living are greatly increased by the loss of neighborhood, leaving people to face calamities alone.

16. A rural community should always be acquainted with, and complexly connected with, community-minded people in nearby towns and cities.

17. A sustainable rural economy will be dependent on urban consumers loyal to local products. Therefore, we are talking about an economy that will always be more co-operative than competitive.*

⊘ ANDREW KIMBRELL *cites the history of the African-American workforce as exemplifying the successive eras of technological displacement of labor and the damage to community that follows, then returns to the idea that the dominant economic sector must be reckoned with even and especially as attempts to develop localized economies proceed:* The African-American experience in the United States almost perfectly mirrors what we're talking about. Through the early 1940s over 80 percent of African-Americans were employed in agrarian work. At that point the introduction of the tractor and the automatic cotton picker led to the greatest exodus of economic refugees in history: twenty-eight million people in a three-year period. They went to the cities where they often did find employment —in the early 1950s around 25 percent of General Motors workers were

*Reprinted with permission from *Another Turn of the Crank,* Washington, DC: Counterpoint, 1995.

African-Americans. However, just as they entered that manufacturing sector, the factories were automated and moved to the suburbs. Because of both racial discrimination and the reality that "first hired's last fired," African-American workers were discarded by technology once again, and left in the inner cities without work.

We should look at the problems this discarded community has: senseless violence, the destruction of the family, drugs, teenage pregnancy. This long-suffering community provides an augury of our future. Regardless of race or ethnic background, studies show that each percentage increase in unemployment leads to an increase in family violence, in suicide, in murder, and in crime. It's an absolute predictor. When we talk about rebuilding community, and rebuilding family, these are the challenges we face.

It's going to take decades to work this thing out. We now have a two-tiered society: We have the new cosmopolitans who work in the international, computerized, high-tech industries and everyone else, people who've basically been discarded just as the African-American community has been. Some have suggested that we develop a vibrant volunteer sector out of the unemployed and struggle to get public and private support for such local organizations. However, we must realize that the corporate sector will not allow such a new volunteer sector to emerge. If local communities and strong volunteer organizations start defending themselves against development, start new economies, and start trying to supplant the national currency, the transnational corporations will destroy them.

Though it is often ignored, the commodification of labor created another casualty: the whole concept of good work. You can do nothing worse to a woman or a man than to alienate them from their work. Very few in the industrialized world can end their workday and feel that they have created something which expresses who they are and what they believe. Recent polls have shown that the number-one thing United States workers want is not more money, not shorter working hours, but more meaningful work. Any movement on work must resurrect the idea of good work.

⊘ RICHARD SCLOVE *explores the relationship between acting on livelihood questions globally and locally and also looks for existing models of locally sustained enterprise:* I agree with the point about not letting the corporations trash the planet meanwhile. On the other hand, building local economies can be a very important part of building the political base for dealing with that higher tier by providing some protection against capital flight and capital strike. By reempowering local communities you can say, "Let's take on the global economy." If you go to them now—prior to such reempowerment—they'll say, "We're fully dependent on it. How can we take it on?"

On the issue of small- and medium-size enterprises polluting more than large corporations, most of our pollution control strategy now remains primitive, capital-intensive; local firms can't afford it and don't have the knowledge to do the research and development. A more advanced strategy would involve less labor efficiency, more material efficiency, and a more renewably based economy. That would shift economies of scale downward. At the moment, however, we lack the social or research infrastructure to support that kind of locally based economy. Among other things, we have to be creating that research, finance, management infrastructure. The Mondragon cooperatives in Spain, while not always the best ecologically, do have a very advanced system of locally controlled background institutions for sustaining locally oriented research, management, and finance. There are interesting models there that could be adapted to building sustainable local economies.

⊘ BETH BURROWS *exhibits her genius for grabbing the thistle, coming up with a thorny question that no one directly answers:* When Teddy was talking about the numbers of homeless with mental diseases—"our mad uncles"—I sat not wondering if I'd be able to take care of everybody else's mad uncles, but would I be a mad uncle in need of care? So that led me to wondering who we are. Maybe that's who sits around this table—the mad uncles. Then I wondered about the people who try to, and want to, stay in the other economy, who have internalized those values. Then came John Mohawk's question, "How will we make our vision attractive so as to seduce them into doing the right thing?" That led me to wonder, "Are we proposing the right thing? Are we simply smoothing the way to what's coming? Are we doing the transnationals' job of making it OK to be marginalized, impoverished, forgotten about? Are we seducing people away from some other less pleasant form of resistance?"

⊘ CHET BOWERS *reminds us that there are institutions behind the economic institutions and that we must take their power into account also. He also comments on the possible cultural imperialism implicit in the idea of reforming the family:* When we operate with double binds we're on the way to despair because we'll never quite get to the effective leverage points. Schools and universities help to confer high status upon forms of knowledge that are the basis of this technologically, scientifically, consumer-driven form of culture that is leading to the problems that we're describing. At the same time these institutions delegitimate local, marginalized forms of knowledge. If we don't give these institutions a more central place in our attention, I wonder whether we're not just building a double bind into the discussion.

The second double bind is more moral than political. It has to do with what I'm hearing about how the new family must meet our Western ideal of egalitarian individualism. I wonder whether we respect cultural differences, or whether we see our mission as bringing enlightenment, and thus Westernization, to these other cultural groups.

To TEDDY GOLDSMITH, *the enclosure of existing economies is all but complete and the hope is that their voraciousness, finally, will put the transnational corporations beyond the pale:* Transnational corporations can obviously take over local economies. That is what they are doing all the time. They are clearly a threat to anything positive we might wish to do. They have simply got to be dismantled one way or another. As it happens they will probably dismantle themselves. If they had taken the trouble to consider the implications of a global economy, they would have realized that it can only be short-lived. If the global economy marginalizes some 80 percent of the inhabitants of this planet, all these people will be forced to live outside it. It will thus have marginalized itself. It is not certain to what extent the corporations will then be tolerated. If they are tolerated today, it is because they provide jobs and sell things that people want to buy. Once they provide jobs to but a few specialists from abroad, and produce goods and services which very few people can afford, why should anyone tolerate them? The growth industry will then be the security services that can protect their installations from hostile popular movements made up of the people they have marginalized. This may actually be one of the main functions of governments in the near future.

In any case global economic development—as already noted—is totally out of control—and processes that are totally out of control can only crash. Many serious students of the world economy are convinced that it is only a question of time before it does crash, and when this occurs, the only available safety net will be the local informal economies that have had time to build up.

JOHN MOHAWK informs us that the desperate future some of our colleagues envision arrived a while back in his part of the world and that the potential for both outlaw and state violence to plague decentralized commu-

nities is real: Where I live, you don't have to wait to live through this economic disaster because most of the people have already lost their jobs. The high-paying construction jobs and the steel plants in Buffalo are all gone. Most of the people are unemployed. The black communities in the Northern cities don't need to wait either—they had the economic disaster twenty years ago. Whenever I go to gatherings of ecologically and economically minded persons, I'm always alarmed that there are no people from those communities representing those communities at the meetings.

The history of capitalist expansion to rural areas is very ugly in lots of places around the world. One of the most powerful experiences I ever had was going to Iran during the revolution and hearing the stories of government repression. Government operatives were demonic and would do horrible things to the populations—it was just an unimaginable nightmare: torture, murder, everything. In order for national governments to play the game of Cold War, they had what they called a "national interest" in keeping the oil flowing. As we move into this period we're talking about, there's going to be all kinds of violence and terrible things happening from two directions. There will be the outlaw cultures that rise among the unemployed people—they'll be a violent group; the drug culture might be an extreme example. It's not going to be everybody just going off to the countryside, looking for a nice farm and putting roses on the patio. It's going to be a rough-and-tumble thing with the helicopters on one side and motorcycles on the other.

In 1929 when the Depression hit, people who were working in the city suddenly had to go someplace. They came back to the countryside. It took about twelve or fourteen years, but they already had the experience of it, and they reconstituted a rural community. I expect to be able to do that. In order to reconstitute community, though, people have got to have a cultural base. Not one single culture—there are thousands of different ones.

⊘ DAVID KORTEN *offers some words in defense of the global communications network, and of the labor-saving potential of new technologies, and speaks to the necessity for a transformation of consciousness at a meta- and metaphysical level, as well as for entirely new political coalitions:* I'm basically concerned with organizations as behavioral systems. Most of my life has been spent in Third World development as part of a foreign-aid establishment. It took me about thirty years to figure out that it was not working nor could it work, and to figure out why, and then to realize that the same dynamic destroying the Third World was destroying my

own country, the United States. So my wife and I moved back to New York City, the belly of the beast, to work on education at home, to change the frame of reference of global awareness. Most of my time now is spent to understand why the global system is self-destructing and how it relates to the local and what we have to do at the global level to create a frame for the kind of localization that Teddy was talking about.

How does this relate to the creation of alternatives? Part of our problem, in bringing about change, is that in general, even among people who are part of our alternative movement, the frame of reference for understanding the nature of the problem is inadequate. The alternative is a fundamentally different way of organizing. As we've seen in Eastern Europe and the Soviet Union, as you begin to build up a new consciousness, change can break through at a very rapid rate, but getting the new idea into the consciousness is an indispensable stage, and we need to do a lot more work on that.

We so often approach the issue of limits as though we're going to have to sacrifice fundamentally. Yet we are talking about improving the quality of life. It comes in the opportunities to have much more free time if we use our technologies properly. For me, the problems are not so much inherent in the technologies as in who controls them and the nature of the institutional systems in which the technologies are embedded.

The transformation also gives us the opportunity to restore human relationships, the social economy. Living in Manhattan, I can see that the issue of automobiles as technology is fundamental also, not just because the automobile is environmentally destructive but because of what it destroys in human relationships. So we are not just talking about survival, we are talking about greater conviviality. Also, there's the possibility of rediscovering a sense of human purpose at a metaphysical level, rediscovering our spiritual nature, and coming to realize that the purpose of life is not merely to consume.

There are two themes for thinking about the restructuring. One is the localization of economies and that includes the restoration of the social economy. I see that being combined with the second theme, the emergence of global intelligence, which is partly a function of our communication technologies. These technologies are being used in many bad ways, but are also creating new potential for the evolution of human awareness and for fundamentally new societies rooted in place but joined through communication.

I was interested in the comment about the juxtaposition of the motorcycles and the helicopters and the discussion about how a number of the same themes are coming out of both the Progressive Movement and the Far Right. We're seeing the whole conventional political system breaking down and new political coalitions emerging. The demagogues who are driving the Far Right are tapping into very real concerns, many of which we're also trying to address. Somehow we need to find a way to capture those energies within a new kind of political coalition.

@ SULAK SIVARAKSA *begins the 1994 discussion of these subjects saying:* I would like to share with you all a minute's silence.

This collective silence is an exceptional experience for many of us, and certainly for this gathering. It is a good prelude to the simplicity and profundity of Sulak's discourse on a Buddhist approach to development.

SULAK SIVARAKSA *continues:* Growth is wonderful, but the Buddha reminds us to be careful! not to have overgrowth. What would a Buddhist concept of development be? You develop your physical body appropriately, not too much. In the West with commercialization and competition the physical body is developed too much. The development of the body must be appropriate with the development of the mind. So when you think, when you breathe, your heart and your head should be synchronized, otherwise you become too clever and wisdom becomes knowledge. Rather knowledge should become wisdom; wisdom, understanding, love, and compassion go together. According to the Buddhist concept of development, you develop your body and your mind, you develop social concern and refrain from exploiting yourself, or others.

Technology means more roads, more dams, more radios, more televisions. What happens? Even though it is spoilt, my country Siam is still a beautiful country. Bangkok is one of the worse cities in the world: with pollution, and traffic jams. Twenty percent of Bangkok's population lives in slums. The people from the country have to migrate to the cities, to Bangkok, Los Angeles, to the Middle East, they become prostitutes in Hong Kong and Frankfurt. For the last fifteen to twenty years when our people suffered, they were told they were nobody unless they caught up with the middle class which had to catch up with the upper class which had to catch up with the West. Now people realize that they don't want that.

What would Buddhist development do with all this consumerist brainwashing? In Buddhism you are taught to confront suffering. In true meditation, you synchronize your heart and your head, you develop yourself physically, mentally, spiritually, and are concerned with your society.

Here is a story of Buddhist development that started with a well-educated, very well-paid fellow. Even so this chap went to the place where his wife came from. The whole place was destroyed: the fish gone, the sea turtles more or less gone, the mangroves destroyed by development, consumerism, all in the name of progress. But this young man restarted it all: with meditation, with listening to the people. People restored the mangroves; the old man who used to look for the turtles' eggs to sell—they're very expensive, you know—started practicing conservation. The turtles came back, the fish, known as the sea elephants, came back. The children are now playing with the fish. They are now enjoying their community. And those of us who are middle class are helping them as they are helping us. They grow rice and vegetables without chemicals, and we pay a bit more for it. So the middle class must learn from the poorer class, the poorer class must learn from the middle class, and we must all confront suffering together. You find out the cause of suffering and greet it. Consumerism, hatred of the old colonialism, technology development, all are illusion. Once you understand that you confront it. The cessation of suffering is through nonviolent thinking, speaking, and acting.

In my country it's working in a small but effective way, and also with the Burmese and Cambodian people. We want to change the system, but nonviolently. It is such a joy for us to learn from them and they from us. That's why we are starting a small ashram and a small school and colleges. Something alternative is taking place in my part of the world. When you come to Bangkok you see a place full of pollution, yet there are signs of hope and they are real. Small, slow, patient is beautiful. Human dialogue, human intercourse, respect, and friendship: that can change the world. Thus we must change ourselves first.

☾ ☽ ☾

So we had solid consensus on the idea that technology will continue, ever more rapidly, to displace human labor, and that massive unemployment will soon result. Almost equally firm was our agreement that rebuilding local economies and vernacular community would be the only truly sustainable solution. How this might be accomplished in the context of a ruthless global market increasingly governed by transnational corporations was the subject underlying most of the discussion, which was largely theoretical, except for Gustavo Esteva and John Mohawk's stories of survival and cultural regeneration in postindustrial, even posteconomic, communities.

Chapter 9

Consciousness and Technology

@ One of the most elusive—and most important—questions before us had to do with the mentality of our age, and that mentality's "coevolution" with technology. A year before, Kirkpatrick Sale had said that speech is a technology, which makes technology and human consciousness almost contemporaneous. In this discussion at Dartington Hall, the various participants cast the net wide, and almost as deeply into the collective past.

It was a kind of contest for the primal human soul, which was assumed to be good, an attempt to pinpoint the expulsion from the garden, and to identify the agency of the fall. There seemed to be consensus that what is wishing havoc on the planet is not the natural mind. More than one person spoke of the distorting effect of literacy and of the tyrannous text. The ideology of our separation from nature, the rise of modernity, and the resistance that paralleled it were sketched for us by Charlene Spretnak. There was talk of the anomie at the core of consumerism. Chellis Glendinning provided contrast to that with her vivid account of the holism of indigenous peoples' consciousness as embodied in their languages, etiquette, and relations to place.

Folks in academe had divergent views on the state of their students' consciousness, self-esteem, and appetite for alternatives. There was a sense that something pernicious of modernity is becoming generalized and that there is resistance to it, both indigenous and intellectual. And finally, concretely, Jerry Mander brought it to our attention that a technology—television—is most definitely globalizing and homogenizing human consciousness insofar as billions *of people around the planet may be passively absorbing the same commercial imagery all at once, this being a complete antithesis of the near infinitely diverse varieties of experience available to human beings that are not estranged from natural community.*

CHARLENE SPRETNAK *begins the session by tracing and linking a great many artistic and political tendencies opposed to the modern mentality and its tenet of our abstraction from nature:* Since technology is a function of modernity, I'm going to say a little about movements that have resisted the modern world view. We don't usually perceive these movements as a heritage of resistance because modern schooling taught us to regard them, if they're mentioned at all, as the endeavors of quixotic losers who fell out along the March of Progress. In fact, these visionaries saw early on what was wrong with modernity, and they created alternatives. It's important that we understand these movements as a lineage. There's a long history of resistance to those aspects of modernity that have proven destructive, and we're the latest manifestation.

Resistance movements within the political economy—whether Marxism or democratic socialism or liberal reforms or fascism—don't ever cure the alienation that they talk about at their inceptions because they remain within the materialist, mechanistic framework of modernity. The deep structure of our age is modernity, not economism. The foundational movements of modernity—Renaissance humanism, the Reformation, the Scientific Revolution, and the Enlightenment—established a radical discontinuity between humans and nature, mind and body, and self and the rest of the world.

This perception of radical discontinuity was probably singular in the history of human cultures. It is eccentric and bizarre, but we're taught it's "progress" and, therefore, natural. Groups that made the most profound critical analyses of modernity focused not only on changing power relations but also on correcting the existential denials of the modern world view. From that ecological and spiritual healing, new social forms could emerge.

Among the first resisters to the "new mechanical philosophy" were the "Radical Sects" during the English Civil War in the mid-seventeenth century. The Levellers, for instance, confronted the commercial revolution that was severing connections to the land. They wanted a decentralized government, more protection for the rights of the small property owner, and an end to the trading cartels. They also urged religious tolerance.

In the years immediately following the Scientific Revolution and the

Enlightenment, the Romantics, especially the major philosophers like Goethe and Coleridge, challenged the *extension* of the mechanistic discoveries of Newtonian physics to our entire sense of being. They advocated participatory consciousness, rather than the harsh discontinuities imposed by the modern, mechanistic world view. Moreover, they concluded from the bloody descent of the French Revolution into the Terror that real political change could not occur without spiritual transformation.

The Utopian socialists like Charles Fourier had some rather odd notions, but Fourier's ideas about collectives and cooperatives were influential for decades, especially in the United States. People were attracted to these group structures as a way to counter the sense of an atomized society of lone individuals, which is the ideological projection at the heart of modern economic theory.

From 1865 until 1920 the Arts and Crafts Movement spread from Britain to Europe, the United States, and beyond. It was based on John Ruskin's critique of modern political economy and William Morris's ecological designs and revival of handcrafted production. Gandhi, among other community-based visionaries, was very much influenced by Ruskin. When Morris was at Oxford, he and his friend, Edward Burne-Jones, the pre-Raphaelite painter, were so concerned about the ugliness and alienation of industrialism, they vowed, "We are at war against our time!" Morris and scores of other Arts and Crafts designers established commercial workshops, exhibitions, communes, and schools that simultaneously addressed core issues of work, home, nature, and consumption. Like Ruskin, Morris believed that the essential dignity of work lies in the unfolding of the person, a concern that is discarded entirely in mass production.

In the United States there were the "maternalist" reformers who challenged the harsh "laws" of modern economic theory. Later, personalism and other Catholic social thought rejected the materialism of both Marxism and capitalism because both deform the unfolding of the person. They insist that the state exists in service to the person, not the reverse.

In the Modernist Movement in the arts—1905 to 1930—much of the thrust was *against* the assumptions of overarching modernity 1450 to the present. Therefore, much of that resistance movement was actually antimodern "Modernism." For instance, D. H. Lawrence sought to recover the cosmological context of our sexuality and all life, which he felt had been shrunken to the solipsistic existence of the modern individual.

To add a negative example here, Nazism astutely manipulated people's discontent with modernity and the upheavals of industrialism and technology that broke up families and communities. Nazism extolled a sentimental reconnection with the soil, the water, and the streams, which was perverted *in service to nationalism*. The sacredness of nature supposedly stopped at the German border. The Nazis emphasized recovery of community until about 1936 and then focused on being a very modern, high-tech war machine.

Today certain truly postmodern developments (not the deconstructionist nihilism) are moving in an ecological direction. They are trying to engage with the core problem of modernity. To me, the problem of various undesirable power relationships in the modern era is dwarfed by the fact that modernity cuts us off from nature and our larger self in a pathological way. It shrinks our sense of being.

⊚ Satish Kumar *talks about Gandhi's embodied vision, nonviolent resistance, and practice of alternatives:* To create a new way of life or restore the proper way of life, Gandhi thought that we need three elements. One is vision. Without vision, meaning is lost. Often contemporary intellectuals lack that depth of vision. We are good at analyzing what's wrong and how we can put it together, but it goes no further. Whereas for Gandhi, a deep ocean of vision and values was essential to build a new way of life.

The second element is resistance. Gandhi not only said, "I don't want British imported clothes," he called upon people to bring out all their British-made clothes and in every city they made big piles of imported clothes and lit bonfires. That was resistance to the global, exploitative economy of Britain. For Gandhi, it didn't stop there. He developed a third element. He called it "a Constructive Program."

Gandhi said, "Don't worry about the British. Start to spin the spinning wheel and we will be independent." Independence was to come not just by cursing the British and writing big articles in the *Times* of India. Gandhi urged, "Build your own alternative economy." The spinning wheel was the symbol of *Swadeshi*, the home economy.

"Resistance" was 10 percent of Gandhi's movement, and 90 percent was "the Constructive Program," where he said, "We have to live and demonstrate that the kind of *Swadeshi* we are creating is joyful." Gandhi said, "Your hands are the greatest store of knowledge." If you don't use your hands and you make other machinery work for you, then you don't use your body. Why not walk half a mile to your field? Why not grind your flour to make bread to keep your hands and your body healthy?

It required the genius of Gandhi to make things simple, practical, and so straightforward: Spin your own clothes and the British will go away.

Vision, resistance, and a constructive program—perhaps we can learn these elements if we want to create a movement against global economy, megatechnology, and multinational corporations.

We seem to think that we don't need families and communities. We are very individualistic: We work in our studies, producing more literature and more ideas, but reaching nobody. So we need to think more how we create the kind of movement which happened at the time of the independence with Gandhi. Perhaps then we can be more effective.

⊘ ANDREW McLAUGHLIN *sees consumerism as the real content of mass culture, regardless of ostensible political ideologies or economic theory:* In terms of consciousness and technological, industrial society, in my book *Regarding Nature* I looked at capitalism to find the market-making part of the process and give reasons why capitalism cannot possibly become ecologically sane. That is a strong claim, but I think it is true. Markets simply cannot make ecologically sound decisions. Markets must be resubmerged within societies for us to achieve ecological sanity. I then turned my attention to socialism. I looked at the history of the Soviet Union. Lenin liked to take hikes. By 1925, there were about 4,000 square miles of nature reserves. By 1929, there were 15,000. The Soviet Union was moving not perfectly, but interestingly. It changed for a number of reasons having to do with science—which needs to be critiqued here as an image of reality—and politics. Because Lenin's centralized bureaucratic socialism could create things, it could undo them pretty quickly. Why? What held them together was a mass culture. When I look at what molds capitalism, I ask, why are the effects the same? They both aspire to achieve a consumer culture. In the United States in this century that's been achieved in a startling way.

In the Soviet Union and its satellite countries, consumerism wasn't achieved, but that's what the government, to maintain its legitimacy, was promising. On both sides of the Cold War, citizens were moving on the consumerist path. The curious and ultimately hopeful thing is that even though an enormous amount of stuff has passed through American lives and into the landfills, people are not satisfied. In my community, people are angry at the idea that they might have to pay more taxes, because then they might not be able to buy something. The American economy is driven by consumer spending. Why? Why do people enthusiastically go into debt? More Americans go to a mall than go to church each week.

What drives consumerism? Television is only one answer. One of the things that people are trying to establish in consumption is personal identity; that drive happens very powerfully once society no longer ascribes identities to its members.

The hopeful part of this consumerist folly is that it doesn't provide real satisfaction. There's supersaturated discontent, and there's no alternative focus for it, so it manifests in the hope for more consumer goods. If we can create alternative visions that people can identify with and find meaningful, then the social movements that we're talking about have some real possibility. I think it's important now to try to devise visions that draw people *forward* toward alternatives to consumerism.

Struggles over place are important. Your consciousness develops because you recognize that what you need to save your place is a viable local economy. You need to disentangle yourself from the global economic web which is destroying the community. Those struggles and the social movements of international dimensions—Deep Ecology, bioregionalism, and ecofeminism—are important as parts of the leading edge of efforts to create ecologically sound communities.

⊘ Enlivening the idea of becoming native to one's place, CHELLIS GLENDINNING *tells stories about learning from the antitheses of technological society—indigenous cultures:* My underlying assumption is that native indigenous cultures are expressive of the full humanity we keep referring to, that they give us a vision of what it could mean to live sustainably on the Earth. We speak of holism or bioregionalism or communal democracy. We have been poking about to find words to identify the sense of the culture, community, spiritual practice, relationship to food, and language that those of us who grew up in mass technological society are bereft of and yearning for.

I've been involved in political movements since the mid-1960s, starting with the Civil Rights Movement in America. I have lived in New Mexico for almost a decade now, and for the last few years I have worked with uranium miners from the Navajo Nation and Laguna Pueblo. As you know, I also live in an indigenous Chicano village. As a result of these experiences, I have come to realize that this sense of holism so many of us seek is *something entirely different* from what we have known before. We may have had glimpses of it in aspects of our lives. We may have had spiritual awakenings that lasted for hours or days. But this integration that we're looking for is something different from these moments. As a person who comes from the dominant culture, I can only *begin* to describe this by talking about what I have seen and learned.

One realization occurred not so long ago. There was an international sovereignty-rights conference for indigenous people in Albuquerque. It lasted five days. I invited my colleague Carl Anthony to attend. Carl is an African-American activist who lives in California, and he is a leader of the Environmental-Justice Movement. Up until this conference, Carl had been mainly exposed to urban ecological issues affecting people of color. He had met native people, but always in settings outside their "real" world. I was hoping he might learn about the uniqueness of the indigenous, land-based political perspective because, to me, it represents what I hope we will all be expressing in the coming years.

For days we sat in the auditorium and listened to indigenous people from all over—Peru, Alaska, Mexico, Colombia, Canada, the U.S. Each delegation spoke of how the loss of sovereignty had destroyed its way of life. The effects included everything from loss of traditional values and ecological destruction to alcoholism and loss of language. The most profound testimony came from a member of the Seminole Nation. He set out to speak and then suddenly began to sob. The man respectfully turned to the Board of Listeners and said he could no longer fulfill his obligation. A Diné man assured him that everyone wanted to hear his testimony and persuaded him to take his full five minutes. The Seminole man turned back to the microphone, and he continued sobbing— for his full five minutes.

After a good while, Carl leaned over to me, and he said with great enthusiasm, "This is *really* something! This is right-on! In about ten years, the cry for sovereignty is going to be mainstream!" I was very happy Carl was feeling so visionary. But I thought his comment missed one of the most important lessons of the conference. "I am elated you feel this way, Carl," I answered. "But when this is mainstream, *there isn't going to be a mainstream!*"

A second realization came to me after a two-day dialogue that took place between a group of Native Americans and a group of non-native new-paradigm thinkers. Our task was to seek out areas of agreement, areas of politics or spirituality or culture that we shared. At the end of the meeting we held a panel discussion, a kind of report-to-the-public.

We were talking about the political struggles of native peoples, and this one European-American woman stood up from the audience and said, "Well, what about *my* pagan roots?! What about *my* indigenous roots?! What about the Goddess and Stonehenge?!" There was a long silence. Finally a Diné man from our group responded, and his response became the basis for a complete reshifting in my own thinking. "That's all very well and good for you to go back to your roots," he said. "You will learn many important things by doing this. But to build an *authentic indigenous culture*—which is your task today—you have to communicate with the rocks and the trees and the birds *here* in this place, *now.*"

There's enormous meaning embodied in the notion of "all my relations." This phrase brings to mind our families, our extended families, the rocks and trees and birds, ancestors. Yet what is it *really* to live with all our relations? Those people who come from an urban environment, who are separated from their families, who do not know where their food comes from, who have no trees around them, do not know much about this. For instance, how do you behave when you enter a still-functioning native community? Western urban people often barge into discussions and relations, and yet I have witnessed in many communities that the task is to sit at the edge until you tune into what is already happening. It is up to *you*, the newcomer, not to disturb relations already in process. There is a subtle etiquette by which you learn to honor relations, and it behooves those of us who come from mass society to learn this etiquette: It forms the basis of the world we want to create.

Language is another arena for our focus if we are going to create a different world. As I have developed an intimate relationship with the natural world in the place where I live, I have realized that the English language does not afford me the opportunity to describe my experiences, except perhaps in poetry. The English language, by its very structure, is distanced from the connectedness of the natural world. It's set up to express separation; there is a subject, a verb, and an object. You are always acting on things when you speak English, always managing, always effecting. A friend of mine who comes from the Lakota world tells me that the structure of the Lakota language is just the opposite: In it, the person is always being *acted upon* by the universe.

☺ *To illustrate the concept of different ways of knowing so crucial to surviving in the natural world, Chellis tells a story of how she came to know when the snow would fall. After a few years of living in northern New Mexico, she heard a particular bird's song. It was mid-August, although she did not know exactly when. Suddenly, she found herself anticipating an early winter. She did not know how she knew about the connection between the bird's arrival in August and the beginning of winter months later—except for having been attentive.*

CHELLIS GLENDINNING *continues:* For me, the gift of being able to have friendships with native people who are living their cultures is the mindfulness that it requires. I can assume nothing, and so I have no choice but to be alert. I think this mindfulness is the very state of mind we want to conjure up as we face the disasters that are befalling us, from unemployment to toxic contamination. We might also ask, "How is it that some native people today—after 500 years of attempted genocide— have such a strong relationship to their culture and such a strong sense of themselves?" Imagine, say in the 1700s or the 1800s, when the most blatant battles were being waged, when the bullets were flying, when the villages were being burned into the Earth. Some people sat in a circle together, and they said, "Our job now is not to win, or to return to how things were. We would wish for this, but we know we cannot. Our job now is to remember our humanity, to pass on our culture and the ways that ensure our humanity. We must do this for future generations." Every native person you meet today who expresses her culture is the product of this historic endeavor. This is an awesome realization.

When I was younger, back in the 1960s during the heyday of the Anti-war Movement, I was certain we were on the horizon of creating a great new world, and I was convinced we were going to win. I will share a very private thought with you: Perhaps our job now is not so much about winning. We would wish for this, but perhaps it is not time for this task. Maybe our job now is about remembering our humanity and passing it on to future generations. It is amazing to me that I do not bring despair or hopelessness to this thought. I bring no less passion to this seemingly lesser task than I have to anything I have ever done.

⊘ Chellis concludes by speaking of traditional prophecies that point toward a world of complete breakdown or a world of harmony—we do not know which. She takes heart from the fact that in North America the long-prophesied white buffalo has just been born. Plains Indian legends have long held that when the white buffalo appears, all the people of the world will come together.

The discussion continues with SANDY IRVINE's *comment on the effects of communications media on his students and some historical correction on the subject of resistance movements:* For about twenty years I've been teaching average-ability seventeen- and eighteen-year-olds. I've noticed in those twenty years that technology is actually impoverishing consciousness at an alarming rate. There has been a dramatic reduction in attention spans, an increase in casual rudeness, and a dramatic contraction in knowledge, despite all the information highways and knowledge stores.

I face students who don't know where Ethiopia is, despite the fact that there are documentaries about it on TV, which suggests to me that there are, indeed, intrinsic problems in the media of communications and computing regardless of their ownership.

In terms of changing consciousness, there's a marked decline in self-esteem and self-confidence. I don't think that the marginalized and the impoverished are going to be the base of any social movement. There's no precedent in European history for that. The Levellers actually were comparatively well-to-do people, from the lesser propertied classes; they weren't the poor of Stuart England. The Bolsheviks drew from the intelligentsia and skilled workers—no unskilled workers, no unemployed, no peasants; Bolsheviks were members of comparatively privileged groups in Russian society. One's got to be careful not to conjure fancies of new social movements arising from those on the fringes. Finally, I've heard it said that we shouldn't be judgmental, but all day today we've been passing judgment on values, lifestyles, and institutions that we don't like. We should ask, then, what business we're about.

Like Gandhi, MARTHA CROUCH *believes that "walking the talk" is powerfully convincing:* My own change in consciousness was precipitated by the practice of neighbors in my community who get along without electricity, grow all their own food, live on two thousand dollars a year, have several kids and a really joyful life. Their home is the community center for our neighborhood. It feels better there. You go there and time changes: You walk into their garden and everything slows down, becomes more sane; they have so much time to be with people. At their home the food tastes better and they make a lot of wonderful wine.

For me it was important to experience, rather than just think about, what it means to have a life that isn't based on consumerism or accumulation, and what it means to not live in a grid of electric lights. The energy feels different. Experiencing that was instrumental in my quitting biotechnology and becoming less accumulation oriented.

I, too, teach at a large university and see hundreds of freshmen. I'm fairly optimistic about their desire to have a more meaningful life, but there's very little support and role modeling for that. It seems easier to get a grant from a philanthropic organization to set up a large program or a demonstration farm or to write a book or publish a journal than not to have electricity in your house in a suburban neighborhood, or to convert your front yard into a subsistence farm. I would like to see more support for these small acts and for there to be many thousands of such acts.

⊘ The futility of consumerism, avers MARIA MIES, *arises from the reality that the deepest human needs cannot be satisfied by mere material:* The kind of addiction which comes with consumerism comes because in spite of all that wealth real human needs are not satisfied. You cannot create a relation buying any kind of commodity. My students and I have discussed this. One woman told me, "I have given no presents to my children for Christmas this year; I have given them time to tell them stories." I'm sure these children will remember their mother, the stories, and the time, and she was happy and the children were happy. It didn't cost anything, so we coined the concept, "the noncommodified satisfaction of human needs."

⊘ RICHARD SCLOVE: In my reading about India and the U.S. I learned that the movements toward *national* self-reliance deconstructed *local* self-reliance.

⊘ CHARLENE SPRETNAK: It's important to realize that these resistance movements faced very difficult struggles, such as the one between Gandhi's community-based model—the Constructive Program—and the state-socialist model of young elite males. Those men, including Nehru, returned from studying in London as smug converts to the ideology of the modern state, with its focus on centralization and on cities. They saw that Gandhi was essential in the independence movement since he was the great leader with the mass following, but as soon as independence was ensured, Gandhi and his community-based vision were marginalized. The London-educated leaders of the new government followed the soft-socialist modern model of the British Fabians. If India had adopted Gandhi's model—bringing economic, cultural, and spiritual renewal to the villages and towns—it would now be far ahead of the rest of the Third World in terms of stability and local self-reliance.

⊘ ANDREW KIMBRELL *suggests that we are educated to see the rest of nature as devoid of spirit and yearns for it to be otherwise, then goes on to ponder the different temperatures of evil:* We often speak of the evils of our times. But the reason many do not see certain technology as evil is that they do not perceive that there are two very distinct evils. There is "hot" evil and "cold" evil. It's hot, purposeful evil that makes the newspapers: rape, violence, and so on. This is intentional evil spawned through heated, albeit distorted or pathological, passions—be they love, hatred, or anger. Megatechnological evil is removed from individual intention or passion: It's abstract power, cold evil. Few of us received evil glee in contributing to air pollution by using airplanes to get here. When I get in my car to drive to Maine with my family, I don't glory in the evil of turning on the air conditioning. I don't shout, "There goes the ozone layer and I've got a greenhouse gas coming right out the back of the car!" No, these evils are inherent in the technologies themselves. They are cold, institution-alized evils. Yet we never hear them condemned in our religions. The moralists ignore this evil which increasingly is becoming far more seri-ous than hot evil. Robert Graves once said that he would become a Catholic when the Pope issued an encyclical against the combustion engine. He'd still be waiting. This understanding of evil allows us to see how our society can continue to speak the language of social justice, even of environmental justice, and yet institutionalized evil keeps hap-pening because we have not addressed technological evil. If evil is abstract, it doesn't require intentionality.

⊘ *Concluding his reflections, Kimbrell takes up the problem of suffering, and the limits that suffering illuminates. There are two very different ways of dealing with limits, he says:* Sacramental imagination, characteristic of traditional societies, consecrates and ritualizes the suffering imposed by the limits of nature and our humanity, whereas the technological imag-ination aims at overcoming and obliterating limits at whatever cost.

⊘ GUSTAVO ESTEVA *introduces the difficult and provocative concept of the "textual mind" and suggests that it need not be the ineluctable fate of every modern's consciousness:* In a conference about technology perhaps it can be of some help to remember the impact of all those specific technolo-gies that modify our consciousness. The text modifies the human con-dition, our perception, our eyes, our full notion of the world. We cannot go back, we are already shaped by text; we have a "textual mind." The "textual mind" is now dominating the world. If I am in a village of illit-erate people, discussing with them an agrarian conflict with their neigh-bors, the elder of the village will rush to his hut and produce a text: the original deed given to them by the Spanish Crown and recognized by the Mexican government. They cannot read that text, but they have been forced to accept its rule over their relations with neighbors and the outside world.

As far as I can see, however, most people on Earth do not have a "tex-tual mind" like modern men and women. They have not allowed the text to redefine and determine their own beings, developing, for exam-ple, the individual selves without which modern men and women can-not face each other. They are not individual selves, but knots in nets of relations, determining their own views of themselves and others. Those of them who become literate may often be reshaped as individual selves, but many of them now are resisting such prospect: They keep a critical distance from the text; they avoid the transmogrification of their soul into a "textual mind."

Both in adopting and rejecting modern technology, we seem to be trapped in the "textual mind": in advertising a technology or in the instructions to use any modern tool, as well as in suggesting anti-megatechnology texts—manifestos, declarations.

The lessons of Gandhi may well be pertinent here. "Be the change that you wish for the world," he said. He did not suggest a program for *them* to do something. He was not disseminating a written catechism. He was spinning his wheel, while talking about its advantages and implications.

⌗HELENA NORBERG-HODGE *suggests that literacy does result in a dramatically different kind of consciousness and that the need for identity can best, if not only, be satisfied by authentic, functional community:* I have lived for twenty-two years with people who are illiterate and have seen some of them become literate. It makes an enormous difference. It has to do with moving away from a direct, unmediated experience of the living world and living community. This unconceptualized, immediate experience provides a deep experiential understanding of the complexity, movement, and shift of life. Within such understanding it becomes evident that the interdependent web of relationship cannot so easily be simplified in a linear and "logical" way. Tolerance, an acceptance of paradox and contradiction, is one of the consequences. We can learn practical things from that: not to push children into literacy too early. There's a lot of evidence that it does make it almost impossible to come back into unmediated direct experience of the world as it is beyond language, category, and rigid conceptualization.

In Ladakh it's been clear that the breakdown of community is a breakdown of identity, too. When you see people consuming, particularly young children who are desperate to have the latest label, the latest toy, what is their motivation? Peer approval; they're looking for community, for love and respect, for recognition, nurturing, and that is precisely what community affords people. It comes back to community and community-based economics. You cannot provide that continuous nurturing and mutual aid without community structures that also provide material—that is, economic—support. There has to be a structural fabric: It can't be just an abstract idea. Today in the West it's often thought that "community" is a group coming together to weep and cry for a weekend to then disband forever.

⌗*Bringing this session to an end,* JERRY MANDER *supplies facts and fig-*

ures about the billions of person-hours spent in the unity of attention to the tube, and the implications for human consciousness are appalling: I would like to cite a few statistics relevant to the question of global consciousness: The average American spends four-and-a-half hours a day watching television—it's similar in Britain and Mexico. Average Japanese and Russians spend even more hours than that watching television. This means that around the world millions and millions of people spend more time watching television than doing anything else except sleeping and working or going to school. Watching American television the average person sees 23,000 commercials per year. Whether it's a car or toothpaste being advertised, the message is the same, which is that buying something is the way to obtain satisfaction and happiness. About 70 percent of the people on the globe now have access to television, very little of which is locally produced. So people in grass houses in Borneo and in the Pacific Islands and people in log cabins in the far North are watching mostly American television.

There are many ways in which to use the term "consciousness," but what these statistics mean to me is that everybody's walking around with the same pictures in their heads, so that their mental imagery or psychological framework is increasingly colonized. Their consciousness is commercialized and globalized.

Chapter 10

The Electronic Revolution: Virtual Empowerment

⊙ How do megatechnology and economic globalization affect the dignity, privacy, and citizenship of persons in modern societies? In many respects, communications technology is not only non-neutral but totalitarian, allowing the expansion of transnational corporations and bureaucracies that would condemn citizens either to dumb passivity or to impotence and frustration. These glamorous technologies extend and integrate cradle-to-grave surveillance, annihilating all concept of a right to personal privacy, and help consolidate the power of the national security state. If every technology, being a form of power, has implicit values and politics, to say nothing of synergistic effects with other technologies and institutional forms, why, we asked ourselves, is there not more wrenching public debate about what technology does to life and polity, as form reduces—really atomizes—content, then hastens to fill this void with semblances and gadgetry?

JERRY MANDER launches this session with a fairly devastating consideration of the totality of the effects of computer technology. It's hard not to conclude that the benefits to individuals are trivial when weighed against the social and ecological consequences: I'd like to explain what I mean by a systemic approach to technology. When a technology is first introduced, consumers get hit by a tremendous burst of propaganda about it, usually emanating from the inventors and corporations that will profit from its sale. Hundreds of millions of dollars have been spent on advertising computers, for example, with the result that computers are now almost universally believed to be a benefit. New technologies are received into a century-old paradigm that holds that technology and progress are always good. And generally, our individual experience of technology is beneficial. In a limited context computers *are* helpful. So are cars.

The question, however, is not whether it does any good, but "What else does it do?" Whether the concern is sustainability or ecology or humanity or even pleasure, how do we judge communications technology more broadly than by asking whether it helps us individually? Sitting at our terminals, sending our e-mail, we say we feel "empowered." In fact, this technology is one of the few subjects that the left and the right agree upon. They all know that technology is neutral, that its consequences just depend on who controls it.

As you know it's my way of thinking that there's no such thing as neutral technology. Every technology has political, cultural, economic, and personal implications. Every technology makes drastic changes in every dimension of society, and your "empowerment" at the keyboard is the least of it.

In the case of computers, for instance, their consequences for personal and community health are seldom taken into account. Computers emit radiation, their use is resulting in workplace injuries from repetitive motion disorders, and their manufacture generates a great deal of toxic waste. Ozone-depleting chemicals are used in making computer chips.

So pollution is a very real consequence of the electronic revolution. Electronics is supposed to be a clean industry. It's anything but. Silicon Valley has become one of the most severely polluted areas in the United States.

Another change brought about by computers, and the ability to link computer networks, is a vast increase in the extent of surveillance of the general population. The credit bureau now knows what you buy, when you bought it, what you spend, what you earn, where you live, and where you used to live. It's got your social security number, your telephone numbers, your fax machine number, and knows what your rent payments have been, and whether you've ever defaulted on a credit card. None of that is possible without computers.

There's high-tech warfare now: The six-minute reaction time of nuclear missile launch-on-warning is a computer process. It means there can now be vast destruction without human involvement, except at the receiving end.

We talk about computers empowering individuals and our activity.

But benefits of computers to corporations are making a quantum differ-ence—the greatest centralization and concentration of power and con-trol ever known. So corporations are "empowered" far more than you and I and our friends. Corporations have higher-quality equipment than citizen activists have and they use it twenty-four hours a day. Because of the links between computers, satellite communications, and other high-speed technology, corporations are able to move information anywhere in the world instantaneously, which enables them to be faster and more flexible. The control of the world's economies envisioned by the transnational corporations would be inconceivable without com-puters. In fact the TNCs themselves could not function without their global computer link-ups.

Another consequence of computers is that they make possible, and perhaps inevitable, a whole new generation of technology, to which computers are integral: genetic engineering, space technology, robotics, nanotechnology, all the new agribusiness technologies, and the like. Without computers these could not happen.

In short, people aren't aware that computers are heavily implicated in the destruction of ecosystems, the homogenization of consciousness, and the loss of cultures; but without computers those things wouldn't be happening anywhere near as widely or rapidly.

⊘ RICHARD SCLOVE *delves a little deeper into the negative aspects of the emerging electronic environment. Then, with discreet sympathy for the devil, Sclove suggests some positive political uses of electronic networks and supplies illustrations from his own experience:* What is this "global information infrastructure"? Nobody knows. To some people, it's U.S. commercial television writ large with 500 channels; to some people it's Internet and e-mail writ large. In the near term, it's an emerging global network in which computer, phone, fax, and television will likely become a kind of single device.

Some of the downside to this is the exaggerated hype about the ben-efits of virtual, nonterritorial communities. There's a moral hazard in that, if our engagement with farflung social networks means we are not aware of our relationships and material interdependencies with, and moral obligations to, the people down the street.

There's also a global, ecological hazard if the consequences include caring less about, or becoming collectively less capable of acting effec-tively on, the local environment because we're so engaged in farflung networks. And if there's a mismatch between bonds of social affiliation —which become global—and political jurisdictions—which remain territorially based, there are political risks to democracy. How are we going to govern political jurisdictions if there are no bonds of affiliation or mutual understanding within them? The answer from the techno-enthusiasts is that we'll change the political jurisdictions, but they are not able yet to describe how that might be beneficially arranged, nor to discuss the problem of making the transition.

Although there's a lot of talk about how electronic networks increase contact with other types of people, my experience doing a lot of Inter-netting is that the people I'm in contact with in Australia and the Netherlands and so on wind up being a lot like me—for example, they're disaffected, ex-sixties people. At the individual level, telecommuting to work can be nice if it's an option that you choose freely, but when it's imposed on you as a condition of employment, so that you're basically forced to have an office at home because it helps the corporation reduce its overhead and you wind up working in solitary conditions, it's not so great. Certainly, microsurveillance of work and work discipline already affects tens of millions of people throughout the world. In fact their finger rate of entry of data is monitored centrally by computer.

Currently, I've heard, the international capital flows are a thousand times greater than the international flow of goods and services, so largely speculative investment dwarfs by many orders of magnitude the formal, material economy. Certainly, there's a reduction in sensuously engaged craft labor. We're seeing human services overtaken by elec-tronically mediated, expert system-dominated interactions. "Produc-tion" increasingly becomes computer-transmitted instructions to auto-mated machinery. Shopping is reduced to clicking a button on a TV remote control. Somewhere else, in a warehouse with no windows, a few people guide automated forklifts to distribution trucks. This is bad for local self-reliance; expanded global trade will tend to swamp the signif-icance of local trade if things continue as they are. In the formal politi-cal domain there is vast potential for manipulating the electorate with results from instant polling, published without any time for deliberation or reflection.

Because people who use computers now do find it seductively fun, really critical voices about this technology are scarce. In the United States, there is a network of activist public-interest groups working on legislation guiding telecommunications and computerization. They want a universally accessible and affordable system, where privacy is protected and civic uses are supported. This would be preferable to a completely commercial information system.

Enlightened political discussion among the public-interest groups in the United States recognizes that users, not just corporations, need to be involved in designing and governing these new systems. And, maybe if the interest groups are really enlightened, they will recognize that *potential* users need to be involved, also. What they don't recognize is that most people are now, or want to remain, nonusers but will be massively affected by this restructuring of the society's economy. So it's especially vital to involve nonusers in deliberations and decisions about these systems.

In addition, many people will be forced to go on this system. As work becomes more and more computerized, an enormous number of people who have no interest in participating in this system for one reason or another are going to have computers forced on them anyway—either because they're told they have to as a condition of employment or because the alternative face-to-face social/economic systems in which they now participate will be eviscerated by these systems. So there may increasingly be no alternative but to turn to online shopping, for instance.

There are, however, some partly compensating human and social benefits and opportunities provided by these systems. Geographically dispersed groups can communicate and coordinate with each other in new ways. Some people who do not do well in face-to-face communication, who are intimidated or socially stigmatized as not attractive, find it refreshing to be able to participate in electronic communication. There is also the technical possibility, if not the political probability, of decentralizing political power relationships with these technologies. That will not happen without enormous political struggle and effort, and maybe not even then—but there is at least some potential.

As a political activist, if you are willing to sacrifice and suffer the negative personal consequences of spending time onscreen and online, you may choose to be politically effective by using these systems—perhaps even to use these systems to coordinate quite new political coalitions, among other things. I have suffered the adverse personal psychological consequences of being online but have been politically effective in ways I couldn't have been other than by participating in the Internet world.

⊘ CHET BOWERS *performs a learned exposition of the ways in which computers amplify certain qualities of thought, language, and relationship that are characteristic of modernity while undermining ways of communication, understanding, and culture that attend to ecological realities and necessities:* Modernity has a number of assumptions about the nature of the individual, the culture-free nature of the communication process, and about the tools that individuals use. I'd like to talk about the cultural and other dimensions of technology and to try to demystify the notion that technology is a tool that we use. My focus here is going to be on computers. We can see how it is that by interacting with computer technology, certain aspects of our experience, among them the cultural, are amplified and others are reduced.

For instance, a stick is not a neutral tool: It amplifies reach, it reduces the tactile, olfactory, and other dimensions of sensory experience. A telephone amplifies voice over distance; it reduces the information and knowledge that is immanent in face-to-face communication. Computers, similarly, amplify certain aspects of knowing and certain cultural forms of knowledge and reduce others.

The forms of knowledge that can be communicated through this print-based technology are explicit forms of knowledge that can be represented digitally. The forms of cultural knowledge that are lost have to do with the tacit, the contextual, and that which is part of memory, that is, the analogues that are the basis of human community, of cultural experience. Computers cannot represent the contextual nature of analogue knowledge, narrative forms of knowledge, nor the forms of knowledge acquired and shared in metarelationships.

Computers enhance the notion that we think with data, that individuals construct ideas with information. This is central to the modern notion that the individual is a rational, self-directed being. Computers reduce our understanding that the thinking of the person is influenced by the cultural epistemology, encoded and reproduced in the language of the cultural group. We are cultural thinkers, and this is hidden by the amplification characteristics of computers which create the notion that we can communicate with people around the world and that we're all using this same language and inhabiting the same reality.

By amplifying the notion of the individual as the basic social unit, the computer reduces the possibility for transgenerational communication. Yet such communication is essential to a culture that's organized in an ecologically sustainable way. With computers, the elder is replaced by the CD-ROM and the hypertext. Interestingly enough, a metaphor used in talking about a person using a hypertext is that he or she is a "navigator," which bears out this notion that individuals are choosing their own course through history, and choosing the way they want the world to be put together.

The computer also amplifies the current, modern orientation toward a highly experimental culture: The assumption is that as we become more experimental with the foundations of our cultural experience we are more progressive—that is, we are increasingly relying upon untested knowledge, on forms of knowledge that may or may not survive in the long term. This characteristic amplifies a cultural view of temporality that frames experience in terms of immediate problem solving. In other words, the computer reinforces the modern sense of temporality by reducing the awareness that we are connected in time with the past and the future.

Computers amplify a conduit view of language, a sender-receiver model of language that has a directly representational function, and that says we simply send our ideas, information, or data through this technology. This view of language reinforces the current myth that the other person then uses data as the basis of what is supposedly individual empowerment. This view of language is essential to the globalizing of modern culture, with its emphasis on the commoditization of knowledge and relationships. Computers reduce the user's awareness that a conduit view of language hides the fact that words have histories, and that they encode earlier forms of cultural intelligence.

Cultures are grounded in mythopoetic constructions of how reality is organized and what the fundamental relationships are. These metaphorical constructions organize how we make sense of the new; there's an encoding of earlier thought processes and thus earlier cultural assumptions. Language thinks us as we think within the language, and this is hidden by the way in which computers reinforce the modern idea that language is neutral.

Computers amplify a moral framework that represents relationships as human centered and essentially instrumental. This statement is based on the increasing recognition that all languages are about relationships and encode the moral templates which govern those relationships. This means that what is lost in communication through this technology is the possibility that one might understand moral relationships as inclusive of human-nature relationships.

Lastly, computers are now becoming a root metaphor that is leading us to remetaphorize fundamental ways of understanding human experience, including life itself.

⊘ HELENA NORBERG-HODGE *pursues the theme of the cultural consequences of dependence on technology and the radical reduction of the sense of diversity that attends the penetration of mass culture, a culture of unfulfillment:* It's important that we see the differences between cultures, but the most urgent and fundamental issue today is that industrial civilization is literally lifting us away from nature. What we call "culture" has grown out of a fundamental relationship to nature. We need to study that process rather than scrutinizing other cultures. Human societies coevolved with specific ecosystems and climates, developing different forms of clothing, food, and architecture, all reflecting local conditions. What we call Western "culture" has become an urban way of living that is now fundamentally shaped by technology and finance.

Dependence on technology includes a relationship to language that is more and more mechanistic. Language removed from direct experience becomes a standardization, a simplification of an infinitely diverse living reality. This is why the difference between oral communication and written is so significant. The latter allows for centralized linguistic control. The jump to the computer age means an exponential use of print-based, written communication and even more centralized control.

The role models in the media today are stereotypically European, blond and blue-eyed. In remote villages in Mongolia, China, and Thailand, people are watching soap operas about rich Californians. In Japan, and in China now as well, women are having operations on their eyes to make them look more Western. In Spain, more and more women on television have bleached blond hair and blue contact lenses. These stereotyped role models rob the individual of self-respect. I come from Sweden where the majority of women are blond and blue-eyed and do look quite a lot like a Barbie doll. It doesn't matter; they can never have that perfect hourglass figure. The result is an obsession with the body, with appearance, so that, according to research, seven-year-olds already hate their bodies. The rise of bulimia, anorexia, and self-hatred actually fuel consumerism. When people are dissatisfied with who they are, they readily turn to the marketplace to find ways of propping themselves up.

The media play a big role even in the increasing divorce rate. You can never live up to the exciting, sexy, rich lives depicted on the TV. Everyday life seems meaningless, ordinary, boring by comparison. This is why even nature programs are not necessarily good. When you present all the wildlife from Africa, or all the butterflies of the world on the TV, it engenders in children a sense that the one butterfly or bit of nature they see outside is boring.

If we were experiencing the richness and diversity that life is, or was, where would we have room for television? That richness starts with the uniqueness of every individual, so who would be the role model? There's no need for television in a healthy, diverse society where people have the freedom to be themselves and to develop an expanded sense of self through their unmediated interrelationships to the cosmos.

⊘ The discussion continues with ANDREW KIMBRELL *characterizing the way the cult of the computer debases human wisdom and saying that this is reflected in the current approach to public education. The ability to track data is prized above understanding:* The transition from oral culture to written culture to the computer culture has taken us from wisdom to knowledge and finally to data. That sad evolution in human thought is nowhere more apparent than in schools and in teaching in the United States and, increasingly, in Western Europe. Teaching is more and more based on computerized test scores. Recently we've abandoned almost all of the essay questions on standardized tests. So the transition from wisdom to knowledge to data is literally being encoded into the thought processes we are teaching our children at every level of school.

⊘ CHELLIS GLENDINNING *suggests that there may not be a middle ground in relation to technologies—at least none that can be reached by comparing aspects of reality that are truly incomparable:* I want to raise the problem of cost-benefit analyses. Because the flow is in the direction of technological progress, as soon as you get into a cost-benefit discussion, meaningful criticism of technologies is simply stopped. Period. *Adios.* As soon as somebody says, "Yes, but *this* study shows the technology doesn't harm anyone," you're locked in stasis. And meanwhile, the technology in question goes forth.

But you cannot weigh dysfunction against function. You always want function or health; you can't say, "Well, I'll take a little bit of unhealth, and a little bit of health," yet this surreal balancing act is implicit in cost-benefit analyses of the risks—or, more properly—*hazards* of technology. The process makes health and profit equivalent; it reduces whole lives into quantities.

⊘ SIGMUND KVALOY *offers a distinction that he has found useful in considering computers and their expanding sphere:* The concept of the *complicated* versus the *complex* and a third quality that we call *pseudo-complexity* proves to be a very good conceptual tool for understanding computers, worldwide computerization, and the vulnerability of these systems.

Nature and society are complex; machines are complicated. Complex entities are processes always containing something new. The complicated is static. Machines are reversible; nature and human societies are not.

Then, in the background, we have the concept of the pseudo-complex, of *imitative complexity,* something created to divert people who are deprived of a genuinely complex life. These concepts allow us to show that this globalization that happens in several dimensions is based on a deep misunderstanding. It mistakes the complex for the complicated. Therefore, this system is highly vulnerable and it will break. It's vulnerable also because it's based on the cheapness of the microprocessor, but that cheapness remains dependent on the continuation of the competitive industrial growth system and its world grasp. Computer experts in America and Europe seem never to have thought about this: that there's a material that might fail—and of course it's bound to; it's based, finally, on mining the deep seas for minerals and requires very costly processes where the costs are hidden in our present system. The materials that you need in chips and microprocessors cannot possibly be locally produced, based on locally self-reliant economies—the way the future societies will have to be based, after the present robber economy has run its course.

𝕯 SANDY IRVINE *offers some hope in the form of reminders of the fragility of these technological systems:* We're attributing superhuman and super-ecological attributes to new technologies. We're talking as if they can cheat entropy, as if they can cheat ecology, as if they're free from any contradictions and vulnerabilities. That's not my experience of the new technologies. If you take the space program, it's quite obvious that it will grind to a halt because there's too much space debris up in space. Nuclear fusion might work in the laboratory, but it might never, ever, become a feasible technology in everyday life.

If we look at computers, they, too, are riddled with contradictions: They require vast quantities of energy which are costly to provide. Many libraries that have been computerized have got huge energy bills. In the long run, the world is bound to face sharply rising energy prices. Despite all the claims about the paper-free office, in the real world computers demand huge amounts of paper. Yet in the future paper will become increasingly expensive. Last, but not least, the things keep breaking down. What's going to happen when there are strikes in Singapore where people make the spare bits for these things?

We shouldn't discount the human capability to resist brainwashing. People do selectively interpret the stimuli they receive. During the Falklands War the British public was saturated, bombarded, with 100-percent pro-Falklands War material in all the press, yet for that period 25 percent, possibly 33 percent, of the British public opposed the Falklands War. In other words, they were not being successfully brainwashed by the media.

Consider the subject of nuclear power: It has been aggressively promoted and heavily state subsidized yet it, too, has ground to a halt. Similarly, we can push up computerization's costs, demand safety standards, slow the thing down, and push it off the rails.

 Martha Crouch and then Andrew McLaughlin each talks about some of the sinister absurdities of computer applications and technologized learning in their respective institutions of higher education.

MARTHA CROUCH: Computer technology is being promoted—just as the first steam-powered tractors were pushed. They were hulking machines far less efficient than the existing forms of farming. But those early tractors were a vision of what could be and were promoted to the point where they took over. Similarly, the first hybrid corn was unproductive and showed remarkably little promise. Yet its proponents kept pushing the research because they could see the corporate advantages in being able to control seeds and farmers.

At Indiana University where I teach, we have a new education school where the idea is that because we need a computer-literate workforce in industry and the military, we need to begin teaching computer skills to the very young. Large corporations are vying to give the university millions of dollars to outfit completely the education building with all the latest computer technology. The university is just licking it up. All these utility bills are being paid by corporations such as AT&T and MCI: It doesn't matter how much it costs because the aim is to get this technology inculcated at the earliest possible age. It leads to ridiculous situations: You walk into the education building and to find out what room someone's in, you have to use a computer instead of just looking at a map.

Computerization facilitates large classes because everything can be computer-graded so you don't have to hire teaching assistants or pay benefits.

Meanwhile few students in the biology department go on field trips anymore because we can't afford the buses and the cars; the classes are too big and there aren't enough teaching assistants to go with them. All the money has gone to buy computers. There's a choice being made. We have spectacular hardwood forests all around Bloomington; there are neo-tropical migrant birds, incredible butterflies. Very few education students go outside and look at actual nature; they sit and look at CD-ROMs of virtual nature. It costs many more thousands of dollars to do that than to go on field trips. So it's not a matter of costs. The technology is being promoted by particular interests in order to train kids in the mode required by the military and industrial complex.

 ANDREW McLAUGHLIN: Computers are like a form of television. If you're writing on a computer you're looking at yourself in the form of your words on the screen. I have a friend who's addicted to Internet. He keeps telling me all the wonderful things one can do. He's involved in saving forests in the Philippines, but he's not involved in saving hardwood forests where we live. He's in this network, and our local community doesn't exist for him.

I've been involved in education at both the elementary and secondary levels and what's coming down, at least in New York State, with real force, is what they're calling "distance learning." The concept is that we can improve education by having a centralized location that will produce a course to be available live or taped for televisions in every school that's linked up to it. They want to put commercials in this material. It leads toward schools without teachers, but with advertisements. This is typical of the way technical innovations are captured and transformed by the dominant economic powers.

⊘MICHIEL SCHWARZ *asserts that these electronic networks* are *qualitatively different from the technologies most humans have experience with hitherto and that the implications are total:* Part of the problem of communicating some of the fundamental consequences and dangers of television, computers, and information networks is that these technologies are unlike others. Most of the impacts of information technologies will be nonphysical. The longer we refuse to talk about "technological culture" as if culture is something apart from this technological world, the more we are in a mode of thinking that technology is something separate—that it's just an instrument. It implies that all things being equal, this machine does the thing that you did before without a machine— and does it better. In reality, nothing remains equal, just about everything changes when you introduce a computer or any of these systems, from the individual level all the way to the level of how people interact. In that sense, it's anthropologically correct to use the word "culture" because the introduction of such technology really changes every corner of what is meant by culture.

Although I agree with Jacques Ellul that "technological culture" is a contradiction in terms because it's not a real culture, I find what Donna Haraway says more useful: that technological culture "is a culture of no culture," but still a culture. Apart from the analytical and conceptual point, if we want to get across that everything changes on all these levels, it is very useful to talk in terms of "technological culture" and the dangers of technological culture.

What we're talking about now, with computers, is something more fundamental and much more integrated than what used to be called technological society. We are shifting, sometimes slowly, sometimes with enormous leaps, many aspects of our culture into modes that are driven and determined by technology. We have to get beyond this perception of technology as an instrument. It's more like technology as culture.

*⊘*Helena Norberg-Hodge *reminds us that there's more to reality than what people like those present know, then talks about technology as a self-feeding proposition, and concludes by raising the necessity for a "strategic embrace":* When Westerners say "we," it often sounds as though they mean all of humankind. Yet millions of people on Earth are not yet living and breathing technology in the way that we are. They still have social systems that incorporate technology rather than vice versa. It is vital that we try to understand what human life is without modern technology in order to have a basis of comparison and therefore a clear understanding of the impact that it's had on our lives. We all gain strength from recognizing this, instead of universalizing our experiences as Westernized, urbanized consumers.

Today, problems push our society in the direction of more technologies, instead of looking for the source of the problems, which often is technological. In a recent article in a U.S. journal, there was a vivid description of how infants in the West don't get enough carrying and nurturing. The average child in the West, it is said, gets something like an hour a day of that. And guess what? The solution wasn't that we should try to ensure that the child does get the cuddling and nurturing it needs; no, this was an advertisement for a new technology—one that is going to provide the child with electronically simulated human touch and movement.

Having very clearly spelled out the fundamental problems that are a result of the technologization of society, I believe that in order to achieve change it is nevertheless essential to have a strategic embrace of certain technologies. The speed and escalating scale that society, partly with public funding, is now embarking on, is of such speed and magnitude that we perhaps need to use the tools we oppose in order to counter that escalation. The car, the computer, and the television may be essential to enable us to get our counter-message out.

⊘ The session concludes with a scatter of insights and observations.

Satish Kumar: In our age we think that things are better if they are done quickly. Speed is the god of the modern age, and in order to achieve "speed" we seek technological progress. If we can say "Slow is beautiful" as well as "Small is beautiful," we will be able to grapple with the problem of technology much more quickly!

🖉SIGMUND KVALOY: Our body and our mind are different from machine systems, including computers: We are complex, and a seamless interface between the complex and the complicated is not possible. They are not on the same logical level. In order to develop creative thinking and inventive doing we need to have continuous and diverse contact between the material world and our material body. With the mechanical typewriter, we are still in touch with the rich qualitative world. I write a little bit, I take out the paper. I am surprised at what "I" wrote; I jot down corrections, using my pen. I have to repair the typewriter, too. I know how it works—it's near to me, it's part of my material world. The computer "imitates thinking," but that is "thinking" modeled on the computer's binary-digit structure, not on the "value/feeling logic" of a human being, presupposing body and history. A computer can have none of these.

🖉RICHARD SCLOVE: The transnational corporations' control of capital —their access to or ability to move capital unquestioned via computer networks, and to mobilize or manipulate a global workforce—are unprecedented. But their enhanced efficacy in the formal political system is less obvious, because corporations are not empowering their full workforce to become political activists. They are insisting on centralized control within the corporation, so central management is still the corporate voice and uses pre-existing expensive telecommunications and public relations methods to try to get out their political message. I'm amazed at how clunky and cumbersome the corporations are in many of their political interventions. At the moment, I see more evidence of political efficacy increasing among a middle tier—including students, professionals, and social activists, not among the underclass or the disadvantaged nor to the enhancement of corporate power. On the other hand, that may change for the worse with accelerating commercial, corporate control of cyberspace.

JERRY MANDER: Corporate power is outside the democratic process. The global economy is rapidly moving beyond public control, so it doesn't matter what political position anyone takes. Effective power will be held by appointive international bureaucratic institutions, rather than by elected governments.

Chapter 11

Women, Patriarchy, and Megatechnology

⊘Throughout the conferences we worked at dissecting the components of megatechnology, or technique. Implicit in all our discussions was that technology is far more than hardware. Tools are integral to human cultures. Megatechnology is indispensable to globalization. We used "North" and "South" as shorthand for wealthy and poor, classes and countries, cognizant that there's a South within the North. One's position in any one of a number of arbitrary hierarchies—civilized or primitive, literate or preliterate, "white" or everyone else, rational or intuitive—determines, to a considerable extent, whether one benefits from (perhaps only apparently), or is wounded by, technology.

If technology is not neutral, if power attaches to technology, then power relationships, patriarchy among them, must come to the fore for consideration. Women know something about this. Feminism, which is not a monolith, keeps questions of justice, equity, and essence in view. Ecofeminists—many of the most eminent of whom were conference participants—are not willing to limit their ambition to mere equality between the sexes. Indeed, to become equal to the players in a system that many of us regard as an artifact of patriarchy is antithetical to ecofeminism. Rather the hope is for equitable, diverse, authentic, and nonexploitative relationships throughout the entire community, more-than-human nature included.

Within this roomy tent, there's plenty of space for nuanced disagreement and, more important, for a synergy of views. Maria Mies, Vandana Shiva,

Martha Crouch, Charlene Spretnak, and Helena Norberg-Hodge constituted the panel, which I moderated.

The panel was a bit impromptu—women attending were called upon to organize it on rather short notice at breakfast that morning. We flirted with departing from the format—which some regarded as rigid and unsatisfactory—of a series of speakers followed by disparate comments. It chagrins me to say that I was among the conservatives on that issue—so rather than a dance, a song, a piece of theater, or a women's council, we remained in the idiom of intellectualism. And the quality of the thinking and sometimes the sharing was high, though feelings were, on the whole, confounded. So be it. What was spoken was some use-tested insight.

STEPHANIE MILLS *makes a brief introduction, then hastens to yield the podium:* Feminism has relevance here because it is a radical analysis of power arrangements and that is what we're about. As someone who's worked in the Ecology Movement, it's been clear to me that patriarchy as internalized in men and women has inhibited our effectiveness. Relegating women to subordinate positions has meant that there's been less intelligence and less diversity of intelligence brought to the work.

If you grant that patriarchy exists, and has for a while, then it has necessarily conditioned our modes of discourse. We may not even know what postpatriarchal discourse is like. We're negotiating that even as we speak. To have a feminist panel is to structure in some attention to these gender-based power relationships. The changes needed may seem like a contrivance—social change is like that. Even something seemingly minor, like nonsexist language—a structural response to a pervasive normal oppression—was awkward at first, but now sounds familiar.

⊘MARIA MIES's *scholarship persuades her that patriarchy was not inevitable, that it had a definite point of origin in prehistory, and that technology was, quite literally, instrumental in its development:* I would like to stress the connection between megatechnology, globalization, and patriarchy—and not only at the present but throughout history and prehistory. As activists we should consider which stages in the development of widespread social phenomena are most relevant. I do agree that the Renaissance and the Enlightenment and their aftermath are more relevant to our present effort. But unless we understand the connection between patriarchy and megatechnology, we can't really understand how to counter it.

In 1977 in a paper called "The Social Origins of the Sexual Division of Labor," I tried to elucidate the connection between conquest, patriarchal religion, weapons and their development, and the monopoly over arms as the cause of the overthrow of whatever balance there had been before. Patriarchy started historically somewhere and some time. It is not universal: History would not necessarily lead to it. Patriarchy began five or six thousand years ago. As soon as hunting technology became the technology of conquest, it was possible to end economic dependence on women. Whereas hunters and gatherers still had to depend on their own women, by warfare and conquest some men could gain independence from their own women and get food and other necessities without work. It is the primary instance of liberation or emancipation of men, if you like, from their own nature—their own women in that case. Through conquest and warfare, more labor—women and men—and bigger tribes can be acquired.

Technologies used in conquest are transport technologies—horses and other animals—and long-distance weapons such as arrows and bows. War technology really is the foundation of the amplifying characteristic of all modern technologies. War technologies reach areas far away from your own. In conquest you don't consider what you do to the conquered territory, you just move on. There's no responsibility for what is left behind. I think this has colored the identity of men in patriarchy since its earliest times.

Most of the modern megatechnologies—like atomic energy, the computer, and biotechnology—are still based on the same world view. They come out of warfare and militaristic research. So warfare is really the father of these technologies, which will reinforce violence against women, nature, and foreign peoples. This cannot be explained as an anthropological given, a drive innate in men, but as the result of this long history, which has its climax in the Enlightenment philosophy of the separation between the mind and the body. Without this drive toward ever farther areas, the whole drive toward expansionist globalization cannot be explained.

Look at the connection between computer technology and its manufacture. It was women in Southeast Asia, in the beginning, who made these chips. Cheap, female labor is really the base of this modern technology. This international division of labor is basically a sexual division of labor—the cheapest labor is female and is being exploited in the creation and production of computers. This is an aspect of the technology that's seldom in the minds of those who use it. When people talk about productivity, they don't mention its real origins in cheap, often coerced female labor. The cheap labor colony for capital and international capital within our own society will be women, housewives—you can be sure of that. It is critical to address this question, even in our discussions about new perspectives: What will be the future sexual division of labor?

⊘VANDANA SHIVA *strides confidently into the divide between two philosophies of feminism—essentialist and egalitarian—and offers some fine distinctions. She then takes up the gender-based politics of population control and finds them Machiavellian. A little colloquy on an upcoming U.N. conference on women follows:* The correlation of men to women as culture is to nature is very old. That correlation between nature and women, as instituted by patriarchy, has been opposed by a large part of the Feminist Movement. Freedom for women is seen as freedom from nature and freedom from anything ecological—not just farming, but everything, including reproduction. Because women are being defined as nature, their bodies and reproduction become part of nature from which they have to escape. Thus feminism adopted the flight from nature as a means of liberation. But there were some for whom connection with nature was an imperative of living properly on this planet. Nature itself was not a problem. Subjugation of nature was a problem. That has been an intellectual split in feminism.

During the preparations for the United Nations Population Conference in Cairo, an ongoing debate raised the issues of excessive consumption, of justice, of people having equal access to the vital resources needed for survival as being the functional issues of ecology. Then a switch took place whereby the Women's Movement began acting as a surrogate for demographic fundamentalism, the idea that every problem will be solved if we can just reduce the numbers on the planet. The key word throughout this was "choice." Feminist movements in the South have argued that far from providing choice, population-control programs are coercive, militaristic, violent systems, which, when backed with the power of money, only violate women's freedom in a basic sense.

Today 97 percent of the sterilizations in India are targeted at women. Family planning is regarded as a women's problem, and the technological control of fertility is the solution. Long-acting, hazardous, new contraceptives are among the favorites of the proponents of population control. This play of forces redefined control into an issue of choice. The word from Cairo was that women had been empowered because reproductive choice had become a legitimate key word in future discourse. But reproductive choice was construed to be the new reproductive technologies and the use of genetic engineering—construed to be contraceptive technologies, which are often hazardous to women; abortion in particular was regarded as essential to reproductive choice, all means of which seem to be targeting the female.

The technological changes associated with cultural changes further devalue women. In a BBC film concerning female feticide, there is a woman in prosperous Punjab who's been to an amniocentesis clinic for sex determination and an abortion. She says, "I'm celebrating the new choice that technology gives me. I choose the color of what I wear; now I can choose the sex of my child."

Choice is being constructed in a patriarchal way. Choice is offered to women as consumers, or as objectives of someone else's decision. But they're not making that choice, nor shaping it, not shaping the world out of which it arises. The larger society would resist genetic engineering and commodifying human reproduction. However, if those technologies can be projected as women's empowerment by creating a new language, a new notion of freedom, the objections are clouded. Something extremely simple and wonderful like having a baby becomes a cycle of capital accumulation. So no matter what you do in this area, there's profit, there are new technologies, and new growth areas.

⊘ MARIA MIES: This whole discourse on choice is very much an American one.

⊘ VANDANA SHIVA: It has been globalized.

⊘ MARIA MIES: It has not taken root yet in Germany to that extent.

⊘ CHARLENE SPRETNAK: Maybe what we should do for the Beijing U.N. Conference is help to frame the development question as the choice between community-based economics or the global market. This will be our choice.

[*Note:* That focus indeed turned out to be a main one at the Beijing Conference. An award was presented to the founder of the Grameen Bank in Bangladesh, which gives scores of thousands of microloans to poor rural women for small-scale businesses. A conference statement also declared that that is the type of development needed to help women, rather than the centralized, industrial model. C.S.]

⊘ BETH BURROWS: One of the most horrible false choices of all is that fetuses are now a natural resource and are increasingly being used to provide materials to prevent aging processes.

⊘ MARTHA CROUCH *tells her own story of unconscious and conscious motivation to learn natural science, of the rigidity and tacit coercion of the research system, and offers her conclusions as to whether or not woman's place could ever be in the lab:* Whether having women more involved in the techno-science industry would help is a real question. Since I decided to quit science completely I have often been accused of wasting my education and being a negative role model for girls.

One of the goals of techno-science is to create novel commodities and to continue expanding the economy. Many of women's functions—in reproduction, like breast feeding, where the relationship with the child and the transfer of nutrients are all of a piece—have been apart from the commodity realm. Science and technology can be used to separate that function into a product that can be cleaved from the process and transferred to men. Men can't breastfeed very easily, but if you can develop a formula—which they're starting to do now by genetically engineering human milk proteins into cow's milk—then that can be cleaved away from the process and men—who are, in general, the ones who run the corporations like Nestle's—can reap the profit. Then women become dispensable.

The female animal is particularly victimized by this. One of the biggest growth industries in biotechnology now is using females of other species—goats, sheep, cows—to manufacture pharmaceuticals in their mammary glands. The factory has been internalized into the female body.

Why should women participate in this as scientists? One argument is that if women participated it wouldn't be this way. Women would be making more of the decisions about the conduct of research. It's naïve to think that women, by participating in science and technology of this type, are going to change it in any fundamental way. What usually happens is that through scientific training women lose any particular perspectives that they may bring. Women who don't end up being completely assimilated into that conventional thinking are unable to keep the products of their creativity and science out of the mainstream of technology development. The diversity that women may bring to science just becomes another asset to the dominant culture.

I'm a good example of doing science in a fundamentally male way as a result of the training. Throughout my graduate work, I was interested in questions to do with natural history: I wanted to know why mushrooms spent all that energy glowing in the dark, and I wanted to know how mushrooms were interacting with other organisms in their environment. Nobody cared; there wasn't any background for it or any money. I tried looking at some of the medicinal herbs, such as henbane. Nobody was interested in that. Finally I came up with a question that everybody patted me on the back for. It was, "If you grow embryos outside of the mother, outside of the seeds, are they normal?" Psychologically the question resonated with me. My mother was severely depressed so I did not have enough nurturing. I was, in a sense, raised by my father, raised without a mother. I wanted to know if I was normal.

What was a pathology for me intersected with the goals of science perfectly. Being able to raise embryos without the mother means that men can raise embryos. And any increase in the ability of men to control reproduction is likely to result in more corporate power over processes related to generation, such as agriculture. This is what happened with my research.

One of the largest transnational corporations involved in the production and processing of edible oils used techniques developed by my lab to regenerate oil palms that were all genetically identical. Such cloned trees were thus more suitable for large, mechanized plantations. In Malaysia, oil palm production became more concentrated in the hands of corporations, rainforest was destroyed to expand the crop, indigenous people were displaced, and water quality near the processing sites deteriorated. My little personal pathology intersected with the male project of science and was amplified into a much more destructive enterprise. For this, I was rewarded heavily.

When I was done with my studies of embryo and pollen development I had a little more self-confidence and wanted to go back to thinking about grandmothers. I simply could not do that within the context of science. When I look at the projects of my female colleagues, it seems they're either identical to male projects or they fail. Someone like Barbara McClintock, who was doing the kind of research that didn't require much money, is the exception. She found a little niche. She was well-respected and could speak the science language. She used a more participatory way of knowing and found out some interesting things which weren't appreciated until they became useful technologically. Barbara McClintock's alternate way of knowing is now the underpinning of genetic engineering, which, I feel, is detrimental to women and nature. How could she have kept it out of that stream? At this point, with the system as strong as it is, I would not encourage young women to go into science. I would not stand in their way. I would argue for equal pay and equal opportunity, but I would not go out of my way to try and mount special programs for women to go into science in order to participate in their own demise.

⊘CHARLENE SPRETNAK *points out the lethal flaw in modern Western culture—that reason, which is but a part of our nature, of nature itself, has come to rule the whole, with understandably distorting results:* If our core problem is disengagement from nature, the solution is re-engagement with nature. So much of Western culture serves to increase that disengagement. Ecofeminism has delineated the linkage between denigration of nature and the female in Western history historically, symbolically, and philosophically. During the witch trials in Britain, some of the leaders of the Scientific Revolution served as inquisitors and used the same metaphors as in the new science: We must torture nature, stretch her on the rack, make her reveal her secrets. One of the key goals of the Scientific Revolution, according to the feminist philosopher Sandra Harding, was the hypermasculinization of thought.

From Kant and other Western philosophers, our society has inherited the sense that rational thought must be free from the "taint" of emotions. Caring and empathy are considered peripheral and often irrational. Even in this age of ecological crises, our call to re-engage with nature is dismissed by the dominant culture as too irrational, too fey, not tough enough. This resistance, which *is* truly irrational, stems, I believe, from the deep roots of modern socialization that shape the modern self as inherently separate from and superior to nature. Now, *there's* a deadly ideology.

⊘ *The final panelist,* HELENA NORBERG-HODGE, *questions the benevolence of exporting, and sometimes imposing, Western-style education, thus equipping the formerly sufficient to become redundant:* A common belief today is that the solution to overpopulation is for Third World women to have power over their own lives through education—by which is meant Western education—employment, and access to financial resources. However, both education and jobs depend upon and support the global marketplace. It is widely recognized that insecurity lies behind the population explosion, but what is not discussed so widely is that jobs in today's global economy are anything but secure. Real security will come about when communities—rather than individuals—have access to, control over, and responsibility for natural resources. The work that will provide security is work that is part of a sustainable economy. And in order to redirect economic activity toward sustainability, we need to examine the nature of modern education.

In talking about engagement with nature, community, or diversity, we have to consider the homogenizing role of what today is called education. Well-intentioned people are, unfortunately, funding schools in Tibet, Ladakh, and Mongolia. To them Western science is neutral, as are numeracy and literacy, and education will empower women. It's a dilemma. Most people around the world today do need education to

defend themselves against the globalization process, much as we ourselves might need computers to be able to defend against the further
expansion of computers. However, the real, enduring solutions involve
reinventing, regenerating, reforming community in human terms, and
in terms of a relationship to nature, a relationship to the place where
you're going to live and from which you will derive your livelihood. We
need knowledge about the bioregion where we practice economic skills
for survival.

It's particularly urgent in the Third World, where millions of people
still have a relatively sustainable relationship to local resources. These
are the majority of primary producers—the farmers, the nomads, and
the fishers who still derive their livelihoods from local natural resources.
The Western-style schools which are being introduced teach the young
nothing about these resources. They teach abstract, specialized skills
that are suited to a larger-scale, urbanized society based on petroleum
and an intensive use of imported industrial resources. This educational
system undermines people's ability to sustain their communities
through local resources.

⊘ The general colloquy begins as S ANDY I RVINE *returns to the raw fact of
overpopulation and argues that it is not, as a rule, presented out of context or
as the sole cause of the world's ills:* I must disagree with Vandana. If you
look at the preparation for Cairo, most pressure groups denied any problem of human numbers. I'm not quite sure who these "demographic
fundamentalists" are. It's a stereotype and travesty to say that people
who think there is a serious population issue have ignored global
inequalities and only focused on human numbers. People like Paul
Ehrlich and John Holdren have always tried to articulate things in the
context of affluence and technological choice. So it's as bad to say there
isn't a problem of human numbers as it is to say that it's only a problem
of human numbers. It is absurd to say that 10,000 is no different from
1,000. There are dramatic differences in impact. Numbers do change the
equation. So let's not blame everything on the population problem, but
it is a problem and it affects many women, as well as the planet as a
whole, very badly.

⊘ R ALPH M ETZNER *discourses interestingly upon a certain gender-based
metaphor and ponders the paternity of invention:* A question which presented itself to me some time ago, and that I've been working on ever
since, as a kind of riddle, is this: "If necessity is the mother of invention,
who is the father?" Different individuals, different groups or cultures,
give different answers. Perhaps there are many possible fathers for the

marriage with necessity, many sources of inspiration and creative innovation.

I've identified six answers to this riddle so far. One answer is in terms
of Darwinian evolution: Since new adaptations are the result of the
interplay of random mutation and natural selection, then *chance* is the
father who interacts with necessity as the mother to invent new adaptations. The answer in the terms of patriarchy, as Maria Mies and other
ecofeminists have been pointing out, is *war and domination.* The "need"
for ever more powerful weaponry and instruments of domination of
"security" is the openly acknowledged driving force of technological
invention. A third answer, associated with capitalism and the free market ideology, is *greed and profit:* As Marx pointed out over 100 years ago,
capitalism is driven by its own inherent logic, the "need" for profit, to
seek ever more inventive and efficient means of increasing both production and consumption. A fourth answer, proposed by some psychologists and philosophers, is *curiosity.* The origin of the word "curiosity" is related to cure and care, the inquisitiveness that drives us to
notice small differences, small anomalies, which can then be applied in
invention when the need arises. Gregory Bateson proposed that an
essential function of mind-in-nature was perceiving the "difference that
makes a difference." A fifth answer, a fifth "father of invention," I suggest, might be that of the artist and the child: *spontaneity or play.* In playing we might discover a new pattern, a noticeable difference, that can be
combined with necessity to generate a creative invention. And a sixth
answer, I suggest, is that given by indigenous people, deep ecologists,
and nature mystics; for such people, the inspiration for creativity and
invention is *mutuality, reciprocity, and relationship,* the desire to preserve
the ever-changing web of living process in which we are all embedded.

 ℗ CHELLIS GLENDINNING *passes around some long-burning Southern California white sage, a gift from a conference held there. She says:* This panel
amounts to a figure-ground shift. What happens to women in relation
to megatechnology and corporate global dominance is suddenly moved
to the fore of our awareness. Yet I see the problem as a whole system.
What if we had a panel of men talking about how all of these same
forces affect them? Men as a class are perceived as the ones with the
power, the ones who are whole. In the early, naïve days of the Women's
Movement, we actually *aimed* to be like the men who we thought were
so complete. Now we realize that men are deprived, oppressed, hurt, and
wounded by the same system. I will tell you a secret thought, and this

thought came out of a conversation I witnessed between Helena and environmental-justice activist Carl Anthony. They were disagreeing about which group of people is the most injured, or if such a designation can even be made. I secretly think that men who grew up within the technological world, the supposed beneficiaries of it, are the most wounded humans in the world. This is not something we as critics of technology should overlook.

⊘ VANDANA SHIVA *describes a question confronting all women on the planet chafing at their oppression. The question is both tactical and strategic and, Vandana says, the past can and should color the answer:* While many of us realize that rebuilding local ecology as a basis of local economy can be the only source of regeneration, there's a whole global structure, primarily economic, with a political base and now a feminist political base that's saying, "We will use all the power in the world to save all the women of the world from their local oppressions." So we are getting into a tense but fascinating conflict between women in different situations having to define for themselves whether they want the partnership of the local patriarchy or of the global patriarchy. Given that terrible situation, you have to rebuild culture from the particularities of history. Those historical particularities, even while you change them, all carry the layers of discrimination. Development made Indian patriarchy worse; colonialism made it worse before that.

⊘ JOHN LANE, *also commenting on the qualities of mind that give rise to megatechnology, says:* Blake was mentioned earlier this afternoon, and Blake, like Jung, divided human capabilities into four parts. He saw that the dominant part was the intellect, and he invented a mythological figure for that called Urizen. With amazing perception he saw that the intellect was always the cuckoo in the nest. The problem with the intellect is its arrogance, its hubris. I find offensive in our culture the male domination, the male concern with intellect, analysis, reduction, those things which are extraordinarily important but which have ranged out of proportion and become the disease. The antidote to megatechnology is not more analysis, intellectualism, or reductionism, but something quite different from it, which is the sacramental imagination.

⊘ *This comment liberates a flock of suggestions that we conduct ourselves differently, however briefly, that we seal the discussion with some kind of impromptu ritual.*

MARIA MIES: I have a problem with calling this one form female and the other form masculine. We all need to be critical of what is happening. Although it is boring we still have not really come to a consensus, so I would not like to have a kind of ritual which pretends as if we had. I'm very touchy with regard to these false harmonies.

⊙ *Despite Maria's reasonable objection, the group did go out in the courtyard to engage in the simplest of rituals: forming a circle, holding hands, and passing a squeeze from hand to hand clockwise around the circle while a bemused Teddy Goldsmith looked on.*

Chapter 12

Concluding Dialogue

☺ *The import of these discussions was serious, not unlike having a fascinating roundtable discussion of mutually assured destruction or nuclear winter. There was a sense in which the form belied the content. There was such a grand sweep of what certainly seemed to me to be bad news and worse trends that it's a wonder we didn't all run gibbering to our rooms after a couple of days listening and talking. Some participants' lives—particularly those directly touching the Earth—kept them grounded. Others of us were really suffering from technological civilization as much as any other creatures.*

The final session begins with JERRY MANDER*'s invitation to several people who haven't spoken at very great length to take the opportunity to share whatever they wish. This unleashes some passions and responses that rise from personal depths. After these stunning comments, the session returns to a more detached mode of conversation, with some tying-up of the loose ends of thoughts.*

CLIFFORD COBB *begins by sharing with the group the emotional basis for his reticence about participating in the conference discussions:* Certain kinds of language are permitted, and if you don't speak the authorized language there are no words. *He invokes dream imagery of suffocation and recalls a truly terrible time in his past when he was feeling suicidal:* It was tied up with both a sense of hopelessness about the world and a sense of hopelessness about myself. I've had difficulty throughout my life separating those two issues.

I understand a kind of rage that comes from being a fatherless man. I think the world is full of fatherless men who are full of rage, unaware of it and taking it out on the world, either by inventing new forms of technology or by never discussing their innermost concerns. So much of what I have seen in Progressive movements and in my own life has been about spreading poison without intending to, doing it in the name of doing good. But the well is poisoned at the source.

It seems to me, then, that civilization is based upon the rage of fatherless men, the rage being directed outward, never focused inward long enough to locate its origins. Along with that rage, there's a pain and a failure ever to earn one's father's love, and a pain of living in a world that is controlled, a world in which feelings cannot arrive. All of the competition that men engage in is connected with this as well. We are proving ourselves constantly. This competition exists not only in the capitalist marketplace that we love to denounce, but among ourselves just as much.

The technologies we are concerned about are like the shadows on the wall in Plato's cave, the outer manifestation of what's going on inside us. To look at the technologies themselves, the things that we have produced, is almost a distraction. I don't think that the technology is inside us, but something inside us is manifested in these waves of technology. All of this seems to me to be tied to a mass psychology of suicide, especially with nuclear weapons, which haven't disappeared. All of the technology that we're talking about seems to be a technology of death to the extent that it is suffocating us and is intended to avoid feeling, to avoid life, and so is a form of dying. The demons seem to me much greater than any of the particular technologies that we're looking at.

⊘ JOHN LANE *also speaks of the soul-wounding character of some modern institutions, then raises the hope that if we can begin healing our split consciousness, a beautiful and worthy technology might emerge:* It's in those years of childhood that each one of us in this room, with a few exceptions, has been branded. We take this branding, this virus, with us, and we are the disease; we are ourselves the poisoned well. Universal education is presented as beneficent, but actually it's lethal. It's in those tragic years that children learn to denigrate their own creativity, their poetic, imaginative, sacramental life. They are taught to value matter rather than mind, to value analysis rather than creativity, to consider the part, the specialist element rather than the whole, the human rather than the natural. It all becomes part of their bloodstream, the nature of their thinking. A tragic split between the skeptical intellect and the imagination within the psyche is the result. This didn't characterize pre-Renaissance society. If you really want to see the outward manifestation of our branded souls, look at the modern cities of the world, with their gridlike buildings and totally dehumanized surfaces. Then compare them with cities like Siena, or the old medieval cities of Europe, which were organic and livable and coherent within their own terms. Or compare Chartres with Heathrow—that is the mirror of our souls. I don't think there will be any fundamental change to technology until the split in consciousness that opened with the Newtonian and Cartesian revolutions of thought has been healed.

There was one contribution over the last two days that moved me most deeply. That was when we were all silent and heard the bird; the bird had been singing, probably for hours, but we had all been so busy talking we didn't hear the bird until that moment of silence. In that wonderful moment, we listened to the Other; we were silent and it entered into the room. That bird, as a symbol of the richer and larger perspectives that we associate with soul, has to enter our hearts. We have to start with ourselves; we have to release the bird in ourselves, encourage and nurture it.

Then we might see the emergence of a rhapsodic technology, where the sacramental and the instrumental were conjoined in the kind of marriage you see in the buttresses and vaults at Chartres. That is allied to something more than the utilitarian. Impossible as it may seem to us today, this kind of rhapsodic technology might someday replace utilitarian, dehumanized technology, which is actually an emanation of our own souls. So we have to start with ourselves in this long process. That was why I said at the first meeting that the antidote to technology is poetry.

Leavening the mood somewhat, JERRY MANDER *says:* Maybe I'm just a bad-news junkie, but these kinds of meetings always give me hope and encouragement. In the context of all the delusion, misrepresentation, and denial, the truth is energizing.

HELENA NORBERG-HODGE *avows that one can't postpone engagement with the world pending one's individuation or enlightenment. She recommends activism as a tonic:* Saying that we have to start with ourselves can lead to a sense that until I've got my inner peace in order, I should not be an activist and working in the world. A change in the social and political framework shapes the self; we can't see ourselves in isolation. We have to start doing the inner work and the outer political work simultaneously. How can I presume to have inner peace if I'm surrounded by competition, pollution, and escalating violence? And if, through my economic choices as a consumer and taxpayer, I actually contribute to that violence, how can I speak of peace?

SULAK SIVARAKSA *offers a philosophical appreciation of what we have heard:* This morning is very, very important. Although we learned a great deal in the last two days, information and knowledge you can get from books. I have learned that slow is beautiful, silence is also beautiful, and smile is beautiful. In discussions like this we should smile more and then, in silence, breathe. I'm very grateful to Clifford. Speaking as a Buddhist, despair is Dukkha, and many of us intellectuals avoid this, but once you acknowledge that the suffering, the fear, the anger, greed, delusion are in us, once you acknowledge it, and understand it and breathe in happily, then they will all go. When I was a famous barrister in a naughty world, a Siamese monk taught me, "The more you breathe in happily, mindfully, anger will go," and then the poisoned well will become fresh water; and then you connect with friendship. In the Buddhist context, the best, outside ourselves, is friendship, because the friend could become your other self, the voice of conscience. We need friends who challenge us, to remind us, and then we become more humble and then we can change the information to knowledge and then change knowledge to wisdom, because wisdom is understanding, and wisdom leads then to love and compassion, the two side by side. We may not change the world tomorrow, but I think we can make ourselves better, so I'm fairly hopeful.

⊚ DAVID KORTEN *acknowledges the vacuity at the core of the situations we decry, a kind of spiritual debasement of human existence, then goes on to some megabusiness reportage that portrays a world financial system whirling mindlessly out of control:* Behind so many of the issues being discussed here, and certainly the technology issues, there's a fundamental loss of sense of purpose, of meaning in living, and of what it means to be human. My own explorations led me to focus on the extent to which our basic institutional structures are fundamentally alienating. Once you become alienated from life, you become alienated from the consequences of technology. Most difficult is trying to understand the inherent nature, the dynamics of the system, and why it leads to that outcome.

The change that's taking place in the whole institutional system is perhaps the most rapid and complex in history. Few of us are even aware that it's happening. The changes are partly driven by technology, but the technology is also driven by the system in which it's embedded. We do have to understand that system. We cannot hope to change the technology or use the technology without changing the system as well. That implies a fundamental change in human consciousness, regaining a much deeper sense of who we are.

The system is on autopilot; there's no one in control. The decisions that are made are totally detached from the consequences. That's key to understanding it. A lot of it has to do with money. The separation of money from values and the fact that the institutions of our society have organized themselves around money. We talk about growth: The more money we create, we think, the better off we are. Absurdly, we even talk about it as creating wealth. Money is a claim on wealth, but it is not wealth. Those who control money replicate it. The shift in equity has come about by moving all the rewards away from the people who produce real worth, to those who are simply playing the money game. The system is shifting power from those who produce wealth to those who are simply extracting wealth, and it's detaching control from those people who have an inherent interest in place, in community, to those who live in a world detached.

The changes in the system that are taking place are being created by an ideology linked to class interest. In the United States it's not even named. Some observers are saying that the power is shifting to the small, and to the local, that more and more employment is in small enterprises, as large firms are breaking up. That's true in a sense, but it's important to be aware of the nature of the relationship. The big firms are shedding jobs at an enormous rate. From 1980 to 1993 the U.S. Fortune 500 firms decreased their total jobs by 4.4 million. Does that mean they're really getting smaller or less powerful? This suggests not: The same firms have increased their sales by 1.4 times, have increased their assets by 2.3 times, and have increased their chief executive officers' compensation 6.1 times!

The monopolization and concentration of power is reflected in a number of ways. Of the largest 100 economies in the world, fifty are corporations. We talk about free markets, but those fifty largest economies are centrally planned.

Economists define a market as highly monopolistic if five firms in an industry account for 50 percent or more of the sales. In a recent article in the *Economist*, the following industries were all characterized as having five firms controlling more than 50 percent of the whole global market: consumer durables, automotives, electronic components, steel, airlines, aerospace. Another three industries in which the top five firms control more than 40 percent of the markets—oil, computers, and media —show strong monopolistic tendencies.

What's happening with downsizing is that you try to cut your core corporation down to the absolute minimum so you're minimizing your obligations and long-term commitments to people. The central focus is on finance, technology, and markets; that's where you get your control. You contract out everything else, so you can squeeze your contractors for every dollar. They have to go out and hire people part-time and externalize the social and environmental costs of their production to the maximum. Through the continuing process of mergers and acquisitions, concentration is becoming greater. The whole antitrust concept is almost completely forgotten.

There are strategic alliances among those core corporations. The big companies agree to share markets and technologies. These are unstable alliances, though. It's a state of quasi-war, while managing the conflict through alliances. That all takes place within the dynamic of the changes in the financial system that push it to demand ever greater short-term returns. More and more decisions are made entirely by computers—based purely on data about historical price movements—and are totally divorced from the actual values of the firms in question.

The people who are managing corporations are themselves trapped by the financial system. They don't plan for the long term—they push to externalize every possible cost. And if you don't, you're going to be bought out or fired. People in the financial system are making massive amounts of money and are themselves evaluated on short-term performance. If they take into account any nonfinancial values, they're out.

⊘RICHARD SCLOVE *asks:* Given that there are some good people in the corporate world, why don't they argue for regulation and politically advocate a system which allows them to be more ethical?

⊘ *Says* DAVID KORTEN: Not many of them have the full picture themselves. The point you raise is underscored by a recent *Fortune* article about top managers who are downsizing and how they come to hate their jobs. They used to be building and creating. Now they're tearing down, they're firing their friends. There were stories about the despair and the depression, about people who can't sleep at night, executives who are getting incoherent in meetings, and experiencing psychological breakdown. You have to pay them outrageous sums in order to focus their attention purely on stockholding so that they will pirate other firms and destroy their friends' lives. We can't just say to executives, "You have to be more ethical." What we can say is, "You're a human being and we share this common problem of our species on a global scale; you see what has happened, this is what we see as why; join with us in changing the system, setting a new paradigm." It's the difference between hope and despair; I have to hope that it's possible.

⊘JOHN MOHAWK: In the middle of the last century, we reached

monopoly capitalism and it didn't work out; it sounds as though we're going round in a circle. So what happens in the long run?

⊘DAVID KORTEN: If it continues on its present course I think the whole thing collapses. We're seeing the social and environmental disintegration. Both are driven by the economic system. From the early process of enclosure, to the process of downsizing, there's less and less place for people. The key is to bring about a change in consciousness; part of this is to understand these institutional dynamics, but the other part is metaphysical: a rediscovery of our spiritual nature and of our connection with the Earth and with one another.

⊘GUSTAVO ESTEVA *suggests that power-from-above may still mystify, but that the actual power to effect change is in the hands of the multitude living on the ground:* Perhaps we are talking of a fundamental change of the nature of power. The metaphor of the king as the person who has the power is still widely used. Most people see the power as something up there when it isn't there any longer.

Just a few months after the Sandinistas took power, after Somoza, we were discussing how to organize the distribution of basic staples. The Sandinistas wanted to use a small, bureaucratic institution created by Somoza. We were suggesting to use all the cadres of the revolution existing in every block in every village. My argument was that power was not at the top but in the hands of the people. The power of Somoza came from the United States, the money of Somoza and his friends, and the National Guard. The minute the Sandinistas entered Somoza's bunker, the money of Somoza was already in Miami and the National Guard had been dissolved and the United States was no longer behind Nicaragua's government. But they thought they had that power in their hands. They didn't understand that the power was in the hands of the people. The Sandinista commanders decided to use the bureaucratic apparatus to distribute food, saying that they cannot trust the people. That was the first tragedy of the Sandinistas.

A friend at Harvard Business School says that Watson, the president of IBM, was the last manager with any real power. When he was offered the possibility to manufacture the first electronic computer and he refused it, IBM required ten years to recover from that decision. Accordingly, Harvard Business School devised organizational systems in which no person in a corporation has any real power; they cannot really do things, and power is the possibility of doing something. In corporations, they are playing the game with the rules dictated to them, which now seem to have gone beyond human control.

Maria Mies tells a story that resonates with Gustavo's—when it comes to matters of survival and the practice of mutual aid the wellsprings of energy and creativity are emphatically neither experts nor institutions: In any case I do not believe that those involved in it at the top will get a chance to change it. Those who really have to survive and who take their own power in their hands, they are the ones who give us the new ideas.

Here is an example: Some very poor women in Brazil came together in a workshop at the U.N. Conference on Environment and Development. First of all they said who they were, what they did, the kind of work they did. Then they started analyzing that system. They said this development is nonsense, it doesn't bring us anything. This world market, we don't want it anymore. When they came out with their new vision of a new society, of a new economy, they asked, "Why don't we start exchanging among ourselves? And also exchange between the women in the city and the countryside?" They have already started negotiating with the trade unions. The remarkable thing was that they were not just an isolated group. They did know about the world economy and they did know about, for example, the Chipko women. [*Note:* Chipko is an Indian village-based movement that takes its name from the Hindi word for "to hug." Villagers, mostly women, interposed their bodies between trees and chainsaws to prevent logging of their watershed.]

That means there is a way and there is hope. In those areas where there is no welfare state, that is where the creativity is, and they don't plow through metaphysics and spirituality, which is rather part of their daily lives. We should share such experiences with each other, be activists, and be involved with such grassroots movements. So it's not something that leads to despair, but to hope. This is happening all over the world.

Vandana Shiva wishes, in effect, that Westerners would mind their own business, tend to their own Götterdämmerung which is having such catastrophic impacts on the peasants and villagers of the world—the multitude who would be happy to continue in their time-tested lifeways: We are talking about a very deep civilizational crisis of the West. The sectors of society that haven't yet been fully destroyed could well be the reserves of healing. However I find myself having to deal more and more with the globalization of the financial system. There's no peasant in India who can say, "My life will carry on exactly the same" when the transfer of all price structures, resource rights, everything into the hands of the corporations is being facilitated. You get all the good people of the West wanting to solve this problem, but they can't solve it internally because it's deeply entrenched. So they want to solve human rights in China; they want to solve patriarchy in India; they want to sort out ethical investment issues, which adds to the exporting imperative for Third World communities that once had self-sustaining economies. So how do we get Northern activists to start fundamentally restructuring internally rather than naïvely becoming the instrument of globalization and destroying the last remnants of sane society?

🔊 SIGMUND KVALOY *questions David Korten as to the stability of the global financial system he has described and wonders whether some market downturn might not accelerate through the system, leading to a worldwide depression that would severely impede the kinds of grassroots initiatives Maria Mies has described.* DAVID KORTEN *responds,* "It's a house of cards."

🔊 MARIA MIES *offers a very sensible caution against irresponsibly mongering doom:* One has to beware of totalizing the disaster. Life will go on. If you spread this gloom, you cannot do anything against the despair of young people. People create not only hope but possibilities and power of themselves. We are in a framework of thinking which is not totally co-opted; it cannot be totally co-opted, as this financial one, because our systems of exchange, our systems of survival, contain this element of hope which cannot be co-opted. We have to make sure this co-optation doesn't happen, because we are still there.

🔊 STEPHANIE MILLS *ventures to speak a word for ecocentricity:* Our context here has been very anthropocentric: In confronting technology and globalization we are of necessity speaking with reference to our own species and its activities. There's been an underlying assumption that peasant society, which domesticates landscapes, is primal society. It grieves me because hunter-gatherer society was more nearly the way of human life that could maintain an equilibrium with ecosystems. Projecting peasant society forward implies maintaining a status quo in terms of the territories of domesticated communities and wild communities. The nondomesticated, living community is the ultimate ground of the intelligence of renewal; and for reasons of our own proliferation by domestication we've distorted that information, that community— it's been what we do as a species.

🔊 TEDDY GOLDSMITH *voices a definition of control as being immanent in living systems rather than something that can be exerted over them:* The key issue is loss of control. Biotechnology, the information industry, all our industry, whatever it may be—nuclear, chemical—everything is out of control. Government is out of control—we don't have democracy any more; politicians and governments do more or less what they like.

In the context of living things, what control means is maintaining the integrity, the basis and stability, of society and ecosystems in time and space—the opposite, in short, of what we're doing today. Individuals do what they like; they're interested in the short term—they're not interested in society or the ecosystem as a whole.

� ☺ ☺

☺ *As in 1993, the last task of the conference was the further development and refinement of a series of questions to serve as a tool for the systemic assessment of technologies. Drawing on notes from the previous conference, and some material drafted at Dartington by an ad-hoc committee, the group ran with the challenge: There were koan-like one-liners, questions about how to question technology, assertions of the true conservatism of Neo-Luddites, and a certain amount of strategizing as well. What follows is a severely condensed (as it had to be) rendition of that last loping time we had together in conversation.*

VANDANA SHIVA *dives right into the question of tactics:* We want to look for the points of action and intervention. That necessarily relates to community issues, because you can't act on technology, you act on societies.

☺ JERRY MANDER *returns to the foundational idea—looking at technology per se is pioneering strategic work:* For a society that has always looked at technology as part of a movement or part of a social dimension rather than as a separate subject, it's important to look at some of technology's intrinsic characteristics: whether it increases the speed or scale of the system, for example. So there's value in evaluating technology as an issue in itself. We need to illuminate the qualities—and politics—inherent to technologies.

☺ TEDDY GOLDSMITH *begins elaborating criteria for technologies. A flurry of other trenchant comments follows:* A technology that is not extremely cheap is totally irrelevant to the solution of the problems facing most people today. I once saw a film about a modern hospital in Tanzania that was brimful of the latest technological equipment—but as pointed out by the commentator, the entire health budget of the country was insufficient to maintain it. That was some years ago. Today, as the highly competitive global economy gets underway, there is likely to be even less money available for maintaining that hospital. God knows whether it is still functioning. I am told that there is a similar hospital in Ethiopia, that is now inhabited only by bats.

Even the setting up of *biogas* [a combustible gas produced by fermentation of organic waste] plants in India, which is seen as the most benign possible technology, has caused a lot of problems for the poor. The reason is that cow dung, which was once available to everybody for free, is now being turned into a commodity which not everyone can afford.

⌕SANDY IRVINE: There's a real danger in that. The environmentally destructive alternatives are very frequently the cheaper ones; and the greener ones are the dearer.

⌕SIGMUND KVALOY: There is an inbuilt tendency in technology to try to arrest the world in accordance with its latest model—static, as all the earlier ones. Inevitably, this inspires both nature and human society to start off in a new direction, entirely unforeseeable by means of mechanistic models.

⌕RICHARD SCLOVE: The political dimensions of technology should be a first-order question, because undemocratic technologies are a severe barrier to deciding what other things matter and acting on them effectively.

⌕BETH BURROWS: We need to state the conditions under which a technology will be disallowed.

⌕MARIA MIES *challenges the notion that technology is somehow an autonomous force:* I was shocked by Andrew Kimbrell's statement that "technology is a primary factor of social change" in our lives, as if technology was the only political, historical, and social subject. Who then could change this if technology is doing everything? In this model "it" is obviously the political subject, and we as human beings have disappeared. In totalizing technology like that, are you not doing the work of those who promote these technologies, and eliminating the human being as a political subject? Technology is the expression of social relations. It is not neutral.

⌕JERRY MANDER *returns to an issue raised by Michiel Schwarz, among others:* I disagree with the idea that you cannot know the secondary effects of technology. The business people who research, develop, and market new technologies spend fortunes of money figuring out every nuance of their impacts, the good news and bad, because they're trying to figure out every possibility for profit. The trouble is they only advertise—or even admit—the virtuous aspects, as we have seen from the tobacco, oil, chemical, and other industries. The bad news is kept silent.

⊘VANDANA SHIVA *notes that the current generation of megatechnological wolves have donned environmentally acceptable sheep's clothing:* While we have to deal, in an abstract way, with the continuities of technology in modern industrial systems, it's more important to focus on the discontinuities. As the cultural markings of the social and ecological impact of an older generation of technologies start to become a social concern, a new generation of technologies is unleashed, with new markings that seem to be addressing the public concern.

If you focus on the new technologies, whether it's the information technologies or the biotechnologies, "dirty," in the old sense of environmental pollution, is disappearing and a false kind of "clean" is getting created. That's the reason 99 percent of the environmentalists of the world are welcoming genetic engineering and so many community organizers are welcoming the personal computer, because there's a façade of autonomy.

One reason these technologies are making such massive inroads is because by the time they connect with the consumer, they are working out to be cheaper; there might be subsidies down the line, but they are not capital-intensive on the face of it. "Mega" is definitely not the scale —it's into the viruses, into the bacteria, into the microchip, and its "mega-ness" is in the nexus.

The old technology problems are already known by the past critique. The new technologies are being offered after a fashion that looks like what we want.

⊘RICHARD DOUTHWAITE *broadens the inquiry in a useful way:* We're trying to get a set of criteria so that we can assess not just the effects of technology on the status quo, but of any change. Perhaps we need a rule of thumb. Gandhi's was, "What are the effects of any change on the last man or the weakest individual in our society?"

⊘JOHN MOHAWK*'s neighborhood is peopled by techno-refuseniks whose basic assumption seems to be that technology is a dubious proposition at best. How to judge it? It's a question of right relationship with nature:* I live next to the most atechnological community in North America—they're located about ten miles from the Indian reservation. The more traditional Indians are philosophically dug in against the idea of technology. And the Amish assume the minimum amount of extended human intervention in the world is how it should be because they're pretty sure that it's probably a bad idea to begin with.

Every bit of technology distances human beings, human society, from nature. Even a stick used as a tool does that. Of course some technologies do it more than others, and there's a place at which it breaks the circle of revival, breaks the bonds between humans and nature, and it is no longer a productive thing.

⊘ ANDREW KIMBRELL *reasserts his sense that technology is a political regime that undermines our ability to be responsible for our actions, and that it saps other vital human qualities as well:* We might knock down the Berlin Wall, get rid of apartheid, but if we're still under the totalitarian regime of technologies we have not really achieved liberation. We can't take responsibility for the technologies that run our lives. I turn on the lights, but I don't know whether or not the electricity's coming from a nuclear power plant. I don't know what they're teaching my kids, but school is compulsory. I don't know where my taxes go, I don't know what's in the air I'm breathing, I don't know what's in the food I eat. I'm completely powerless because megatechnologies have centralized all of our basic functions and so we can't control our lives. That's totalitarianism. The fact that we don't seek liberation from that just shows the degree of technology's entrenchment and our entrancement. We have become servile in a technological state, and we don't even know it. We need to foster awareness of this technological oppression, and that will lead to the historic struggle against it.

Another two points concerning the impact of technologies: First, technologies have destroyed the sense of hearing. We seem to have given up the fight over noise pollution: Machines create havoc with hearing. The daily cacophony of traffic, factory, construction, TV, and other media is oppressive. Overall, machines almost never make beautiful sounds. Nature is full of them. The second point is about craft: Technology's principle objective is convenience. It constantly seeks to make work easy. This exacts a hidden cost. Anybody who's ever tried to master a craft knows that the difficulty of the thing is what teaches discipline, hope, and accomplishment. Overcoming this difficulty shows how much you care whether you are a musician, artist, or activist. By gaining convenience we lose craft.

⊘ CHELLIS GLENDINNING *'s concerns center on technology's bearing on the psyche:* I'm concerned about the relationship between technology and psychological dysfunction — in technology's invention, production, manufacture, and disposal, and in its effects. I'm concerned about the relationship between technology and the very structure of our thinking. And I'm concerned with the relationship between technology and the beliefs of people and now, in the postmodern world, our beliefs about beliefs.

⊘TEDDY GOLDSMITH *wonders why these criteria wouldn't be ignored by the powers that be. He extols the virtues of gerontocracy and of a cultural coherence that can withstand the incursion of technological anathemas:* Drawing up a list of criteria that new technologies would have to satisfy in order to be acceptable is a good idea, but these criteria would have to be pretty tough, and the corporations would never accept them. Attempts have been made to prevent nuclear proliferation, but they have failed miserably. Attempts have also been made to control the biotechnology industry, but they have failed even more dismally. Today, one can say that the biotechnology industry does exactly what it likes. There are no effective controls on its activities, even though those activities could be disastrous for life on this planet.

Embeddedness of the technologies in human relations, conviviality, meaning, knowledge, the question of power, of compatibility with beliefs: All these are criteria more or less satisfied when the context is a communal economy, and they cannot be met in the context of a global economy.

In the traditional community, the technologies serve the power, largely of the elders, over the young. This power is essential, because if the old cannot exert power over the young, the culture will have no continuity. So it's legitimate power. Conviviality is totally absent in the global economy. People complain that the things we do no longer have any meaning. Well, if you're working for your family and your community, doing things that make sense like producing food, making artifacts that are useful to you in your daily life, rather than working for some massive organization producing parts for some strange apparatus, then your life has meaning again.

In the traditional community, technology is accepted only as it fits in with your system of beliefs and knowledge. The Japanese samurai couldn't accept the musket: The musket was introduced by the Portuguese, and the Japanese couldn't take it because it interfered with their system of beliefs. They couldn't countenance an instrument which enabled a six-year-old child to kill a samurai who'd been training in the martial arts since infancy. Muskets did not fit in with the Japanese view of things.

⊘ANDREW MCLAUGHLIN *also speaks an ecocentric piece, and a lovely word for a touchstone of virtue:* It seems important to reject emphatically the concept of the environment. Whenever you talk about "environment," you automatically slip into an uncritical anthropocentrism. "The" environment is a fiction. There are as many environments as there are centers of life. We are, for example, part of the trees' environment.

"Flourishing," I would say: Let life flourish! including both humans and the rest of nature. We humans have gone too far and are crowding out the rest of life. If that's unfair, what ethically follows? First you stop doing harm. That's the beginning of questioning technologies: Do they do harm? If so, then stop them, resist them, unwind them, break them down. Then, concurrently with ceasing to harm, which may be a project that carries through to our great-grandchildren, what we'd like to do is restore. Restoration technologies become something that you might want, cautiously, to endorse.

⊘JOHN LANE: One of the most harmful effects of technology is ugliness.

⊘MARTHA CROUCH *tells a story whose punchline is a good criterion for technology assessment:* At a conference at a camp in Kentucky last month I was in charge of feeding 150 people for a week. People were complaining about a lot of things, one of which was that the water was highly chlorinated. The camp manager said, "We get our water directly out of the creek, and we just upped the chlorine because there's *Giardia* present." I wondered whether to buy bottled water. Someone offered to get a filter for the water machine. So we put it on the machine, the water tasted great, and everybody forgot about the creek.

That technology allowed us to be more comfortable. If we had had to drink that chlorinated water—and it was truly awful—or if we had all gotten really sick with *Giardia*, or we had had enough power to act, we would have figured out how to make the creek more healthy and everything would have benefited. The fact is that that technology—even if it had been made by a communal, local economy by meaningful work—acted as a shield between us and what was happening in the world. So my question is, "What does the technology allow us to ignore?"

⊘TEDDY GOLDSMITH: In such situations technology merely serves to accommodate such undesirable trends rather than reversing them, and that is what most of our technological devices are used for. Mahatma Gandhi once said that people fall sick because they eat badly and do not take exercise. To take modern medicine may make us feel better, but that merely encourages us to go on eating badly and not taking exercise.

⊘SATISH KUMAR *alludes to the extremism of megatechnology and reminds us of Schumacher's proposal of a more modest, accessible technology:* We might consider E. F. Schumacher's principle of the disappearing middle. Because when we have new technology, certain intermediate tools which you can use, and can repair, tend to disappear. So you are left with either a sickle or a great combine harvester, and nothing in the middle. For this reason we need intermediate and appropriate technology.

⊘ PAUL BLAU *reminds us that if tools are not neutral, neither are societies, and that certain technologies would not stay revoked without a sea change in the societies currently dependent on the power of their tools:* I want to draw your attention to one fact which haunts me very much: that you can't dis-invent the engines of technologies, which means you must have a long-term perspective about the impacts of technology on society. If we can't dis-invent technologies, they exist as long as this civilization exists, somewhere, maybe hidden, but there. It boils down to the problem that when we discuss the question of technology, we have to go back to the program of an entirely different view of life and of society. To try to tame technology is not enough.

⊘ JERRY MANDER's *question illuminates the way megatechnology works to entrap us in an ahistorical present:* Does technology cause the loss of a sense of historical time? Sense of time, of continuity with the past, is different, I think, from the acceleration of tempo.

⊘ MICHIEL SCHWARZ *also talks about the solipsism of experience within megatechnological surrounds:* Perception has lots of layers. I want to mention these two: First, how does the technology affect perceptions of our needs? We think we need certain technologies and they become self-fulfilling, self-referential, and reinforcing. That is one of the points in Langdon Winner's early work; the autonomy of technology is not in the technology but in the perception that we need more of it, and that we cannot do without it. Second, because of technology, technology-based virtual realities are created that become so real that actual reality starts to mirror artificial reality.

⊘ ANDREW MCLAUGHLIN *suggests another reason that technology seems to render its users useless:* Technologies become opaque to us. We can't take them apart to see how they work. More and more, we can no longer repair things in our lives. We must throw them out when they stop working.

⊘ TEDDY GOLDSMITH *expands on the consequences of the opacity of megatechnologies:* We cannot adapt to the world that the new technologies are helping us to create. For instance, we are just not equipped biologically to contend with such things as chemicals and radioactive particles in our food. We have no means of directly apprehending such things. To find out if there is dioxin in the banana I am eating I would have to have it examined in a distant laboratory—at an exorbitant cost. Even if I could apprehend the presence of this poison in my banana I would not be able to understand the full implications of allowing it to enter my body—nor, for that matter, would my doctor, who has not been trained to do so.

⊘JOHN MOHAWK *suggests, pragmatically, that a full cost accounting of prospective technologies might reveal them as unprofitable and nip them in the bud:* We've only been successful in stopping megadevelopment projects on the basis of what their proponents cared about, not what we cared about. One of the things that is wrong with some specific technologies is that some are not cost-effective. That is an argument that will get their attention.

⊘VANDANA SHIVA *regards the synergy of megatechnology and global trade as a calculated effort to annihilate the self-reliance of persons and communities by monopolizing every aspect of economic life:* That integration of technology and commerce creates the system of modern-day slavery. It doesn't allow people to act: You can't give up your car because the supermarket is too far to walk. The disintegration of communal society and capacity is the outcome of a very carefully crafted integration of technologies in different sectors. The same company now selling the seeds is buying the crop, doing the processing, and the marketing.

⊘BETH BURROWS: . . . and taking the germ plasm, and donating to the favored environmental organizations.

⊘HELENA NORBERG-HODGE *points out that technologies now implicate citizens of the North in the destruction by proxy of lifeforms and lifeways around the world:* Modern technologies enable us to have an impact, completely unaware, on the other side of the world. Whether it's spraying DDT in your garden or pushing a few computer buttons, the separation between the agent and the impact is dramatic and dangerous. It leads to irresponsible acts. When our technological arms have become so long that we can't see what our hands are doing, we have created a situation which prevents responsibility, accountability, and compassion.

⊘ *Because the aim of this session is to develop some criteria for analyzing technology as a thing in itself and, secondarily, to propose actions that might follow on those analyses,* JERRY MANDER *offers this strategic counsel:* Very few groups have attempted consciously to identify all the full dimensions of the impacts of technology and to articulate a set of questions to clarify long-term thinking.

Strategy is difficult in a subject area like this, because we're not focusing on a specific issue. We're criticizing, challenging a whole world view. So it's not surprising, even if it is unfortunate, that not a single American environmental organization has a position on technology as an issue in itself.

While I agree with John Mohawk about reaching out to the opposition, they're the most difficult to reach. It's also important to work in the circles that you are part of.

At Public Media Center, when we approach a political problem or a campaign we start with the inner circle of people, those most likely to understand and support the cause. We convince and involve them first. Then we go out to the next circle, people who really don't understand what we're talking about but aren't against it. Finally, there's the circle of people who do understand the problem but oppose the campaign. They're the people we have to confront, more or less.

Another advertising precept is to start from where the audience is, not where you are. You don't start with what you know, you start with what they know, and you build a bridge to there and then from there. Accordingly, we should be raising the question of whether consumption is actually satisfying people. What people really want is peace, security, pleasure, family, spiritual contentment, and community. In essence, that's what *we're* "selling," but they don't know that. They think we're taking away what they want. So we have to make it clear that it's all the shiny new objects that are replacing, and undermining, the genuine sources of human satisfaction.

*⊘ A basic misunderstanding surfaces—*DAVID KORTEN *says he's on board for advocating an improved quality of life but not that we need to do away with technology.*

JERRY MANDER: There has been no proposal that we do away with all technology. Our discussion has been to illuminate what's good and what's bad about technology as a whole, and possibly about specific technologies. The issue of banning technologies is a next step.

⊘ SATISH KUMAR: Is there a perception out there that we are against technology as such? I am not against technology. But I am against megatechnology. Technology for profit is a wrong use of technology.

⊘ SULAK SIVARAKSA *brings his own clarity and experience to this discussion of making our arguments certain and conveying them to general audiences:* It does make sense for me that we convince ourselves, we are clear what is good, what is bad, what we should be critical of, what we should be aware of. These messages are intellectual at a high level, but once you are convinced you can make them into language, you can convince the people; and once you convince the people you are on the right track.

About six years ago they were going to build a wonderful technological advance, a beautiful sky train up to a distant city. The environmentalists and the university professors were very angry, but they didn't know what to do. They said species will disappear, the butterfly and so on. The government said, "No, the big company is ready, the contract is about to be signed." I said, "What about the people, and the Sacred Mountain?" They didn't know what I was talking about. That is, they did not understand about sacredness, so I had to bring in the monkhood. The monks want to preserve the sacredness of the mountain, and together the monks stopped the sky train which would be useful only to tourists.

This is a bit more concrete, but I'm pretty sure that in my area they realize now that technology, development, and progress aren't any help. Once we are convinced, they are convinced; but you must always have the spirit of tradition to help; that is the stronger part that we can use strategically to overcome something which is big and not very helpful to the people at large.

⊘ TEDDY GOLDSMITH *advocates a more oppositional stance toward technology if only to propound the truth that technology can't solve problems caused by a whole system gone wrong:* We have got to be Luddites for a host of reasons. One of them is that we cannot control technologies once they are introduced, and we will become ever less capable of doing so as the corporations that make use of them become more powerful and ever less controllable. Another reason is that technology does not provide a means of solving the sort of problems that confront us today, which are largely caused by the breakdown of natural systems like the family, the community, and the ecosystem. There is no gadgetry, however elaborate and sophisticated, that can bring together a family that has broken up or can restore the cultural pattern of a society that has disintegrated. Burglar alarms, armored cars, and the rest of the paraphernalia used for fighting crime do not help us address the real problem involved. Today's increasing crime rate is but a symptom of the breakdown of the family, the community, and our society in general. There are many other symptoms of the same problem, such as the high rate of drug addiction and alcoholism, increasing violence, and the growing incidence of many mental problems. If we are really to address the problem of crime, and at the same time all these other associated problems, we clearly must restore the family and the community. However, we can only do this by abandoning our present economic priorities, which no one in authority is willing to do.

Technology cannot provide us with a clean environment. Environmental technology is big business today. The term itself is very misleading; it includes waste disposal technology—which mainly consists of burying chemical and nuclear wastes in holes in the ground or dispersing them over the countryside via incinerators or cement kilns. The only

beneficiaries of this process are the chemical companies and the industries that generate the waste and, of course, the waste management companies, many of which are run by the Mafia. The only policy, as I have
already noted, is not to generate industrial wastes in the first place.

⊘ CLIFFORD COBB *points out that as conservatives of a sort, we Neo-Luddites wind up with some right-wing bedfellows:* Liberals and Progressives are
often more of a problem than Conservatives. True Conservatives have a
skepticism about progress that is the whole basis of their philosophy. For
example, many Fundamentalist Christians in America have a skepticism
about progress that does not exist among liberal Protestants and liberal
Democrats. My associates are often the most difficult to convince about
these ideas. Pat Buchanan, who ran for president as a Republican and is
somewhat of a fascist, just wrote a newspaper piece criticizing Conservatives for embracing progress. We need to recognize that the world is
more ambiguous than good guys and bad guys. The people we thought
of as friends in the past, the altruists, really are the most dangerous people in the world.

⊘ VANDANA SHIVA *suspects that although self-proclaimed critics of technology may be few, a fundamental objection to technological totalitarianism
is an underlying motive in much activism:* Technology has been made more
opaque than any other part of a destructive system. Technological
progress has become the ultimate justification. Whereas the Environmental Movement runs to hundreds of thousands of participants and is
in some ways part of the megatechnologies' structure, there aren't very
many technology critics save those around the table here. Still, if you
consider criticisms around dams, for instance, people give reasons like
the displacement of communities, but it's the ugliness of the technological structure that is the real mobilizing force for most activists. The
tribals, of course, are very clear that they don't want to move; but every
urban activist who joins an anti-dam campaign is basically intervening
in a technological shift.

⊘ SIGMUND KVALOY *addresses the subject of urbanization, a process he
regards as being neither inevitable, as many world figures claim, nor desirable
as a mode of existence:* Modern urbanization and technology are two
sides to the same coin. The Brundtland Report asserts that the future will
predominantly be urban—90 percent living in enormous megalopolises.
As though it were a natural law. But our deepest-thinking, most wide-
ranging ecologists, like Barry Commoner, George Borgström, Gösta
Ehrensvärd, Lewis Mumford, et al., have for thirty to forty years been
amassing data and analyses to show that if humankind is to survive, the
future must predominantly be a rural one. This fantastic culture that we

have invented in Europe and spread all over the world is a product of urban society; yet the cities or towns of Goethe, Schiller, and Beethoven were more like small villages in the countryside today. They cannot be compared to modern cities at all. You might even say that the culture we are so proud of might never have happened in an urban setting of the modern type.

⊘ JOHN MOHAWK *returns to the necessity of getting our message to groups other than the choir and urges readiness to seize strategic moments—like Chernobyl—where megatechnology's full consequences are disclosed. He also reveals himself to be free from idealism where human nature is concerned:* Our work has to reach those people who at this moment wouldn't have anything to do with us. We also need to find engineers, writers, or otherwise influential spokespersons in the media, people in the medical profession, people who are not thinking about any of this stuff, and get them to read it. The easy part is to get my friends to go along with this; the tougher part will be to get people in business and other areas to even consider that some of the things that we see might have some validity.

There is nothing in my experience that leads me to believe that people are basically good-hearted—they're good-hearted when they think it's good for them to be good-hearted. People can be persuaded if the arguments follow the sense of things that they understand. The biggest battle that we've won was with the nuclear power industries. We were skating up a glass hill, right up until the time that the Chernobyl accident happened. We had the communities out there, we had people blockading, going to jail, big movements; the students were on our side; the little grandmothers would carry flowers at parades against the new power plants; the women, the Indians, the minorities were there, all mobilized against the new plants which the utilities were still building like crazy.

When that Chernobyl accident happened, the people who were running that anti-nuclear movement started making a good, solid argument. They stampeded the financial community, contracts were canceled, the whole thing collapsed in months. You have to look for those openings and you have to exploit them—you even have to create them. Goodness and light against badness and evil isn't enough!

We're proposing to wage the most impossible fight anybody could have imagined: the fight against the major dream of the last 500 years of Western civilization.

⊘ BETH BURROWS *suggests that the fight might be more possible if we ourselves were living the solution with manifest delight:* I think we need to consider building our own small community, that is a joyful place, to be liv-

ing happily there and being attractive people. Perhaps in the Third World you don't need to do this because you still have communities, but we may need to do it as here as a model and to stop people from going to your communities to see what they're like, or to fix them.

⊙ TEDDY GOLDSMITH *opines that questioning technology is necessary but not sufficient, that the magnitude of the problems we confront demands a dramatic worldwide political devolution:* I do not think that an anti-technology movement by itself can provide the basis of a successful political movement. It has got to be part of something bigger than that. As I have intimated, to solve our problems we must move in exactly the opposite direction to that in which we are moving today. Political and economic policies must be reversed in just about every field. What we need to create is a network of largely self-sufficient, self-governing communities, loosely organized into larger social and political confederations. This is precisely what Mahatma Gandhi wanted for India. However, the best model for us is the Swiss Confederation. Until recently real power resided with the communes, only residual powers being delegated to the governments of the cantons and the Swiss Confederation itself. Unfortunately this system could not survive economic development, which by its very nature had to transfer power to the central government and the corporations.

My feeling is that the increasingly alienated members of the atomized society in which we live will yearn more and more for a community-based society. That is certainly the view of that remarkable man, Wendell Berry. He sees the conflict between the global economy and the local economy as being the main political issue of the next decades. Proponents of the latter, made up of those who have been marginalized by the global economy, must eventually become the majority. They should form a new political party, which should be above all the party of the community. There is no reason why such a party should not eventually come to power—that is if the normal electoral process is allowed to survive.

⊙ MARIA MIES *attests the value of unequivocal opposition to certain technologies and affirms the competence of ordinary people to make judgments about technology, given sufficient information. Hers is a fine simplicity:* Ten years ago when we started our movement against genetic engineering and reproductive technology we started asking, "Why do we need all this?" Technology is meant to solve problems; the promoters of this technology promised they could solve the problems of hunger, disease, infertility, and so on. We analyzed and proved that this is rubbish: Technology cannot solve these problems. There are ways and means to solve these problems without technology. We said "no" to this technology—radically no; and that has been the correct strategy so far. Those who want to promote these technologies, they have these kinds of discussions on the bad and good sides of technologies all the time. This is not our job. We have to say "no" to this. We were able, then, to mobilize many people and have coalitions: with trade unions, with the church people, the students, the peasant women; and the ethical question is alive in people's minds and hearts. Although as lay people we do not understand everything—we had only the literature which any citizen can read—that is enough to form a judgment about whether we need these technologies. And we came to the conclusion that it is not us as people who need gene and reproductive technology, but capitalist corporate interests who need new areas of investment and new markets so that "growth" can go on.

Biotechnology, nuclear technology, and computer technology are war technologies. They are not problem-solving technologies, they are problem-creating technologies; that is why we don't want them. I'm against these problem-causing technologies.

We have also to look at other technologies and ask not only qualitative questions but also quantitative ones. For instance, the car: How many cars do we need is the question, not only if you are against any car or any kind of improvement in them.

The main thing is that people should be informed, as we informed ourselves. Then the acceptance of these problem-creating technologies would be undermined. I don't want to waste any more time on these pro and con questions.

⊘JERRY MANDER *also talks about the ethical and educative value of the "radical no":* I personally am very comfortable with Maria's position. *Four Arguments for the Elimination of Television* is still selling quite briskly fourteen years after I wrote it, which I take as meaning that there are a lot of people out there who don't find the idea of eliminating some technologies to be all that alarming. Sometimes taking an extreme position is the most positive approach: First of all, it's what you actually believe. Secondly, you bring to light a community of other people who might share that belief. Third, you move the argument in your direction; even the compromisers have to deal with your position. You broaden the spectrum of discussion. In my experience, I found that the idea of the elimination of television had to be included in a lot of debates from then on. So I'd be willing to say no to several technologies right now.

⊘HELENA NORBERG-HODGE *provides an eloquent summation of the sys-*

temic causes of our civilizational problems and a plea to persist in our effort to articulate the connections between science, technology, economic growth, and the raft of human and ecological problems now plaguing the world: It's so important for us to distinguish between the work of opposition—including a clear analysis of the monolithic globalizing process—and the work of finding a multitude of sustainable solutions in specific locations. We need to look at Western science, technology, and economic growth as one system—one system which claims to be the formula for the whole world. It's true that it's almost sacrilegious to talk about technology, but science is the real heart of the problem. Western science has become an unspoken world religion. The blind respect for narrow expertise, the fear of looking at change, relationships, and connections because you can't be waffly or unclear is a major consequence of reductionist science. We need to continue the discussion, which started long ago, about the divided, compartmentalized mind that our society imposes, even on young children.

Millions of people on this planet have not yet undergone the process of "education" that leads to a loss of vision and a consequent loss of economic control. However, development and globalization are pulling more and more people in. The majority end up in shanty towns.

There is an inextricable link between specialization and the large-scale, economic production that's leading to a mass culture, a global monoculture. While specialization shapes the compartmentalized mind of the individual, economic specialization promoted as comparative advantage encourages every individual, every local community, every nation state to specialize its production. Greater and greater specialized education and specialized production lead to an increased dependence on the highly exploitative global economy.

People keep saying, "We know the problem. We've heard enough. Let's get on with solutions and do something." Yet the understanding of the connections is perhaps poorer than ever before. In other words, an understanding of the root causes of the vast number of problems we face is lacking. It looks as though ozone depletion, climate change, unemployment, and increased cancer rates are all separate problems when, in fact, the economic system—which promotes ever greater industrialization and trade, and competition—lies behind it all. Once this is recognized, it becomes quite clear that solutions lie in economic diversification and decentralization. There are thousands of local projects that are rebuilding local economies and communities with great success. These tend to be win/win strategies—leading to reduced pollution, secure employment, and increased community ties.

Conclusion

Every time I attempt to put my finger on the reason why we should turn away from technology-as-matrix-and-answer, the reasons are either so many that I wind up with a cloud of horror stories and appalling prospects suffocating me or so ineffable that I find myself groping to name the qualities of life, mind, and spirit that seem to be going extinct in this *fin-de-siècle*. I may have stumbled into the newly fashionable fuzzy logic, or possibly just succumbed to apocalyptic hysteria. More likely, burning in my animal heart, the abhorrence of a world where everything is humanmade, for sale, captively bred, under "ecosystem management," and a society where everything that is not expressly regulated is no longer possible, cannot be voiced but in a howl.

Our species evolved on Earth over millions of years in natural surroundings. Sounds self-evident in our post-Darwinian time, but we don't take being organisms very seriously. However, technological, mechanical, and fossil-fuel advances, as well as synthetic chemistries, have for the last 250 years or so functioned in lieu of a biological base for the expansion of the modern enterprise.

An exponentially growing population dependent not only on non-renewable resources but on "ecosystem services"—soil fertility, O_2–CO_2-exchange—is in trouble long before the last drop is sucked out of the last oil well, though. No end of technological fixes—like the Green Revolution, nuclear energy "too cheap to meter," fiercer antibiotics, a hydrogen economy, genetic engineering, and nanotechnology—have been offered as the next steps, the latest solutions to the problems that inevitably followed on the attempts throughout history to transcend our organic essence and to treat the Earth as an economy rather than an ecosystem. It's an epistemological problem. However new the technology, it's still more of the same misunderstanding. Thus we find ourselves at a singular moment: Not that civilizations haven't collapsed before, leaving deserts in their wake, but because this civilization is now global, there's nowhere left to turn. Except away from the mechanical to the organic, to restore what we can of culture and place. Or, in a final, climactic techno-fantasy, to designate other solar systems as Enterprise Zones. Bizarre as it may seem, the global market is poised to lift off, by technological means, leaving denuded fields and hillsides, festering *favelas*, flooded coastlines, and billions of redundant human beings light years behind here on poor old Mother Earth.

Insofar as the value of any existence, whether it be that of a student or of a forest, is articulated in economic terms, we've allowed life to be regarded as a machine. And because the vast majority of humanity— peasants and farmers included, to say nothing of nerds and policy wonks—no longer participates in, or knows the spontaneity of, wild nature, the metaphor of mechanism and the ethic of instrumentality are reinforced throughout human consciousness. Why would we feel any filial responsibility toward life on Earth? The market paradigm, the idea that everything and everyone on the planet can rightly be treated as a potential commodity, threatens the complete de-souling of the world.

Feminists worked hard to advance the understanding that the personal is the political, that the gender-based power relationships of everyday life are a significant expression of our values and very often a promising, if difficult, arena for change.

The technological also is the political. Every technology concentrates and extends power, amplifies some effort or effect. Even the least technology is no unqualified boon. Technology determines the politics of our species' relationship with the rest of life on the planet, for one thing, to the extent of reshaping the terrain and the composition of the atmosphere as well. Military technology—from the war club to the geostationary reconnaissance satellite: All armed force trumps politics. Advanced medical technology and artificial intelligence would like to change the politics of mortality. Neuroscience would objectify the mystery of the self and all otherness out of existence, arguing that it's all genetically determined.

This is, as the organizers of these international conferences put it, "a state of extreme technological excess."

In some regions, perhaps there is a maldistribution of certain appropriate technologies—bicycles, sewing machines, efficient cookstoves—basic tools for a decent subsistence. Among the world's well-to-do, though, there's a bankruptcy, a pathos evident in all the frivolous gadgetry—from electronic haircurlers and video games to reclining chairs that give massages, to children's toys with treacly voices that offer good, if insipid, counsel—consumer items as surrogates for some of the most elemental and affective human capabilities. These technologies—and their more sinister big brothers—are so excessive that the line between the human and the synthetic has long since begun to blur.

For now the vast majority of urbanites and suburbanites continue in ways of life utterly dependent on the good functioning of a megatechnological infrastructure from power plants to transmission grids to sewage treatment facilities to electronic banking to supertankers to elevators to agribusiness to interstate highways. Either the common sense to recognize the precariousness of our situation has been engineered out of us, or our personal and social imagination and memory have been stupefied by the last half-century of technological excess.

In the voices captured on these pages, you heard dozens and dozens of thoughtful, courageous people utter words to break that trance, to reawaken the imagination, to encourage you to think some "unthinkable" thoughts, such as, "Nothing is inevitable if we say no." That such nay-saying is the antidote to despair. That there is a vast and diverse community of sane and decent people arguing that there must be alternatives to the totalitarianism of trade and technology.

It was the purpose of the two meetings to attempt a systemic analysis of technology, to make it possible to debate technology as a whole.

Then as the suspense and terror of the Unabomber story mounted, the hip press and major media characterized all technology critics (many of whom participated in these two conferences) as Luddites, or Neo-Luddites. Rather than acknowledging the vast destruction that ensues on technological advance, the press focused on the violence committed by an alienated intellectual, or failed to consider the greater, nonviolent resistance to the technologically implemented incursions of mass markets, or noticed the contradictions—that technology critics sometimes do their criticizing on word processors, or fly in jets to address audiences interested in these ideas.

In all of this was a quick disservice being done to a long-standing body of philosophy and pursuit of alternatives. Dozens of serious, economically disinterested scholars, authors, and activists have, especially during the last quarter-century, been developing their analyses of, and responses to, what political scientist Langdon Winner has termed "autonomous technology." And just like those mycorrhizal citizens' groups—the invisible threads linking the lives of places, keeping the planet vital—their thought remains underground. The breadth, detail, and compassion—for human community and nature's integrity—that characterize the turn away from technology cannot and will not appear in media which are either servile to the interests that prosper by mass technology or which are simply embarrassed by the prospect of a devolution of the global economy and a reclamation of lifeways that are not enervated, governed, or poisoned by technology but enhanced by skillful means.

Unlike the proponents of mass technology and economic globalization, the activists and thinkers mounting this critique don't stand to profit from their brand of advocacy. These are lifetime civil society folks. Their concern is Gandhian, for the least person. They don't confuse a juggernaut's momentum with progress. Cynicism and vested interest and sheer faddishness mostly prompt the mainstream media's dismissal of persons, pointing out the shadow side of technological development. Even the Luddites did not regard technology as a monolith; then as now the wish was to exercise discernment, to have some choice in the matter. The people you met in these discussions are Conservative, even Fundamentalist, in that they seek to conserve, as a basis for humane conduct, the fundamental matrix of nature, family, culture, and community. Most of the necessary work in the world does not involve "symbolic manipulation," but looking after children, digging in the soil, or seining the sea, and dealing with plants and animals—direct engagement with living beings. And in the world outside the steel and glass campus, community does not consist of like-minded people e-mailing themselves, but of small groups bound together by vicinity, economy, and mutual aid. It is not on fusion power or fiber optics, but on just such work, in just such communities, that the human future depends.

By the mid-nineties, when these conferences were held, the market-driven, technologically implemented attack on the very basis of subsistence threatened traditional village and peasant communities around the world. Conferees John Mohawk, Chellis Glendinning, Sulak Sivaraksa, Gustavo Esteva, Helena Norberg-Hodge, Vandana Shiva, and Satish Kumar all related firsthand experience of development's depredations: structural adjustment programs; attempts to privatize what remains of the commons—from wild land to local varieties of crop plants; construction of megadams; the introduction of toxic, capital-intensive commodity agriculture; industrial forestry; wage slavery; satellite broadcast of generic "cultural" imagery; forced migration to urban slums; and the ascendance of the cult of expertise.

Thus what you found here was something of a dialogue between pre- and post-modern societies and the formation of a common understanding which included the sense that the citizens of the North have plenty of devolutionary work ahead. There was a shared sense that the dignity of humanity is being ground away and the diversity of life pulped by this megamachine, and that drastic environmental change as a "side effect" of commonplace technologies like the automobile is already upon us, to say nothing of what might result from a bioengineered bug going native or a launch-on-warning missile system going haywire.

Just about anybody *but* a rocket scientist should, on confronting these realities, appreciate the urgency of turning aside this megatechnological trajectory. It seems reasonable enough that human communities ought to look before leaping into absolute technocracy. Simple justice and civic responsibility really require a well-informed public empowered and considering what technology is doing in our lives and what good we would wish for ourselves and for posterity. At the very least, we should shun systems and technologies that will make it impossible for us ever to change our minds and arrive at ways of living in place more respectful of, and suited to, the biological reality that made and sustains us. The wonder is that despite the power and pervasiveness of the propaganda for megatechnology, a great many people understand that technology will not solve problems caused by technology and that transnational corporations provide a living for the multitude. It looks like something simpler, more basic and human, is required and is transpiring.

The megamachine may or may not have a linchpin or a diagram that shows where its wires cross. Even if there's no main switch, there's getting to be a lot of grit in the gears, dust blown into the circuitry.

Just as this intelligentsia of technology critics does its work around the edges of the official version of reality, thousands of citizen groups everywhere in the world are dug in and defending the lives and souls of their places and communities, even beginning to restore their lands and livelihoods. None of which generates so much as a headline, unless there's a riot. And then we hear about that effect, but rarely the whole story of the cause. Still, the word gets around.

Every day my roadside mailbox fills up with newsletters from dauntless little outfits, bands of women and men working hard to stop the logging of old-growth forests or to prevent the expansion of roads; to create new political parties or to outlaw factory farming; to restore big predators to big ecosystems or to organize study circles; to preserve genetic diversity in agriculture or to learn the demanding arts of nonviolent conflict resolution; to start a cohousing project or blockade a train carrying nuclear waste; to raise awareness around human overpopulation, institute local currencies, challenge the legality (or brigandage) of corporations. None of which, be it noted, is a technofix; virtually all are working on problems that, if not caused by technology, are exacerbated by it.

Evidence, then, that right here in my country, down on the ground, there are countless cultures of resistance and regeneration whose members, located in real places, will never be on the talk shows. These citizens have their counterparts all over the planet, in places where the stakes are even greater and the sanctions are severe. These are people, numbering in the hundreds of thousands, who will resist with their last ounce of strength rather than allow the natural world and the dignity of the person to disappear forever into the market and the machine.

In support of those campaigners and defenders, and in hopes of helping inform such efforts, are the intellectual labors of the participants at these meetings: professors, philosophers, journalists, organizers, physicists, anthropologists, psychologists, economists (several of whom refer to themselves as "deprofessionalized"), poets, and a couple of farmers, Most operate at the margins: of academe, of nongovernmental organizations, of media, and of the economy. Many came of age in the sixties, have been peaceniks, Greens, feminists, ecologists, have been active in Native American treaty rights struggles, the Civil Rights Movement, and even psychedelia.

Most of them are idealists enjoying the mixed blessings that that state of mind and way of life bestows. They take positions conventionally deemed to be impossible—like Jerry Mander arguing for the elimination of television or Teddy Goldsmith campaigning over the years against the Maastricht Treaty, the World Bank, and the FAO (Food and Agriculture Organizations). Such is the prophet's weird lot of being forced by conscience or vision to stand apart from the present moment and speak from a timeless standpoint, to bear witness for the future, even if the hard sayings are drowned out by whatever's playing on the Walkman. A person can indeed become cranky and isolated under such circs; and however vigorous their intelligence, rigorous their scholarship, and voracious their appetite for real information, a person still only holds but a piece of the truth.

It was the gift of these conferences to bring together scores of such people holding diverse, carefully reasoned, sometimes conflicting positions. We were able to sit at the same table and work together with astonishing accord. I am loath to oversimplify, but we seemed to agree that a simpler life of communal responsibility serves humanity and nature best and that megatechnology undermines and overturns this authentic, more equitable existence. The reductionism of science was roundly condemned as a violently disintegrative force. Ecological conscience, a sense of the sacred, a passion for biological and cultural diversity inspired our communion.

Such can be the synergy of face-to-face encounter. And believe me, it cannot and will not be televised. I only hope that these pages bespeak the breadth of concern for human community and nature's integrity in the voices—thoughtful, ardent, sage, subtle, and fierce—of our meetings. The meaning was not esoteric.

Yet this endeavor and all the efforts of all those citizens' groups, and all the everyday work of subsistence, remain somewhat mycorrhizal. The mycorrhizae, unseen, are the subterranean threads that connect the roots of the plants of prairie and forest. They gather and distribute the essentials of flourishing.

So this body of thought, and these cultures of resistance, are inconspicuous, not on the surface. It is no good to the world for them to remain obscure, though.

Nevertheless, it is rare for the content of these conversations to be reported. The benefit is to the participants' thinking and may eventually bear fruit. Our care was to disseminate these unthinkable thoughts more widely. Therefore much gratitude is due the Foundation for Deep Ecology for its support in producing the manuscript and to Sierra Club Books for publishing this work.

I never felt less crazy or less alone than I did at these conferences, among these heroines and heroes, colleagues, and friends. We saw the same Big Picture, mourned many of the same losses of beauty and interest, felt the same vocation to *do something* in our dozens of different ways. Now the hope is that this talk, these voices of criticism, dissent, and affirmation will offer reasons and a sense of participation in the turn toward a worthy way of living premised in respect for human capability, and for every living thing on the Earth.

78 Reasonable Questions
to Ask About Any Technology

As articulated, debated, and refined by the participants in the 1993 and 1994 Mega-technology conferences, 78 tools to be used in dismantling the megamachine and restoring organic reality. Designed to be comfortable to everyone's grasp and to provide a lifetime of service if honed with hope and polished by imagination.

Ecological

What are its effects on the health of the planet and of the person?
Does it preserve or destroy biodiversity?
Does it preserve or reduce ecosystem integrity?
What are its effects on the land?
What are its effects on wildlife?
How much and what kind of waste does it generate?
Does it incorporate the principles of ecological design?
Does it break the bond of renewal between humans and nature?
Does it preserve or reduce cultural diversity?
What is the totality of its effects, its "ecology"?

Social

Does it serve community?
Does it empower community members?
How does it affect our perception of our needs?
Is it consistent with the creation of a communal, human economy?
What are its effects on relationships?
Does it undermine conviviality?
Does it undermine traditional forms of community?

How does it affect our way of seeing and experiencing the world?
Does it foster a diversity of forms of knowledge?
Does it build on, or contribute to, the renewal of traditional forms of knowledge?
Does it serve to commodify knowledge or relationships?
To what extent does it redefine reality?
Does it erase a sense of time and history?
What is its potential to become addictive?

Practical

What does it make?
Whom does it benefit?
What is its purpose?
Where was it produced?
Where is it used?
Where must it go when it's broken or obsolete?
How expensive is it?
Can it be repaired? By an ordinary person?
What is the entirety of its cost, the full cost accounting?

Moral

What values does its use foster?
What is gained by its use?
What are its effects beyond its utility to the individual?
What is lost in using it?
What are its effects on the least person in the society?

Ethical

How complicated is it?
What does it allow us to ignore?
To what extent does it distance agent from effect?
Can we assume personal, or communal, responsibility for its effects?
Can its effects be directly apprehended?
What ancillary technologies does it require?
What behavior might it make possible in the future?
What other technologies might it make possible?
Does it alter our sense of time and relationships in ways conducive to nihilism?

Vocational

What is its impact on craft?
Does it reduce, deaden, or enhance human creativity?
Is it the least imposing technology available for the task?
Does it replace, or does it aid, human hands and human beings?
Can it be responsive to organic circumstance?
Does it depress or enhance the quality of goods?
Does it depress or enhance the meaning of work?

Metaphysical

What aspect of the inner self does it reflect?
Does it express love?
Does it express rage?
What aspect of our past does it reflect?
Does it reflect cyclical or linear thinking?

Political

What is its mystique?
Does it concentrate or equalize power?
Does it require, or institute, a knowledge elite?
Is it totalitarian?
Does it require a bureaucracy for its perpetuation?
What legal empowerments does it require?
Does it undermine traditional moral authority?
Does it require military defense?
Does it enhance, or serve, military purposes?
How does it affect warfare?
Does it foster mass thinking or behavior?
Is it consistent with the creation of a global economy?
Does it empower transnational corporations?
What kind of capital does it require?

Aesthetic

Is it ugly?
Does it cause ugliness?
What noise does it make?
What pace does it set?
How does it affect quality of life (as distinct from standard of living)?

The Jacques Ellul Society

Readers may be interested to know that there is an organization dedicated to the ongoing pursuit of the issues and concerns raised by the Megatechnology conferences. The Jacques Ellul Society is designed to be a home for the world's leading activists, thinkers, and writers struggling against megatechnologies and technocracy. It is named after the distinguished French philosopher whose writings on technology have been seminal in creating the current resistance movement against modern technology. The society had its inaugural meeting in May of 1996 and will continue to hold regular international meetings, seminars, and conferences. The Jacques Ellul Society will be publishing a journal and a series of white papers on key technology areas. The permanent address is 310 D Street NE, Washington, D.C. 20002.

Bibliography

The initials after some of the entries indicate which person(s) recommended them.

Abbey, Edward. *The Monkey Wrench Gang*. New York: Avon Books, 1975. (S.M.)

Abelson, E., ed. *A Mirror of England*. Devon, England: Green Books, 1988. (J.L.)

Adbusters (quarterly). Vancouver, British Columbia: The Media Foundation. (D.T.)

Akwe: Kon Journal. *Indigenous Economics: Toward a Natural World Order*. Ithaca, NY: Summer 1992. (C.B.)

Alpbach Symposium. *Beyond Reductionism: New Perspectives in the Life Sciences*. London: Hutchinson, 1969. (S.Kv.)

Annas, George. "Outrageous Fortune: Selling Other People's Cells," in *Standard of Care: The Law of American Bioethics*. New York and Oxford: Oxford University Press/Clarendon, 1993. (B.B.)

Apffel-Marglin, Frédérique, ed. *Dominating Knowledge: Development, Culture, and Resistance*. Oxford: Oxford University Press/Clarendon, 1990. (M.C.)

Apffel-Marglin, Frédérique and Steven A. Marglin, eds. *Decolonizing Knowledge: From Development to Dialogue*. Oxford: Oxford University Press/Clarendon, 1996. (M.C.)

Bachofen, Johann Jakob. *Myth, Religion and Mother Right: Selected Writings of J.J. Bachofen*. Princeton, NJ: Bollingen Series, 1967. (E.H.)

"A Basic Call to Consciousness: The Haude no sau nee Address to the Western World," in *Akwesasne Notes*. Rooseveltown, NY: Mohawk Nation, 1978.

Bateson, Gregory. *Mind and Nature: A Necessary Unity*. New York: E. P. Dutton, 1979.

———. *Steps to an Ecology of Mind*. New York: Ballantine Books, 1972.

Beck, Ulrich. *Risk Society: Towards a New Modernity*. London/Newbury Park, CA: SAGE, 1992. (M.S.)

Bender, Gretchen and Timothy Druckrey. *Culture on the Brink: Ideologies of Technology*. Seattle: Bay Press, 1994. (M.S.)

Berman, Morris. *The Reenchantment of the World*. Ithaca, NY: Cornell University Press, 1981.

Berry, Thomas. *The Dream of the Earth*. San Francisco: Sierra Club Books, 1988. (S.M.)

Berry, Wendell. *Watch with Me*. New York: Pantheon Books, 1994.

———. *Entries*. New York: Pantheon Books, 1994.

———. *Another Turn of the Crank*. Washington, DC: Counterpoint Press, 1995.

———. *A World Lost*. Washington, DC: Counterpoint Press, 1996.

Blake, William. *The Portable Blake,* edited by Alfred Kazin. New York: Viking Press, 1946, 1968.

Bookchin, Murray. *Our Synthetic Environment*. New York: Colophon, 1974.

———. *The Ecology of Freedom*. Palo Alto: Cheshire Books, 1982.

———. *Toward an Ecological Society*. Montreal: Black Rose, 1984.

Borgmann, Albert. *Technology and the Character of Contemporary Life: A Philosophical Inquiry*. Chicago: University of Chicago Press, 1984. (R.S.)

Borsodi, Ralph. *This Ugly Civilization*. Philadelphia: Porcupine Press, 1975. (J.L.)

Bowers, C.A. *The Culture of Denial: Why the Environmental Movement Needs a Strategy for the Reform of Universities and Public Schools*. Albany: State University of New York Press, 1995.

———. *Educating for an Ecologically Sustainable Culture: Rethinking Moral Education, Creativity, Intelligence, and Other Modern Orthodoxies*. Albany: State University of New York Press, 1995.

———. *Elements of a Post-Liberal Theory of Education*. New York: Teachers College Press, Columbia University, 1987. (C.C.)

Brodsky, Joseph. *Less Than One*. New York: Farrar, Straus & Giroux, 1986. (G.R.)

Brook, James and Ian A. Boal, eds. *Resisting the Virtual Life: The Culture and Politics of Information*. San Francisco: City Lights Books, 1995.

Burnham, David. *The Rise of the Computer State*. New York: Vintage Books, 1980. (J.M.)

Burrows, Beth. "Ethics and Other Irrational Considerations," in *Boycott Quarterly*, Vol. 1, No. 4, Spring 1994.

Burrows, Beth with Jack Kloppenburg, Jr. "Biotechnology to the Rescue? Twelve Reasons Why Biotechnology Is Incompatible with Sustainable Agriculture," in the *Ecologist*, Vol. 26, #2, Mar/Apr 1996, p. 61 ff.

Capra, Fritjof. *The Tao of Physics*. Boston: Shambhala, 1975.

———. *The Turning Point: Science, Society and the Rising Culture*. New York: Simon & Schuster, 1982.

Carson, Rachel. *Silent Spring*. Boston: Houghton Mifflin Company, 1962, 1987. (K.L.)

Catton, William R. *Overshoot: The Ecological Basis of Revolutionary Change*. Urbana: University of Illinois Press, 1982.

Coates, Gary. *Resettling America.* Andover, MA: Brick House, 1981. (J.M.)

Colborn, Theo, Dianne Dumanoski, and John Peterson Myers. *Our Stolen Future: Are We Threatening Our Fertility, Intelligence, and Survival?—A Scientific Detective Story.* New York: Penguin Books, USA/Dutton, 1996. (S.M.)

Crouch, M.L. "Biotechnology Is Not Compatible with Sustainable Agriculture," in *Journal of Agricultural and Environmental Ethics,* Vol. 8, No. 2, 1995.

——. "Why Science Can't Save the Earth," in *Branches,* Vol. 8, No. 3, July-Aug. 1995.

Dasmann, Raymond F. *A Different Kind of Country.* New York: Macmillan Publishing Company, 1968. (S.M.)

——. *Environmental Conservation,* 5th ed. New York: John Wiley and Sons, 1984. (S.M.)

Davidson, Art, ed. *Does One Way of Life Have to Die So Another Can Live?* Bethel, AK: Yupik Nation, 1974. (J.M.)

deSola Pool, Ithiel. *Forecasting the Telephone: A Retrospective Technology Assessment.* Norwood, NJ: Ablex, 1983. (J.M.)

Diamond, Stanley. *In Search of the Primitive.* New Brunswick, NJ: Transaction, 1974.

Dostoevsky, Feodor. *Notes from the Underground and "The Grand Inquisitor."* New York: Dutton, 1960. (G.R.)

Douthwaite, Richard. *The Growth Illusion: How Economic Growth Has Enriched the Few, Impoverished the Many, and Endangered the Planet.* Tulsa, OK: Council Oak Books, 1993.

——. *Short Circuit: Strengthening Local Economies for Security in an Unstable World.* Devon, England: Green Books, 1997.

Drengson, Alan. *Beyond Environmental Crisis: From Technocrat to Planetary Person.* New York: Peter Lang Publishing, Inc., 1989. (A.Mc.)

Drengson, Alan and Yuichi Inoue, eds. *The Deep Ecology Movement.* Berkeley: North Atlantic Books, 1995.

Dreyfus, Hubert L. *What Computers Still Can't Do: A Critique of Artificial Reason.* Cambridge, MA: MIT Press, 1992. (D.T.)

Ehrenfeld, David. *Beginning Again: People and Nature in the New Millennium.* New York: Oxford University Press, 1993. (S.I., D.T.)

——. *The Arrogance of Humanism.* New York: Oxford University Press, 1978. (S.I., D.T.)

Ellul, Jacques. *The Technological Bluff.* Grand Rapids, MI: W.B. Eerdmans, 1990. (D.T.)

——. *The Technological Society.* New York: Alfred A. Knopf, 1964. (G.R.)

Emerson, Ralph Waldo. "Nature," in *Nature/Walking.* Boston: Beacon Press, 1991.

Esteva, Gustavo. "Development as a Threat: The Struggle for Rural México," in *Peasants and Peasant Studies,* Teodor Shanin, ed. Oxford: Basil Blackwell, 1987.

——. "Tepito: No Thanks, First World," in *In Context,* Number 30, Fall/Winter, 1991.

————. "Hosting the Otherness of the Others," *Systems of Knowledge as Systems of Power*, S. Marglin and Frédérique Apffel-Marglin, eds. Helsinki: UNU-Wider, 1993.

————. *A New Source of Hope: The Margins*. Montreal: Interculture, 1993.

Ferry, W.H. *The Corporation and the Economy*. Santa Barbara, CA: Center for the Study of Democratic Institutions, 1959.

————. *Mass Communications*. New York: Center for the Study of Democratic Institutions, 1966.

————. "Must We Rewrite the Constitution to Control Technology?" in *Saturday Review*, March 2, 1968.

Foreman, Dave and Howie Wolke. *The Big Outside: A Descriptive Inventory of the Big Wilderness Areas of the United States*. New York: Harmony Books/Crown, 1991. (J.D.)

————. *Confessions of an Eco-Warrior*. New York: Harmony Books, 1991. (J.D.)

Fowler, Cary and Pat Mooney. *Shattering: Food, Politics, and the Loss of Genetic Diversity*. Tucson: University of Arizona Press, 1990. (B.B.)

Franklin, Ursula. *The Real World of Technology*. Toronto: CBC Massey Lectures Series, 1990. (S.M.)

French, Marilyn. *Beyond Power: On Women, Men and Morals*. New York: Summit Books, 1985. (P.G.)

Gahrton, Per. *Låt Mormor Bestämma 2000—Talet*. Stockholm: Bonniers, 1993.

Gandhi, Mahatma. *Man v. Machine*. Bombay: Bharatiya Vidya Bhavan, 1966.

Garrett, Laurie. *The Coming Plague: Newly Emerging Diseases in a World Out of Balance*. New York: Farrar, Straus & Giroux, 1994. (S.M.)

Gill, Eric. *A Holy Tradition of Working: Passages from the Writings of Eric Gill*. West Stockbridge, MA: The Lindisfarne Press, 1983. (J.L.)

Glendinning, Chellis. *My Name Is Chellis and I'm in Recovery from Western Civilization*. Boston: Shambhala, 1994.

————. *Waking Up in the Nuclear Age*. Philadelphia: New Society Publishers, 1987.

————. "Notes Toward a Neo-Luddite Manifesto," in *Utne Reader*, March-April 1990, No. 38.

————. *When Technology Wounds: The Human Consequences of Progress*. New York: William Morrow, 1990 (available only through Ned Ludd Books, Box 1399, Bernalillo, NM 87004, 1-505-867-0878).

Goering, Peter, Helena Norberg-Hodge, and John Page. *From the Ground Up: Rethinking Industrial Agriculture*. London, Bristol, and Atlantic Highlands, NJ, and Berkeley: Zed Books and the International Society for Ecology and Culture, 1993.

Goethe's Faust. Translated and with an introduction by Walter Kaufmann. New York and London: Anchor Books, Doubleday, 1961. (S.M.)

Goldsmith, Edward. *The Way: An Ecological World View*. Boston: Shambhala, 1993.

————. *Blueprint for Survival*. Harmondsworth, England: Penguin, 1972.

Goldsmith, Edward; Martin Khor; Helena Norberg-Hodge; Vandana Shiva; et al. *The Future of Progress: Reflections on Environment and Development*. Devon, England: Resurgence/Green Books, 1992, 1995.

Gorz, André. *Capitalism, Socialism, Ecology*. London and New York: Verso, 1994. (A.K.)

———. *Ecology as Politics*. Boston: South End Press, 1980.

———. *Paths to Paradise: On the Liberation from Work*. London: Pluto Press, 1985.

Greco, Thomas H., Jr. *New Money for Healthy Communities*. Tucson, AZ: Thomas H. Greco, Jr., 1994. (S.M.)

Griffin, Susan. *A Chorus of Stones: The Private Life of War*. New York: Doubleday, 1992.

———. *The Eros of Everyday Life: Essays on Ecology*. New York: Doubleday, 1995.

———. *Woman and Nature: The Roaring Inside Her*. New York: Harper & Row, 1978.

———. *Pornography and Silence: Culture's Revenge Against Nature*. New York: Harper & Row, 1981.

Gross, Bertram. *Friendly Fascism: The New Face of Power in America*. New York: M. Evans and Company, 1980. (S.M.)

Haraway, Donna J. *Simians, Cyborgs, and Women: The Reinvention of Nature*. London: Free Association Books, 1991. (M.S.)

Howard, Sir Albert. *The Soil and Health*. London: Industrial Christian Fellowship, 1946 (W.B.)

Huxley, Aldous. *Brave New World*. New York and London: Harper & Brothers, 1946. (S.M.)

Hyde, W. Lewis. *The Gift: Imagination and the Erotic Life of Property*. New York: Vintage Books, 1983. (M.C.)

Illich, Ivan. *Energy & Equity*. New York: Harper & Row, 1974.

———. *Tools for Conviviality*. New York: Harper & Row, 1973, 1980. (L.W., G.R., G.E.)

———. *In the Mirror of the Past: Lectures and Addresses, 1978–1990*. New York: M. Boyars, 1992. (G.E.)

———. *In the Vineyard of the Text*. Chicago: University of Chicago Press, 1993. (G.E.)

Irvine, Sandy. *A Green Manifesto*. London: Macdonald Optima, 1988.

Jackson, Wes. *New Roots for Agriculture*. San Francisco: Friends of the Earth and Salina, KS: Land Institute, 1980. (W.B.)

Jünger, Friedrich Georg. *The Failure of Technology*. Chicago: Gateway Editions, 1956. (A.K.)

Kass, Leon R., M.D. "Patenting Life: Science, Politics, and the Limits of Mastering Nature," in *Towards a More Natural Science: Biology and Human Affairs*. New York: The Free Press, 1985. (B.B.)

Kimbrell, Andrew. *The Human Body Shop: The Engineering and Marketing of Life*. San Francisco: HarperCollins, 1993.

Kloppenburg, Jack R., Jr. *First the Seed: The Political Economy of Plant Biotechnology, 1492–2000*. New York: Cambridge University Press, 1988. (B.B.)

Kohr, Leopold. *The Breakdown of Nations*. London: Routledge & Kegan Paul, 1957. (G.R.)

Korten, David. *When Corporations Rule the World*. West Hartford, CT: Kumarian Press and San Francisco, CA: Berrett-Koehler Publishers, 1995.

Kropotkin, Petr Alekseevich. *Fields, Factories, and Workshops*. George Woodcock, ed. Montreal and New York: Black Rose Books, 1994. (L.W.)

Kumar, Satish, *No Destination: An Autobiography*, Devon, England: Green Books and Tulsa, OK: Council Oak, 1992.

Kvaloy, Sigmund. "Complexity and Time: Breaking the Pyramid's Reign," in *Wisdom in the Open Air*. Peter Reed and David Rothenberg, eds. Minneapolis: University of Minnesota Press, 1993.

———. "Green Philosophy," in *The Green Fuse*, J. Button, ed. London and New York: Quartet Books, 1990.

———. "Inside Nature," in *The Future of Progress*, Goldsmith, Khor, Norberg-Hodge & Shiva, eds. Bristol, England, and Berkeley, CA: International Society for Ecology and Culture, 1995.

La Chapelle, Dolores. *Sacred Land, Sacred Sex, Rapture of the Deep: Concerning Deep Ecology and Celebrating Life*. Durango, CO: Kivakí Press, 1992. (J.D.)

Lane, John. *The Living Tree: Art and the Sacred*. Devon, England: Green Books, 1988.

———. *Ants in the Snake's Tail: Aesthetics and Ecology*. Devon, England: Green Books, 1996.

Latour, Bruno. *Aramis, or The Love of Technology*. Cambridge, MA: Harvard University Press, 1996. (J.Mo.)

———. *We Have Never Been Modern*. New York: Harvester Wheatsheaf, 1993. (J.Mo.)

Lawless, Edward W. *Technology and Social Shock*. New Brunswick, NJ: Rutgers University Press, 1977. (J.M.)

Leopold, Aldo. *A Sand County Almanac and Sketches Here and There*. New York and Oxford: Oxford University Press, 1949. (S.M.)

Liedloff, Jean. *The Continuum Concept*. Reading, MA: Addison-Wesley, 1985.

Lyon, Oren and John Mohawk, eds. *Exiled in the Land of the Free: Democracy, Indian Nations, and the U.S. Constitution*. Santa Fe, NM: Clearlight Publishers, 1992.

Mander, Jerry. *Four Arguments for the Elimination of Television*. New York: William Morrow & Company, 1977, 1978. (J.D.)

———. *In the Absence of the Sacred: The Failure of Technology and the Survival of the Indian Nations*. San Francisco: Sierra Club Books, 1991.

Manes, Christopher. *Green Rage: Radical Environmentalism and the Unmaking of Civilization*. Boston: Little, Brown & Co., 1990. (J.D.)

McKibben, Bill. *Hope, Human and Wild: True Stories of Living Lightly on the Earth.* Boston: Little, Brown & Co., 1995. (J.D.)

McLaughlin, Andrew. *Regarding Nature: Industrialism and Deep Ecology.* Albany, NY: State University of New York Press, 1963.

——. *Ecology and Philosophy*, special issue of *Philosophical Inquiry*, Winter-Spring 1986. (D.T.)

Merchant, Carolyn. *The Death of Nature: Women, Ecology, and the Scientific Revolution.* San Francisco: Harper & Row, 1980. (M.C., G.R., P.G.)

Metzner, Ralph. *Maps of Consciousness: I Ching, Tantra, Tarot, Alchemy, Astrology, Actualism.* New York: Collier Books, 1974.

——. "Pride, Prejudice, and Paranoia—Dismantling the Ideology of Domination," in *World Futures* (in press).

——. *The Well of Remembrance: Rediscovering the Earth Wisdom Mythology.* Boston: Shambhala Publications, 1994.

Mies, Maria. *Ecofeminism.* London and Atlantic Highlands, NJ: Zed Books, 1993.

——. *Patriarchy and Accumulation on a World Scale: Women in the International Division of Labor.* London and Atlantic Highlands, NJ: Zed Books, 1986.

Miller, Henry. *The Time of the Assassins: A Study of Rimbaud.* Norfolk, CT: J. Laughlin, 1956. (G.R.)

Mills, Stephanie, ed. *In Praise of Nature.* Washington, DC, and Covelo, CA: Island Press, 1990.

——. *Whatever Happened to Ecology?* San Francisco: Sierra Club Books, 1989.

——. *In Service of the Wild: Restoring and Reinhabiting Damaged Land.* Boston: Beacon Press, 1995. (J.D.)

Mohawk, John. "Deconstructing Utopia," in *The Permaculture Activist*, Vol. 8, No. 2, 1992. (M.C., S.M.)

More, Thomas. *Utopia*, H.V.S. Ogden, translator. New York: Appleton-Century-Crofts, 1949.

Muir, John. *John of the Mountains: The Unpublished Journals of John Muir.* Boston: Houghton Mifflin, 1938. (D.T.)

——. *My First Summer in the Sierra.* Boston: Houghton Mifflin, 1911. (D.T.)

——. *Travels in Alaska.* Boston: Houghton Mifflin, 1915. (D.T.)

Mumford, Lewis. *The Myth of the Machine.* New York: Harcourt, Brace & World, 1967–70. (C.G.)

——. *Technics and Civilization.* New York: Harcourt Brace Jovanovich, 1934, 1963.

——. *The Pentagon of Power.* New York: Harcourt, Brace & World, 1970. (L.W.)

Naess, Arne. *Ecology, Community, and Lifestyle: Outline of an Ecosophy*, translated and revised by David Rothenberg. Cambridge, England: Cambridge University Press, 1989.

——. *Is It Painful to Think? Conversations with Arne Naess* by David Rothenberg. Minneapolis: University of Minnesota Press, 1992.

Nandy, Ashis, ed. *Science, Hegemony, and Violence: A Requiem for Modernity.* Tokyo,

Japan: The United Nations University and Delhi, India: Oxford University Press, 1988. (S.M.)

Nietschmann, Bernard. "The Third World War," in *Cultural Survival Quarterly* (11) No. 3, 1987. (J.M.)

Noble, David F. *America by Design: Science, Technology and the Rise of Corporate Capitalism*. New York: Alfred A. Knopf, 1977.

———. *A World Without Women: The Christian Clerical Culture of Western Science*. New York: Alfred A. Knopf, 1992. (M.C.)

———. *Progress Without People: In Defense of Luddism*. Chicago: Charles H. Kerr Publishing Co., 1993. (M.C.)

Norberg-Hodge, Helena. *Ancient Futures: Learning from Ladakh*. San Francisco: Sierra Club Books, 1991.

Noss, Reed F. "The Ecological Effects of Roads or The Road to Destruction." Missoula, MT: Wildlands Center for Preventing Roads, 1995. (S.M.)

Noss, Reed F. and Allen Y. Cooperrider. *Saving Nature's Legacy: Protecting and Restoring Biodiversity*. Washington, DC, and Covelo, CA: Island Press, 1994. (J.D.)

Orr, David. *Ecological Literacy: Education and the Transition to a Postmodern World*. Albany: State University of New York Press, 1992. (S.I.)

———. *The Global Predicament: Ecological Perspectives on World Order*. Chapel Hill: University of North Carolina Press, 1965. (S.I.)

Orwell, George. *1984*. New York: Harcourt Brace Jovanovich, 1949. (S.M.)

———. *Coming Up for Air*. New York: Harcourt, Brace, 1950. (S.M.)

Polanyi, Karl. *The Great Transformation: The Political and Economic Origins of Our Time*. Boston: Beacon Press, 1957.

Postman, Neil. *Technopoly: The Surrender of Culture to Technology*. New York, Alfred A. Knopf, 1992. (D.T.)

Quinn, Daniel. *Ishmael*. New York: Bantam Books, 1992. (J.D.)

Redd, Peter and David Rothenberg, eds. *Wisdom in the Open Air: The Norwegian Roots of Deep Ecology*. Minneapolis: University of Minnesota Press, 1993.

Rifkin, Jeremy. *Biosphere Politics: A New Consciousness for a New Century*. New York: Crown, 1991.

———. *Time Wars: The Primary Conflict in Human History*. New York: Henry Holt, 1987.

———. *The End of Work: The Decline of the Global Labor Force and the Dawn of the Post-Market Era*. New York: G. P. Putnam's Sons, 1995.

Romanshyn, Robert. *Technology as Symptom and Dream*. London: Routledge and Kegan Paul, 1989.

Roszak, Theodore. *The Cult of Information*. New York: Pantheon/Random House, 1986. (D.T.)

———. *The Making of a Counter Culture: Reflections on the Technocratic Society and Its Youthful Opposition*. Garden City, NY: Doubleday & Company, 1969.

———. *The Voice of the Earth*. New York: Simon & Schuster, 1992.

———. *The Memoirs of Elizabeth Frankenstein*. New York: Random House, 1995.

Roszak, Theodore, Mary Gomes, and Allen Kanner, eds. *Ecopsychology: Restoring the Earth, Healing the Mind*. San Francisco: Sierra Club Books, 1995. (R.M.)

Sachs, Wolfgang, ed. *The Development Dictionary: A Guide to Knowledge as Power*. London: Zed Books, 1992. (C.B.)

———, ed. *Global Ecology: A New Arena of Global Conflict*. London: Zed Books, 1993. (C.B.)

Sale, Kirkpatrick. *Human Scale*. New York: Coward, McAnn & Geohegan, 1980.

———. *Rebels Against the Future: The Luddites and Their War on the Industrial Revolution—Lessons for the Computer Age*. Reading, MA: Addison-Wesley, 1995. (C.G., J.D.)

Schaef, Ann Wilson. *Women's Reality: An Emerging Female System in a White Male Society*. San Francisco: Harper & Row, 1985. (C.C.)

Schumacher, E.F. *Good Work*. New York: Harper & Row, 1979.

———. *Small Is Beautiful: Economics as if People Mattered*. New York: Harper & Row, 1973.

Schwarz, Michiel. "The Technological Culture: Opening the Political and Public Debate" in J. Durant and J. Gregory, eds., *Science and Culture in Europe*. London: The Science Museum, 1993.

Schwarz, Michiel and Michael Thompson. *Divided We Stand: Redefining Politics, Technology, and Social Choice*. London: Harvester-Wheatsheaf and Philadelphia: University of Pennsylvania Press, 1990.

Sclove, Richard E. "Town Meetings on Technology," in *Technology Review*, July 1996.

———. *Democracy and Technology*. New York: Guilford Press, 1995.

———. "Putting Science to Work in Communities," in *The Chronicle of Higher Education*, 31 Mar 1995.

Sclove, Richard E. and Jeffrey Scheuer. "On the Road Again: If Information Highways Are Anything Like Interstate Highways—Watch Out!" in *Computerization and Controversy: Value Conflict and Social Choices, 2nd ed.*, Rob King, ed. San Diego: Academic Press, 1996.

Sessions, George, ed. *Deep Ecology for the 21st Century*. Boston: Shambhala Publications, 1995. (A.Mc., J.D.)

Shallis, Michael. *The Silicon Idol: The Micro Revolution and Its Social Implications*. New York: Oxford University Press, 1984. (S.K.)

Shelley, Mary. *Frankenstein, or, the Modern Prometheus*. New York: E. P. Dutton & Co., 1933. (S.M.)

Shepard, Paul. *Nature and Madness*. San Francisco: Sierra Club Books, 1982. (S.M.)

———. *The Tender Carnivore and the Sacred Game*. New York: Charles Scribner's Sons, 1973. (S.M.)

Shiva, Vandana. *Staying Alive: Women, Ecology, and Development*. London: Zed Books, 1989.

———. *The Violence of the Green Revolution*. Penang, Malaysia: Third World Network, 1991. (M.C.)

———. *Monoculture of the Mind: Perspectives on Biodiversity & Biotechnology*. London and Atlantic Highlands, NJ: Zed Books, 1993.

Simons, G. L. *Eco-Computer: The Impact of Global Intelligence*. New York: Wiley, 1987. (S.Kv.)

Sivaraksa, Sulak. *Seeds of Peace: A Buddhist Vision for Renewing Society*. Berkeley, CA: Parallax Press, 1992.

Smith, Adam. *The Wealth of Nations*. New York: E. P. Dutton & Co., 1934–37. (A.K.)

Smith, J. Russell. *Tree Crops: A Permanent Agriculture*. Washington, DC, and Covelo, CA: Island Press, 1987. (W.B.)

Snyder, Gary. *The Practice of the Wild: Essays by Gary Snyder*. San Francisco: North Point Press, 1990. (J.D.)

———. *A Place in Space: Ethics, Aesthetics, and Watersheds*. Washington, DC: Counterpoint, 1995.

Spretnak, Charlene. *Green Politics: The Global Promise* (with Fritjof Capra). New York: Dutton, 1984, and Santa Fe, NM: Bear & Co., 1986.

———. *The Spiritual Dimension of Green Politics*. Santa Fe, NM: Bear & Co., 1986.

———. *States of Grace: The Recovery of Meaning in the Postmodern Age*. San Francisco: HarperCollins, 1991.

———. *The Resurgence of the Real: Body, Nature, and Place in a Hypermodern World*. Boston: Addison-Wesley, 1997.

Suzuki, David. *Time to Change: Essays*. Toronto, Canada: Stoddart, 1994.

Suzuki, David and Peter Knudtson. *Wisdom of the Elders: Sacred Native Stories of Nature*. New York: Bantam Books, 1992.

Tarr, Joel A., ed. *Retrospective Technology Assessment—1976*. San Francisco, CA: Francisco Press, 1977. (J.M.)

Thoreau, Henry David. *The Maine Woods*. Boston: Ticknor & Fields, 1864. (D.T., G.S.)

———. *Wild Apples: A History of the Apple Tree*. Worcester, MA: A. J. Stonge, 1956.

———. *Walden, or Life in the Woods, and On the Duty of Civil Disobedience*. New York: Harper & Row, Publishers, 1965. (D.T., G.S.)

———. "Walking," in *Nature/Walking*. Boston: Beacon Press, 1991. (D.T., G.S.)

Tickner, J. Ann. *Self-Reliance Versus Power Politics: The American and Indian Experiences in Building Nation States*. New York: Columbia University Press, 1987. (R.S.)

Trainer, Ted. *The Conserver Society: Alternatives for Sustainability*. London and Atlantic Highlands, NJ: Zed Books, 1995. (S.I.)

Whyte, William Foote and Kathleen King Whyte. *Making Mondragon: The Growth and Dynamics of the Worker Cooperative Complex*. Ithaca, NY: ILR Press, Cornell University, 1988. (R.S.)

Winner, Langdon. *Autonomous Technology: Technics-Out-of-Control as a Theme in Political Thought*. Cambridge, MA: MIT Press, 1977.

———. "Do Artifacts Have Politics?" in *Daedalus*, Vol. 109, No. 1, Winter 1980.

Reprinted in *The Social Shaping of Technology*, Donald McKenzie and Judy Wajman, eds. London: Open University Press, 1985. (J.M.)

————. *The Whale and the Reactor: A Search for Limits in an Age of High Technology*. Chicago and London: The University of Chicago Press, 1986. (S.M.)

Winner, Langdon, ed. *Democracy in a Technological Society, Vol. 9* in the series *Philosophy and Technology*, Paul Durbin, general editor. Dordrecht, Netherlands and Boston: Kluwer, 1992.

Wordsworth, William. "Ode: Intimations of Immortality from Recollections of Early Childhood," in *The Works of William Wordsworth*. Hertfordshire, England: Wordsworth Editions Ltd., 1994. (S.G.)

¡Zapatistas! Documents of the New Mexican Revolution. New York: Autonomedia, 1994.

Zerzan, John and Alice Carnes, eds. *Questioning Technology: Tool, Toy, or Tyrant?* Philadelphia, PA, Gabriola Island, British Columbia, and Santa Cruz, CA: New Society Publishers, 1991.

Index